cities in transition

Cities

in

Transition:

From the Ancient World to Urban America

Edited by:
Frank J. Coppa and
Philip C. Dolce

 Nelson Hall Chicago

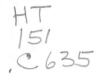

To our wives and daughters

Rosina, Francesca, and Melina Coppa
Patty and Susan Dolce

Contents

Preface

The extraordinarily rich and varied urban life that men and women have experienced throughout the ages has played a crucial role in the evolution of the modern world. From the start, city life has excited interest and provoked controversy. The city represents the triumph of man's creative genius and is unquestionably the home of most advances made in his civilization. Unfortunately it also has produced enormous psychic and physical problems which have yet to be resolved. While some have seen the city as representing art, learning, and modernization, others have viewed it primarily as the center of corruption, crime, and decay. The dispute continues to this day, and the proliferation of urban problems has aroused prejudices and produced fears which can be better understood when examined in historical perspective.

The aim of this book is to survey important aspects of city life from the ancient world to contemporary urban America. Following a broad sweep of European urbanization and its consequences, this volume stresses the varied forces, institutions, groups, and attitudes which form a vital part of urban America. The twenty-four original essays presented here combine the perspective of scholars from a number of disciplines. By utilizing the expertise of artists, literary figures, sociologists, mass communications experts, biologists, anthropologists, and historians, the editors have sought to present a multidimensional view of the city. The excitement and diversity of urban life is reflected in the wide spectrum of views—some traditional, others highly controversial—found within the covers of this book.

The present volume is an outgrowth of a television series entitled "The Evolution of Cities: From the Village to Megalopolis and Beyond" which was produced by St. John's University for the Columbia Broadcasting System.

We would like to express our appreciation to Dr. Thomas Curran, the academic coordinator of the series, for his cooperation. A special word of thanks is also accorded Winston Kirby, the director of the Television Center of St. John's University. His interest and assistance helped make this work possible.

F. J. C.

P. C. D.

Part I

EARLY URBANIZATION AND THE DAWN OF CIVILIZATION

1. Cities as a lure for intellectuals

Anne Paolucci

There have been two ages of great cities in the Western world—our own age, of course, in which there are hundreds of gigantic cities across the face of the earth and the ancient world of Hellenistic Greece and Imperial Rome when several major cities (notably Alexandria, Carthage, and Rome) numbered well over a million in population. Size alone, however, does not explain the lure of the city for the intellectual; there are other, more important considerations. We must look beyond numbers for the essential elements which define the complex social, economic, and political structure which has, throughout history, attracted cultural and artistic expression.

First of all, we must remind ourselves that it takes leisure to permit the existence of scholars, scientists, artists, and intellectuals generally. It takes money to provide leisure. And it is a fact, of course, that money tends to concentrate in cities; so that it is possible to say that leisure on a large scale can be sustained only in cities. This observation is not new; the city has long since given its name to the composite cultural achievements which we call "civilization"—a word that is derived etymologically from the Latin for city: *civitas*. To be civilized has meant, traditionally, nothing more than to have taken on the habits of city life. As one writer puts it: "Cities remain the symbols and carriers of civilization wherever they appear. . . . the story of civilization may . . . be told as the story of cities."

Leisure is all-important for the exotic flower which we call culture to bloom. But cities do not have to be big sprawling metropolises or megalopolises to provide the leisure which produces the life of intellect. On the contrary, the two cities that have produced the greatest number of poets, painters, philosophers, scientists, historians, and architects have been relatively small cities by modern standards: Athens in the fourth and fifth centuries before Christ and Florence in Renaissance Italy. In the span of less than a century, Athens could boast of the presence within its limits of the philosophers Socrates, Plato, and Aristotle; of the historians Herodotus and Thucydides; of the tragedians Aeschylus, Sophocles, and Euripides; of the greatest author of comedies, Aristophanes; of the scientist Democritus; of the sculptor Phidias; and scores of poets, painters, and architects. A list of the intellectual giants of Renaissance Florence is equally impressive: one need only mention Dante, Boccaccio, Petrarch, Michelangelo, Machiavelli, Giotto, Cimabue, Fra Angelico, Marsilio Ficino, and Galileo.

Some scholars argue that when cities become very large they cease to be centers of civilizing activity, that there is a golden mean beneath which there are not enough people for a truly civilized existence and above which there are too many. But it is rather a broad mean. Cities can become large indeed before they become incompatible with civilized existence. Yet there is a limit. And it is the tension of that limit that has historically both attracted and repulsed the intellectual. We should perhaps call it the dialectic of the city. The ideal situation for intellectuals has always been, we are told, to be disciplined by the tension of the one and yet have an escape to the tonic of the other.

For the intellectual and the artist, being in the city is like being caged; but that is exactly what our great theaters, concert halls,

4

scientific academies, museums of art, major universities, newspapers, and publishing houses are—great aviaries of talented people protected, nourished, and treasured. It is the isolated poet in the city who most longs to escape, who cries after the soaring bird, "No hungry generations tread thee down." But when an intellectual is forced to live forever in the country, how tiresome it can become unless, of course, he is someone like Henry Thoreau, who could absorb himself completely in his own thoughts.

Life in the city, it has been said, is a psychological stimulant for cultural activity because it forces on us an intensification of nervous stimulation. The sociologist George Simmel, early in this century, wrote:

With each crossing of the street, with the tempo and multiplicity of economic, occupational, and social life, the city sets up a deep contrast with small town and rural life with reference to the sensory foundations of psychic life. The metropolis exacts from man as a discriminating creature a different amount of consciousness than does rural life. . . . Precisely in this connection the sophisticated character of metropolitan psychic life becomes understandable—as over against small town life which rests more upon deeply felt and emotional relationships. . . . [City] life thus underlies a heightened awareness and a predominance of intelligence in metropolitan man. . . . Intellectuality is emphasized to preserve subjective life against the overwhelming power of metropolitan life, and intellectuality branches out in many directions and is integrated with numerous discrete phenomena.

It takes great psychic energy to survive the nervous stimulation of the city. Without such energy, the subjective life of the would-be writer or artist, philosopher or scientist can indeed be overwhelmed, and the lure of the city for the intellec-

EARLY URBANIZATION AND THE DAWN OF CIVILIZATION

tual can end up being like the lure of the flame for the moth that hovers around it—an invitation to be consumed as the mythical Icarus was consumed when he flew too close to the sun and as Semele was consumed in the lightning glance of Zeus.

It is not difficult to understand how this nervous excitement of the city can breed excesses and how these excesses, in turn, can force the intellectual to take up the opposite kind of existence by way of reaction. There have been whole movements in history and in literature dedicated to the return to nature, to the natural environment of country life, to the simple values and tasks, to the tonic of such life.

The eighteenth century, with its highly rational and formalized social structure, inspired such a reaction in the poets of the nineteenth century. The so-called Romantic Movement of that age was characterized by the exaltation of the simple life, the return to the internal man and the immediacy of nature. Ironically, the philosophical base of that major literary movement, which produced some of the greatest poetry ever written in any language, is to be found in the philosophy of Jean Jacques Rousseau—a product of the most highly sophisticated culture of the eighteenth century, the culture of the French encyclopedists and their patrons. In 1749, Rousseau wrote what was to become a famous essay on the notion of man's perfectibility and the corrupting influence of society, explaining that, in order to realize his true potential man must turn to nature and give up the artificial life of society, particularly the demands of formal education with its external, restrictive rules and standardization.

The poets and writers of the early half of the nineteenth century took up this challenge, each in his own way: Wordsworth, Shelley, and Keats in England; Leopardi and Manzoni in Italy; De Vigny, Lamartine, Victor Hugo in France; the early Goethe in Germany. Their main thrust was the insistence on simplicity—and in the terms we are considering, this meant a return to the simple life, to nature and closeness with nature, to the source of true being. With intensified industrialization later in the century, this commitment to nature and the natural life took on new meaning and became a harsh criticism of urban life with all its tensions, abuses, and dehumanizing demands. The novels of Dickens depict that criticism in its most vivid and compelling terms.

In America, there were a number of unique experiments on the part of intellectuals to put into practice the ideal of returning to nature and the simple life: Henry Thoreau at Walden Pond; the Alcotts and their friends at "Fruitlands"; the experiment at Brook Farm, which Ralph Waldo Emerson for a time considered joining. All of these were efforts to establish self-sufficient economic communities, where the members lived together and worked the soil, sharing the fruits of their labors. It was a kind of economic communism.

Today we have a new kind of experiment among our hippies who, dissatisfied with our capitalist society and with the "establishment" as a whole, seek a return to self-sufficiency. Theirs is a kind of social communism, but it is not a commitment to nature in the sense that it was for the New England intellectuals or for the poets of the Romantic Age. The hippie communes often exist right in the middle of the big cities. Their justification for existence is not a positive affirmation of the superiority of life close to nature but simply protest—rejection of the political structure which, paradoxically, allows them to indulge in their hand-to-mouth existence. Their retreat from society is not a preference for the natural life but simply the undermining of political life.

There is one other exception which should be mentioned: the religious orders. The Trappist monks, for instance, have for centuries lived within a well-regulated private community, economically self-sufficient, close to nature, and dedicated to work, prayer, and meditation. The order is made up of all kinds of people—including intellectuals like Thomas Merton, who became famous as a writer. But all of these communities—the

EARLY URBANIZATION AND THE DAWN OF CIVILIZATION

New England intellectuals, the religious orders, the hippies of our day—simply dramatize the fact that city life is tense and that its stimulation repels as well as attracts. Ultimately they point up the fact that such experiments in withdrawal are themselves artificial, running counter to the natural tendency of the intellectual to find the means for expression in the diversity and rich stimulation of the city.

History shows that for the producers of cultural life, the general trend has been toward the city. From the beginning of recorded time, intellectuals have sought the city and the life of the city. Let us return to the example of that cultural city par excellence—the Athens of Pericles. In retrospect, it is no exaggeration to say that Athens itself became a work of art in the fifth century before Christ—the physical city with its magnificent array of temples and public buildings like the Parthenon, and the spiritual city which nurtured the great community of intellectuals who found in it the inspiration for their work.

Even a harsh critic like Aristophanes cannot be separated from the city that enabled him to flourish, that provided him with the intellectual excitements, the nervous milieu, the very themes of war and peace which brought out his full potential. Athens in the fifth and fourth centuries before Christ was a great city-state, and its political history inspires awe; but it was also, as we noted, a great patroness of the arts, of science and philosophy; a place where the foundations were laid for all subsequent Western culture. It enabled the nobleman Plato to choose as his teacher the lowly Socrates; and it produced an Aristotle who was not only the great disciple of Plato but also the teacher of Alexander the Great. And if Socrates, the first authentic voice of Western thought, provoked a confrontation with the city that had nurtured him and had allowed him to teach there all his mature life, that same city—it must be remembered—was also the place where every citizen was encouraged to submit his works of art for public prizes. Athenian citizens were invited to attend the great public performances of the prize-winning plays of Aeschylus, Sophocles, and Euripides, and an Athenian who could not afford the price of a ticket received the money for it out of the public treasury.

Imperial Rome was concerned more with governing, with legislating and enforcing world peace, than with exciting the sensibilities of intellectuals. But the city of Romulus—of the fratricide who civilized a band of outlaws to the point where the sense of law was their supreme value—nevertheless remained for centuries the mecca for all the intelligence and talent of the ancient world. Even in its decline, when barbaric kings repeatedly threatened to raze it to the ground, aspiring intellectuals in the ranks of the barbarians themselves preferred to restrain the wrath of the invaders and to preserve at least a semblance of the grandeur that was Rome.

Procopius, the historian of the Emperor Justinian in the East, warned the Germanic kings that while they could probably level Rome in a matter of weeks, it would take them a thousand years, if ever, to build the like of such a city again. Rome, as the proverbial expression has it, was not built in a day. Into its making had gone the talents of hundreds of thousands of builders, thinkers, legislators, statesmen, poets, dreamers, painters, sculptors, entertainers, scientists, philosophers, saints, and sinners.

Rome did fall, as we know; and for many centuries it remained the equivalent of a small town or village. But the imperial government survived for a while longer at Ravenna, on the Adriatic coast, where it was able to hold off the barbarians. It was to Ravenna that artists, writers, and intellectuals came in the fifth and sixth centuries. What they wrought can still be seen today in the magnificent architecture of its churches and in the superb mosaics of St. Apollinare Nuovo and St. Apollinare in Classe—not to mention those beautifully preserved mosaics of San Vitale. It is worth mentioning, at least in passing, that Ravenna and the great family of Da Polenta welcomed the exile Dante Alighieri in the fourteenth century, offering him physical

9

and spiritual haven. The first great poet of the modern world is, in fact, buried in Ravenna.

Gradually, the power of Ravenna diminished and Europe entered into a period of relative barbarism when cities, or towns, if they survived at all, ceased to have an intellectual life. Learning fled to the hills and to hidden valleys, to the monasteries of disciplined monks, who patiently copied manuscripts, preserved old treasured books and paintings, and kept alive—through some of their members—the continuity of intellectual life. In the great monasteries like Monte Cassino, not far from Naples (wholly destroyed in World War II and then completely rebuilt, according to its original design), intellectual life found a haven and a sanctuary.

Eventually the cities came back. No one can say precisely how—for where there are no cities there cannot be precise history —but they came back in central and northern Italy, first, then in various parts of France, the Low Countries, and Germany.

Culturally, it was in Sicily—Germanic Sicily, the Sicily of the German Hohenstaufen emperors so dear to the poet Dante— that city life first flourished again in the Middle Ages. In the eleventh and twelfth centuries, poets and artisans from France and Germany found their way to the court of the Fredericks— Frederick Barbarossa, his grandson Frederick II, Conrad, and Manfred. It was there that Italian lyric poetry received its first great impetus and the vernacular came into its own. Frederick II, perhaps the greatest of the Hohenstaufen rulers, invited Provencal troubadors to his court-city, welcomed German *minnesingers*, fostered arts and letters in every way. In 1224 he founded the University of Naples. That city flourished for a long time thereafter as a center for science, philosophy, mathematics, medicine, astronomy, and poetry.

When the imperial rule of the Hohenstaufens failed ultimately and the city-states of northern Italy began to assert themselves through their guilds and unions, the writers, artists, and intellectuals found there the kinds of milieu and encouragement they needed to carry out their work. One need only mention the city of Florence under the great leadership of the Medici family— Cosimo first, then Lorenzo his grandson. It was Cosimo de'- Medici who founded the famous Medici Library and set up the academy for Greek studies, headed by the Platonist philosopher, Marsilio Ficino. His patronage and protection of such artists as Brunelleschi, Donatello, Luca della Robbia, and Ghiberti was the glory of Renaissance Italy—matched only by the patronage and interest of Lorenzo. Lorenzo was himself a brilliant scholar and an excellent poet; he spent huge sums on Greek and Latin manuscripts, and also on his many friends—poets like Poliziano and Pulci and philosophers like Pico della Mirandola and Ficino.

Florence was at that time the financial capital of Italy and of Western Europe. It is no accident that Italian, as we know it today, is in effect the Florentine dialect. The language was formed by the poets and writers of the time of the Medici, having been given its initial great impetus earlier, by Dante. It was in the Medici household that Michelangelo came, early in his teens, to prove his genius. And it was at the papal court in Rome that he found recognition for his mature talents. Money does not define genius; but one wonders if the magnificent Moses now in the Church of St. Peter in Chains in Rome would ever have been conceived if Pope Julian II had not commissioned Michaelangelo to execute a statue for his tomb; or what the Sistine Chapel might have been like if Michelangelo had not been asked to paint its ceiling.

Papal Rome flourished long after the decline of Florence; but with the Reformation and the invasions into Italy by the French and Spanish, intellectuals—preceded by the wealth of Italian merchants—fled to the city-states of Germany and the Netherlands. And from there they went to England—an England full of confidence and power, an England full of enthusiastic and daring explorers, of poets and artists dedicated to the new-found

11

EARLY URBANIZATION AND THE DAWN OF CIVILIZATION

power of their sovereign, an England on the brink of complete autonomy, an England emerging from victorious confrontations with Spain and Rome. The life of this England was centered in London, where, at the end of the sixteenth century, we find a society of mixed elements coming together in the unity of a prosperous and proud nation.

There was, as one writer has put it, "a great industrious class standing between the noble and the peasant, running over with individual originality of character and infusing their spirit into the sovereign, the statesman, and the soldier." When Shakespeare left his native Stratford for London around 1585, the hegemony of Elizabeth was well established, and with it came the full flowering of arts and letters.

In London, Shakespeare found not only the facilities required to enable him to develop as a playwright, but the writers and scholars of Europe, the storytellers of Italy, the lively milieu in which he was able to see, hear, and read firsthand poets, dramatists, artists, men of letters, adventurous explorers. Shakespeare's London was the London of Edmund Spenser, Thomas More, Philip Sidney, Francis Drake, Walter Raleigh—the London of Christopher Marlowe and Ben Jonson, the Blackfriars Guild, and the Court with its wealth and its patrons.

Today we have our Ford Foundations and our Carnegie Institutes—much more money perhaps than was available at any one time to the writers and artists of Elizabeth's time or the ancient Athenians or the Florentines of the time of Medici. But we have lost much in the impersonal kind of subsidies and grants which exist in our age for artists and writers.

So far, we have discussed the lure of the city for intellectuals from a positive point of view. We must not forget, of course, that there have been periods of history when the city inspired more criticism than praise, more pessimism than optimism, despair rather than enthusiasm. But even at such moments, the lure of the city is discernible—indeed, the fascination of the city at such periods is even greater.

How do we explain the phenomenon? We noted earlier how, in many respects, it is like the suicidal lure of a blazing flame for the fragile-winged moth. As Jacques Ellul expresses it in his recently published, brilliant book, *The Meaning of the City*, the great metropolis is a parasite:

> Like a vampire, it preys on the true living creation. . . . We cannot repeat too often that the city is an enormous man-eater. . . . The city devours men. [Its] very character is to receive from the outside; to consume, and to produce things usable only inside the city and to her gain. . . . There is something magical about her attractiveness, and it is impossible to explain men's passion for the city. .\. . The irresistible current flowing in long unconscious waves to pull men toward her dead asphalt, without giving a thought for her force, her seductive power.

What the city best produces for itself and most ravenously consumes are, of course, the works of civilized leisure. An endless flood of newspapers, magazines, books, television and radio scripts, lectures in teeming universities, paintings, sculptures, sonatas, symphonies, operas, and countless works of architectural ingenuity and genius to house, or store, or display them in. Again in the words of Ellul:

> It is understandable that the city produces, and singularly so, in the intellectual life. Nowhere else do ideas evolve so rapidly. And today is not the first time historians have concluded that intense intellectual and artistic development coincided with the appearances of cities. It is obviously permanent contact with other men which frees the human mind, which facilitates the exchange of ideas, which permits the accumulation of enormous quantities of human raw material whose synthesis is the glory of human intelligence. But what is not often noticed

13

is that the city is there first, *she* is the antecedent. The city is the condition (by her creation of the necessary environment) for great ideological developments.

The lure of the city for the intellectual is thus a creative lure. When a would-be writer or artist feels drawn to the city, he has only potentially what he aspires to be. He must let himself be drawn in or he will realize nothing. Ellul insists:

> It is maddening perhaps, but we cannot conceive of Plato without Athens, or Racine without Paris. I am not trying to set the city up as an invariable conditioning factor, but we must recognize that the intellectual life cannot exist outside the city. It is true that Montaigne withdrew to the country to write his *Essays*, but it cannot be denied that their substance was taken from his life in Bordeaux.

And, we may add, the readers of those *Essays*, like the readers of Henry Thoreau's *Walden*, are, today as yesterday, mostly city bred and educated. Man's greatest work is the city. The more energetically and fervently he yearns for anything on this earth, the more he works, consciously or unconsciously, to build the city. It is useless for the urbanists to wail: "We drew up beautiful plans for your cities, and you did not build them." The city of civilized man is itself its own builder. "The tractors, bulldozers, cement mixers, and air-compressors, announcing the heavy clouds of factory smoke, a job, getting up joylessly to a sunless sky and dirty air—" all are drawn into being by the lure of city life, which is there, at least in spirit, long before any of them can make an appearance. And for all its pride, the same must be said of the life of the intellect.

We often ask ourselves these days: What will man's intellect devise for his happiness tomorrow? In our wildest dreams and flights of imagination, it is always a metropolis that we envision.

Anne Paolucci

Heaven itself is conceived as a glorious city of God. And for those who prefer the company of the devil in eternity, there are authorities enough who say that hell too has its city. Damned or blessed, in hell or heaven as on earth, therefore, our intellects are held more or less fixed by the lure of the city.

2. the Medieval city

Craig Fisher

With few temporary setbacks Western Europe has experienced a continuous expansion in population, agricultural production, technology, trade, and industry since the year 1000. Accompanying this expansion has been a continual development of cities; these cities have been the result of both social and economic growth and at the same time the cause of further progress. It is not surprising that modern theorists who advocate the end of social and economic expansion view the modern city with alarm. The city has been the laboratory for political experimentation, social mobility, racial solutions, and economic discoveries. We have come to assume that the city is by nature an everchanging, innovating institution, constantly upsetting established tradition.

However there have been and are other cultures where urban life has been highly developed but where the cities have ceased to be progressive centers, where the cities do not question or disturb the basis of the larger society, such as in the Roman Empire, Byzantium, Islam, China, and India. In these cases powerful, centralized governments have tamed the city to the ideals of an older, more conservative society.

The modern city of Western Europe has maintained its progressive, innovative character at least in part because of its peculiar origin and early development in the Middle Ages. The modern European-type city is descended not from the Greek or Roman city but from the medieval city.

Between the fall of the Roman Empire of the West in the fifth century and the beginning of social and economic expansion in the eleventh century, there was a period of six centuries during which the city ceased to be the most important social unit in Western Europe. There has been much debate as to how far the city as an institution disappeared, but it is clear that the most important, most complex social unit in these centuries was no longer the city but the monastery. The early medieval monastery essentially took over the cultural role of the ancient city: it maintained education, libraries, medicine, the crafts, hostelries for travelers, and even a basic civic structure with elected abbot, council, and assembly of all the monks. However, in economic terms, the monastery was closer to the manor or estate than to the city. Unlike the city, which gained its food from the countryside by exchanging its imports and manufactured goods and which has reciprocal trade with other cities, the monastery lived off its own land and sought to be as economically independent as possible.

In these six centuries of the first half of the Middle Ages, society worked out a three class system on the basis of function— the clergy as spiritual leader, the feudal lord as warrior, and the serf as farmer. This six hundred year break in the development of cities is most important, because when cities began to reappear in the eleventh century the urban class was a new element in a strongly organized society, an element which could not be easily fitted into traditional society. This new class of merchants and artisans came to be called by a special term, the bourgeoisie. If a citizen of an ancient Greek or Roman city-state were able to study the medieval city's structure, he would remark that this society was upside-down, the very reverse of his own. In the ancient city-state the rural aristocrat and the free farmer were regarded as the foremost citizens. They only tolerated the city craftsman in politics during democratic regimes and often, as in Athens during the democracy, excluded the usually foreign-born merchant from active participation in government. In the medieval city, the merchant was the foremost citizen, the artisan and laborer came next, while both the farmer and the rural aristocrat were excluded from citizenship. Even in Italy, where nobles resided in the cities, they were sometimes excluded from politics. Thus the merchants and artisans really dominated the medieval city and made it impossible for the city to be integrated into either the feudal military system or the manorial agricultural society.

Initially, kings tried to deal with these new cities as vassals. But the feudal lord-vassal relationship was an extremely personal contract between two men; while it might be regarded as a corporate body, the city could not easily fit into this personal contract of allegiance. More importantly, the merchants and artisans of the city did not want to render knightly military service, which was the basis of the feudal contract. On the other hand, the feudal nobility regarded the upstart bourgeoisie as unfit for real warfare and socially excluded the merchant from knighthood.

While the city merchant or artisan did not become a member of the feudal order, he could not be realistically included in the class of the manorial serf, though churchmen and knights often tried to consider him as serf. During the later Middle Ages when parliaments were organized, both city men and farmers were put together into the Third Estate. In order to pursue a trade or a craft, the city resident sought official privilege to be distinguished from the serf. To gain such privileges cities went to the traditional authority of justice, the king. They negotiated by appealing to mutual interests or by using political pressure, gifts, and even violence for charters of privileges. These charters, in varying degree, freed city residents not only from serf status but also in part from public authority itself. Nineteenth century historians like to picture the serf fleeing from the manor to freedom in the city. It would perhaps be more realistic to observe that the manor's lord and the serfs were probably glad to get rid of a young serf impoverished by the overpopulation of the manorial village.

Among the first privileges the city resident sought was a guarantee of his own personal freedom which would be extended to his descendants. He also negotiated for the right to own and bequeath property. The serf did not enjoy these rights, but the merchant or artisan could hardly have carried on his occupation without such guarantees. The merchants of the city would further seek by charter freedom from tolls and even the right to set up certain monopolies against outsiders. A more developed city sought the concession to administer justice within its walls and over its residents. This was needed because the merchant law of sales and contracts was a novelty and required specially experienced judges. Also, the men of the city did not trust the social justice of royal judges drawn from the class of feudal knights. Finally, justice was extremely profitable in the days when there were no prisons but when the fine or corporal punishment was exacted immediately. For these reasons cities sought the freedom to administer justice and were willing to pay a high price for it.

If the monarchies of Western Europe had been more powerful and effective in the eleventh and twelfth centuries, the new cities might not have been able to gain such privileges. However, the kings of that period found it difficult to force their will on a walled and resolutely defended city. Further it was often to the king's advantage to support cities. They provided royal outposts in the territories of unruly vassals and could supply the king with able administrators. Most important, cities could furnish money to the king in the form of taxes or loans.

When central governments collapsed in northern Italy and later in Germany, the medieval city achieved autonomy and became a city-state. It subjected a rural territory to insure its food supply, taxed citizens and subjects, and waged war on rival cities. Even in this enlarged area, the merchants and artisans, organized

19

in guilds, controlled the politics of the city. Thus the chartered city springs from the medieval period as does our tradition of bourgeois hostility toward both nobility and farmers. In short, the evolution of the middle class stems from the medieval city.

The medieval city, like its modern counterpart, occupied and developed a site. A consideration of the plans of several cities will illustrate some of their main features and will point out some of the differences between them and ancient or modern cities.

In the case of Trier, the relationship between a Roman city and its medieval successor can be traced (figures 1 and 2). Trier, situated on the Moselle River, a western tributary of the Rhine, was founded as a Roman colony by Augustus about 13 B.C. The colony was to provide a Roman stronghold, settled probably by veterans from the army, to help control the newly organized frontier of the empire. The city was laid out in a grid pattern; the Romans as engineers appreciated an orderly city with square or rectangular blocks. An open space, or forum (F), was provided, and later an aqueduct and amphitheater (A) were built, while the main north-south street was decorated with colonnades. The following centuries were a rare period of security for the Roman Empire, and no walls surrounded the colony. However, in 275 Germanic invaders sacked the city.

Trier was rebuilt after 300 by the Roman emperors as a military capital for the western provinces. Now a larger area was walled, a palace complex (P) was added with its baths (b), and a new Christian cathedral (C) was built. The population may have reached as high as 60,000. Shortly after 400 the Rhine frontier collapsed and Trier was sacked four times in the following century. By 800, the city had been changed in form. Its center was now the cathedral (C) where the archbishop, who was the lord of the area, still had his capital. There were three monasteries (M) beyond the Roman walls. In fact there was no longer a city within the walls but rather six rural villages (V) whose inhabitants were attracted by the religious establishments

Craig Fisher

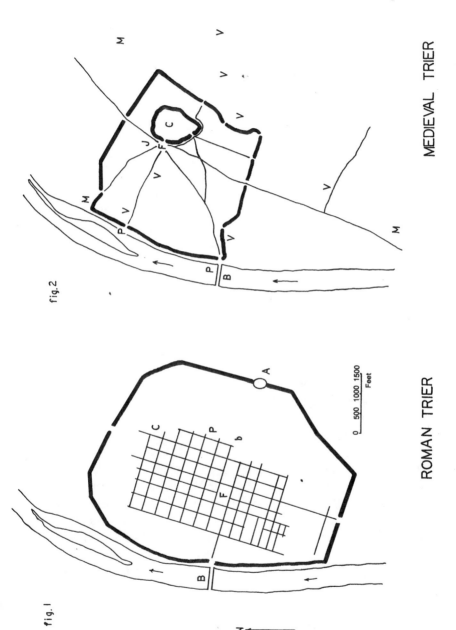

MEDIEVAL TRIER

fig.2

ROMAN TRIER

0 500 1000 1500
Feet

fig.1

and the good land of the area. The Roman walls were in decay with too few people in the villages to man them.

In 882, the Vikings coming up the river sacked churches and villages. The archbishops rebuilt the cathedral in the 900s, erected new walls around their church, and set up a regular market (F) at the gate. A Jewish quarter (J) also came into being. The trade of the city grew: salt from up the river, a major local wine industry, and some manufacturing of glass. The plan shows that the streets no longer followed the Roman grid but rather the paths of traffic: the main road from north to south and other roads from the market to the bridge (B) and river ports (P). Clearly there had been a long break in the inhabitation of the city for the ancient streets and property lines no longer existed. About 1120, during a period of prosperity, the archbishop began to build new, more extended walls using the Roman walls for half of the course. When the walls were finished in 1150, it was the citizens of Trier who finished them; the archbishop had been temporarily driven from the city. Trier had a limited economic role. In 1300, its population was only 8,000, one seventh the size of the Roman provincial capital; as late as 1850, the city was still within the medieval walls.

East of the Rhine beyond the frontier of the Roman Empire, where no cities had been built, the medieval city was completely new. The counts of Zahringen, who had recently built their castle (figure 3, B) on a small eastern tributary of the Upper Rhine, needed a merchant center for supplies. In 1120 they chartered a "free city," Freiburg, at the foot of their castle hill. Each merchant who wanted to settle there was guaranteed certain liberties and was rented a lot 50 by 100 feet for his house. The count had laid out a broad street for the merchant houses and for a market. An area for the parish church (P) was set aside to the east of this street and a plot for a hall of justice (C), later the city hall, to the west. (In medieval symbolism, east was spiritual; west, secular.)

As merchants filled the main street and as artisans were

attracted to the new settlement, they built up side streets. Apparently they preferred curved streets because they cut down the wind and thus made the heating of houses easier. Curved streets also increased the sense of security because it was thought that they would confuse an invading enemy, and they were regarded as more beautiful since they emphasized the variety of house fronts. Straight streets were unnecessary since the medieval city had no rapid traffic. Walking or horseback riding were the normal means of transportation. Large carts were rare since most goods were carried by porters or beasts. Later in the twelfth century, the settled area was enclosed by a wall. As at Trier, the walls were an indication that the citizens were undertaking their own defense even against their landlord-count.

By the thirteenth century, European kings were powerful enough to build new cities. In 1248, the French king, Louis IX, began to build the port city of Aigues-Mortes (figure 4) in the Rhone River delta as a staging point for his crusade to the Near East. The city walls were finished by the end of the century. The city was laid out on a grid of five streets each way; the French king could control the street pattern better than the German count at Freiburg. The royal tower (t) was located at a point to command the rectangular fortifications of the city, while a parish church (c) was set up on the main square. Though medieval Aigues-Mortes probably never had more than 4,000 inhabitants, the size of the modern population, in the predominantly agricultural society of its day it had far more political and economic importance than a modern town of the same limited size.

What clearly distinguished this city from a village of that period was its walls. The city walls were the most expensive civic project and were designed both for security and stark beauty. Unlike the ancient Roman city with its temples, public baths, theaters, arena, aqueducts, and colonnaded main streets, the medieval city had few civic monuments other than its walls and parish churches. The medieval businessmen who paid the taxes preferred utility over monumentality. Walls also closed

23

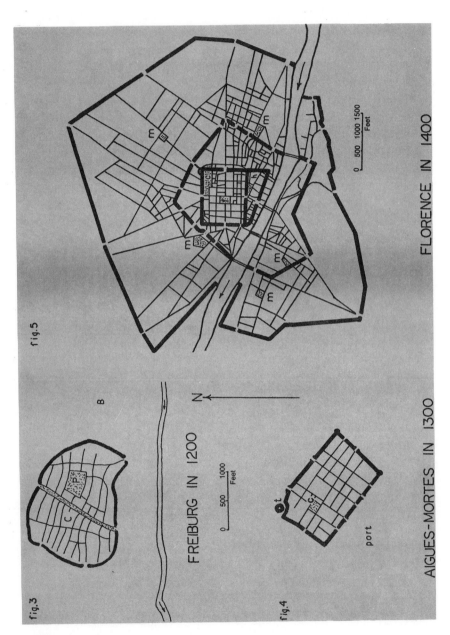

FLORENCE IN 1400

fig.5

0 500 1000 1500
Feet

FREIBURG IN 1200

0 500 1000
Feet

fig.3

AIGUES-MORTES IN 1300

fig.4

port

in the city-dwellers; at the end of each street there was to be seen either a gate, always locked at night, or the wall itself. The residents seemed to have preferred to see nature outside the walls. There were few open squares and no parks inside the city, though most houses had gardens—usually for vegetables.

Florence is often regarded as a city of the Renaissance. But the fifteenth century architects only decorated the facades of a medieval city (figure 5). Here in Italy it is clear that Roman cities were often continuously inhabited well into the medieval period. The grid pattern of streets within the first rectangular Roman walls was essentially maintained in later Florence. The site of the ancient forum (f) was still the main market of the medieval city. Here, unlike the case of Trier, the early cathedral (c) did not become the center of the city.

By the 1000s Florence was outgrowing the Roman walls, and a triangular area between the walls and the Arno River, known as the merchants' quarter, was added. With each new series of walls, the now useless stretches of walls were dismantled and normally were transformed into streets. In 1172, an entirely new circuit of walls was begun, now enclosing a territory across the river. When the new religious orders, such as the Franciscans and Dominicans, appeared in the early thirteenth century, with their urban mission of preaching and social service, they established their houses (m) outside the main gates of the city. At the gates they could find both cheap land and the poor they were pledged to aid.

The suburbs outside the walls of the medieval city were the closest thing they had to modern slums; here only those who had nothing to lose or who were protected by religion were secure enough to live. Within the city the generally cramped quarters led to a mixture of classes and of residential, commercial, and industrial establishments.

In the medieval city only the poor commuted to work. The artisan worked in the front room of his house, the merchant stored and sold his goods in the street floor of his house, and even the chief officials of a city like Florence moved with their families into the city hall during their terms in office. Incidentally, these occupational residences increased security and lessened the need for large police forces.

When a third and much extended circuit of walls was being built, Florence was a metropolitan city, one of the most prosperous and populous cities of Europe with a population of 90,000 in 1328. As a wealthy and powerful city-state it was then building a monumental cathedral and campanile (c) and had just finished a new city hall (h), today called the Palazzo Vecchio. Such city halls were built for defense as well as monumentality. Each night the doors of the hall were locked by the magistrates against faction and rioting, even as the city gates were locked against outside enemies.

The medieval city came of literary age only late in the Middle Ages. By the thirteenth century most Italian cities had their more or less literary chronicles. Dante set his *Divine Comedy*, a fund of urban attitudes and animosities, in the year 1300. But it was not until the next generation that Boccaccio developed the short story as the peculiar literary form for an urban society. In his *Decameron* he still extolled the nobility and caricaturized merchants and artisans. However, the tragic story of a young man who falls in love with a weaver girl is revolutionary in suggesting that the lower urban class can love and can be worthy of tragedy (IV:7).

Modern urban theorists in criticizing the city of today are currently romanticizing and idealizing the medieval city. In fact, many a modern theorist would find a medieval city without sewers and with tanneries more unbearable than a modern smog-plagued metropolis. And while the medieval city to maintain its position presented a united front to the outsider and definitely had a sense of identity, internally the city was racked by factions, rivalry, and violence. Any glance at the police records of an

Craig Fisher

Italian city in this period reveals an amazing degree of personal assault. While the smaller size of the medieval city made contacts more personal than the largely impersonal nature of the modern city, enmities were at the same time more violent and less avoidable.

Clearly the medieval city was exposed to many of the problems of its modern counterpart. An abbot wrote of the French city of Laon in 1112, "No one was safe going into the streets at night."

3. the Italian Renaissance city: the city of Man

Edward J. Manetta

The Renaissance was an age of exploration, and the major discovery was a renewed appreciation of humanity itself. At this time a new spirit prevailed which stressed the importance of the individual, and there was apparent an extraordinary appreciation of men of merit. In this respect the Renaissance was not the rebirth of classical culture but the beginning of modern individualism and civilization. The new attitude quickly found expression in the art and architecture of the period, which visibly demonstrated a heightened consciousness of life and the beauty of this world rather than a medieval preoccupation with the afterlife.

In Italy the art of the Renaissance was supported by prosperous merchants and the ruling classes of the cities. Undeniably one of the major factors in the emergence of Renaissance culture and cities was the development of a middle class composed of craftsmen, professionals, and merchants. This element became sufficiently powerful both in numbers and wealth to effectively check the influence of the feudal aristocracy and challenge the ideals of the culture which this noble group championed. The triumph of the middle class over the feudal aristocracy represented the victory of the city over the rural countryside.

Throughout Italy the expansion of city culture accompanied the rise in trade. Florence, in particular, was noted for her finished cloth, which was sold throughout Europe. In more ways than one her economic expansion provided the basis for her cultural leadership. As her wealth increased, the guilds of the city commanded ever greater influence and wealth. Eventually the city, and with it much of the patronage of the arts, fell into their hands. Secular support of art, architecture, and urban renewal had a profound impact on the nature of artistic production of the period.

During the early sixteenth century Italy began to furnish the modern world with a cultural leadership comparable to that exerted by Athens during later antiquity, setting the pace in art, architecture, literature, and fashion. In the years that followed almost the entire European world consciously discarded the style and spirit of the late Gothic age and adopted the worldly style of the Italian Renaissance.

Venice and Rome were jewels in their own right, but of the various cities, Florence set the standard, assuming cultural command of Italy and the continent as well. Nowhere else, with the possible exception of ancient Athens, were the inhabitants of a city so involved with ideas, so intellectual by nature, so keen in their perception, so immersed in art. The Florentines developed a culture that stimulated the imagination of all of Europe and has continued to command admiration and respect to this day.

Florence's artistic primacy was carefully nurtured by her merchants and political figures. Not only painters, but artists, sculptors, philosophers, and poets were generously subsidized and made to feel important. The business and political classes of the city had a sincere love of learning, considering it the best road to cultivation and true happiness. In line with this belief, academies were established for the various arts, and public libraries were opened. During a period of some thirty years Cosimo de Medici spent the equivalent of *twenty million dollars* for manuscripts and books alone. He expanded the functions of the various academies and spent lavishly for public buildings, festivals, and pageants. He, like others of his house, subsidized and endowed the Renaissance. The embellishment of the city had political implications as well for it tended to demonstrate the well-being of Florence during Medici control. Civic pride, ambition, and competition all worked to make Florence the showcase of the world.

The Renaissance produced not only great and beautiful cities but a cluster of artist-geniuses who could well be called "universal men." Included in this category were such figures as Leonardo da Vinci, Michelangelo Buonarroti, Donato Bramante, and Andrea Palladio. Within the Renaissance city artists were accorded a high position in society; their work was highly valued. It was under their inspiration and direction that the cities of Italy were transformed into artistic masterpieces that still inspire awe and admiration.

Since Renaissance culture flourished in the cities, the wealthy commissioned the building of palaces, town houses, and private chapels in the urban centers of Florence, Rome, and Venice. Municipalities called for fountains, public squares, and new city halls, while the secular and the regular clergy called for new churches and places of worship. One of the greatest architects and city planners of his generation was Donato Bramante. Under the influence of Brunelleschi, Alberti, and Leonardo, he developed the high Renaissance form in architecture, achieving a powerful symmetry in his works which invited imitation.

The Renaissance cities were made up of buildings which presented a completely balanced and symmetrical aspect. Like a three dimensional essay in rational order, all the parts were placed in harmonious relation to one another and to the whole; yet each part was complete and independent, an entity unto itself. In many respects the Renaissance cities expressed the ideals of classical antiquity. While valuing the individuality of the new age, they also revealed their debt to the classical concern for regularity, simplicity, and above all dignity.

The influence of Greek art upon Renaissance architecture is well known. Equally important was the adoption of the Greek style in the construction of buildings and cities. Architecturally speaking, the Greek concept of building structure is dealt with in sculptural terms—that is, to visualize the completed building and city as a totality, setting the masses each with a familiar geometric pattern arranged in such a manner that each has an equal exterior or some other mathematical scheme of easily comprehended regularity.

To this love for regularity and order the Renaissance man brought his preoccupation with individuality and competition. As an example of the intense competition which existed among the guilds within the trades and crafts, some craftsmen such as stonemasons had their individual trademarks. These identified the mason, and the particular grid design identified the guild in which he served his apprenticeship. The same quest for personal identity which exists today is but one of the legacies of the Renaissance city.

In order to comprehend the development of the Renaissance city we must appreciate that it often expressed the feelings of the individuals who created it and who believed that man could realize the highest good by being true to himself. Everything depended upon the individual's confidence that his body, his mind, and even his personality constituted an artistic form. The shape it took in this case was architecture, as the city itself became an artistic concept. The activities of the everyday life of the people were reflected in monuments, passageways, and public places as the entire city became an ambience of art.

For many artists of the Renaissance, philosophy was as important as form. As Alberti explained, the manual work done by the artists (architects and city designers were artists, not

31

merely engineers and politicians) was directed not only by craft rules but also by principle comprehensible only to the most precious of human characteristics, the intellect. Perhaps the most important artistic idea put forward by Alberti was his notion that beauty was a philosophical reality beyond the reach of taste and fancy.

Among the great Renaissance figures was Michelangelo, whose career covered all those Renaissance ideals that we conceptualize as "inspired genius" or "universal man." Although he was an architect, painter, poet, and engineer, he thought of himself as a sculptor first, since sculptors shared in something like the divine power to make man. In his view the artist was not the creator of the ideas he conceives; rather he finds them in the material world, and they are the reflections of the absolute idea which is beauty.

Michelangelo's entire inspiration came from the human body, which was for him the visible aspect of the soul. In his own words, "The parts of a structure and plan follow the forms exemplified in the body." Beauty is attainable through the relationships of the parts in perfect harmony one with the other; art is produced through the total harmony of the spiritual and the physical, the perfect mixture of the material and the conceptual. The cities of the Renaissance attempted to follow this prescription, and some succeeded.

Rome, for example, which had been a spiritual and political capital, was turned into a symbol of power and majesty through its architectural achievements. To further portray her strength and spirit, Michelangelo was commissioned to reorganize the Capitoline Hill, the facade of the Palazzo dei Conservatori, and St. Peter's. To this day these are monuments of imaginative planning, with lasting beauty and permanence. City planning and development was undertaken by the artist rather than the bureaucrat or administrator, and the enduring results are the eloquent testimony of their achievement. Nonetheless, credit

32

must be given to the political class of the age for their vision in the selection of artists for this urban renewal and beautification.

Another important aspect of city development was the planning and redesigning of the *piazze* or city squares which adorned most Italian cities and which formed an important center of urban life. Traditionally these squares had been designed as roomlike enclosures, and this had been the practice right to the time of the Renaissance. Michelangelo, however, with his imagination and foresight, chose to ignore tradition and structured his city squares in such a manner as to leave one side completely open. A classic example of the new style is St. Peter's Square in Rome, which has its main entrance free of all obstruction. The design rapidly became the prototype of squares throughout the European world. The Latin countries of Europe, and especially Spain and France, imported the Italian standards of city design and were influenced not only by Michelangelo but also by the master architect Andrea Palladio.

The architectural influence of Palladio is so important that one cannot possibly do justice to his greatness in a few sentences. The value of his books on architecture alone influenced designers and builders in cities throughout the Western world. These works contained precise information and directions with accurate drawings for construction of moldings, columns, doorways, and porticos. Some of the finest buildings in Renaissance Italy were designed by Palladio, and countless others were inspired by his work. Innovative concepts such as the covered market places not only found immediate acceptance but have continued to illustrate the permanence and genius of his work. His plans for country houses, palaces, and churches demonstrate a modernity and a versatility that places him in the ranks of men such as Michelangelo and Da Vinci. His influence transcended Italy, indeed Europe, and reached the shores of America as well.

EARLY URBANIZATION AND THE DAWN OF CIVILIZATION

In art, architecture, and city planning, Renaissance men brought about changes which have had an amazing power of persistence. Indeed, most of the buildings which predominate in our urban environment today in one way or another trace their genesis to the age of the Renaissance—the period which ushered in the modern urban world.

4. the preindustrial city: a view of the World we have lost

Frank J. Coppa

Perhaps the most remarkable feature of the world's history since 1700 has been the extraordinary expansion of its human population. From 1600 to 1900 it tripled, and it has almost doubled in the twentieth century. Intimately linked to this population explosion has been an unprecedented and, in the eyes of some, a dangerous concentration of people in cities the world over. The creation of an urbanized society, having from one-third to one-half its population in cities, has frightened as well as fascinated observers and has captured the imagination of historians, economists, and social scientists. City life is almost as old as civilized man, and it is no exaggeration to say that to understand the latter, one must have some knowledge of the former.

Undeniably the village contains in embryonic form many of the features found in the city including houses, religious shrines, and craftsmen. It also takes the first steps toward the establishment of organized morality, law, and government. What the village lacks is the concentration of population found in urban areas, the same degree of social and economic stratification, and finally the same sense of separation that the city has from the countryside. The ancient Egyptians depicted the

EARLY URBANIZATION AND THE DAWN OF CIVILIZATION

city as a cross within a circle. The circle indicates a moat or wall, or even some nonmaterial, moral means of keeping strangers out and the inhabitants together.

The cross represents the convergence of roads which bring in men, goods, and ideas for exchange, examination, and exposition. The crossroads is a reminder of the important role played by commerce in the evolution of cities, but one should not neglect to cite the industrial development that took place within their walls—an experience which decisively determined the nature of more than one medieval town.

Indeed, urban economic evolution has provided a convenient means of classifying towns both in the capitalist and communist world. Social historians in the Soviet Union classify towns in terms of Marxist categories. They speak of the slave-owning city, the feudal city, the capitalist city, and their culmination, the socialist city. In the West scholars of urbanism have pointed to different types of settlements on the basis of their economic functions. They speak of the stockade city, the agrarian city, the market city, and the industrial city. Within this second system of categorization, the first three types of urban phenomena are all preindustrial and therefore share certain common characteristics.

The precise manner in which towns originated is still being debated. According to one view, that of Lewis Mumford, the historic role of transforming the village into the city was undertaken by its dynamic, masculine population. In his opinion their activity turned the community away from the more feminine village concerns of nutrition and reproduction. A citadel or stockade was built, and in it were hoarded the supplies and goods of the community, part of which, very likely, was plundered. In this manner there was created a species of scarcity in the midst of plenty. Mere physical power and coercion, however, did not suffice to legitimize their arbitrary action. To create a more general compliance, the hunter-chieftains turned to religion, and shared their spoils in order to secure priestly sanction. Thus Mumford claims that the first cities, the stockade cities, were created by an alliance of military, political, economic, and religious interests.

The stockade has appeared at various times and places. When seafaring Norsemen established their dominion over the Slavs, they congregated in groups in order to insure control. They also huddled in fortified enclosures called *gorods* in the Slavic language, and these entrenched camps gave rise to the oldest Russian cities. Similar walled enclosures in the west were called *burgus*, a word preserved in all the modern languages: *burg, borough, bourg,* and *borgo*. These burgs, which were originally military establishments, soon became administrative centers as well.

Although the stockade town appeared at the dawn of civilization, it survived in colonial and frontier areas to quite recent times. Such towns were the spearhead of the American frontier, serving as forts or trading posts far in advance of the line of settlement. They secured the west for the approaching population. The stockade proper enclosed the control towers of the district, some housing, and the all important storehouse. This central area did not serve as a place of general residence. The entire population of the district gathered in this space only on special occasions, such as religious holidays, when threatened by some natural or man-made calamity, or when a special fair was held. The stockade also served as a center of exchange for ideas and goods.

When the landowners of the district supervised by the control towers established themselves permanently within the stockade, the agrarian city was born. They came into the center because they craved the security, comfort, and prestige of dwelling inside the walls. They were able to come because they had dependents outside the wall to till the soil and bring their harvests into the city. In turn, they were followed by merchants and artisans, who catered to their needs within the city. Since these individuals depended upon the consumption of the urban landowning class, trade and manufacture had but a limited market and little potential for expansion. Not surprisingly, within the agrarian city, the proprietary or landowning class set the style of life which the productive class slavishly emulated, hoping someday to likewise shun economic pursuits and enjoy a life of leisure.

Most of the urban areas of the ancient world were of this type, but agrarian cities survived to the modern period. During the sixteenth century Spanish urbanization in the new world displayed a number of striking features characteristic of the agrarian city. For one thing, such Spanish colonial centers in the new world lacked extensive industrial development, in part because the Law of the Indies forbade any form of manufacturing that might compete with the economic development of peninsular Spain. Furthermore, town life was largely controlled by the landed oligarchy that commanded the rural supply of goods. Finally, these towns were divided not only on the basis of class and occupation but also along racial lines. After initial confusion a form of apartheid was practiced. In the Spanish cities of America there were two distinct sectors: that designed for the white population and the Indian barrios that supplied most of the lower class services.

The mood and nature of urban society changed dramatically when the merchant replaced the landowner in determining the pace of city life, that is, when the market city appeared. Such a city did not emerge simultaneously with the market, which was to be found in the agrarian and even in the stockade city. Rather it appeared when market and public square became one, when the merchant became the most important individual in town. This occurred in more than one area, but nowhere was the transformation as sweeping as western Europe and particularly Italy from the tenth to the fourteenth centuries.

This urban transformation was in large part due to the agricultural revival in the countryside. Just as the Industrial Revolution and the industrial city were made possible by an agricultural revolution, the urban revolution of the eleventh to the fourteenth centuries was in large measure dependent upon changes in the countryside including the immense extension of arable land throughout Europe, the application of more adequate means of husbandry, and the widespread use of irrigation. Italy assumed a commanding position in the revival of agriculture, trade, industry, and urbanization. She was not only geographically closer to the advanced civilizations of the east but also virtually surrounded by the remnants of Roman civilization with its strong urban tradition.

A number of factors enabled the Venetians to assume a singular place in the economic history of Europe. In her drive for commercial supremacy, Venice was assisted by the agricultural revival on the continent which increased her trading prospects. She took advantage of this development by obtaining permission from the German emperors to trade with the whole of Italy. At the same time her close relationship with the Byzantine Empire, and its capital, Constantinople, the greatest city of the Mediterranean basin, contributed to her trade and prosperity. The residents of Venice also proved to be inventive, developing a new type of city based on the differentiation and zoning of various urban functions. These different areas were separated by waterways and open spaces, but tied together by bridges and boats. Modern city planners can still learn from the Venetians, whose division of their city into industrial and residential areas did not destroy the unity of the "Queen of the Adriatic," but kept its core from becoming blighted and congested.

Venice's success inspired rivals, and Pisa and Genoa contested her commercial supremacy. By 1300, Genoa, known as "the haughty one," was a dynamic market town. Her population of 100,000 made her the fourth largest city in Italy, and outside the peninsula only Constantinople surpassed her. In her quest for profits she was the first city in the west to have used arabic numerals in business transactions, first to have equipped her seamen with navigation maps, and earliest to provide her merchants with maritime insurance contracts. Her government was a model of mercantile efficiency, keeping accounts in accordance with the latest principles of banking, Its consolidated public debt was so well administered that it sold above par in the open market.

Genoa belies the old cliché that the life style of all preindustrial cities was leisurely and time was not of import. Indeed the time element was so important there that contracts were dated not only by the day but by the hour. Nor was its population ignorant or passive. Rather it was competitive, if not aggressive, and illiteracy was all but unknown, as even the lower elements in the city were drawn into its economic and commercial ventures. Nor is it true that religion dominated every aspect of life in this preindustrial city. Rather the laws of business were supreme in their own sphere and not even shunted aside for the principles of canon law. This preoccupation with the profit motive excited the envy and criticism of their contemporaries who charged that the Genovese violated every tradition, displayed an insatiable greed, and engaged in ruthless competition with their neighbors.

The legal status of the individual within a city such as Genoa was that of freedom. The air of the city makes one free says the German proverb, and indeed even the serf who lived within its walls for a year and a day was entitled to freedom. Whatever the difference in wealth and social position, men in the cities enjoyed the same civil status. With freedom of the individual there was a freedom of the land, which could easily be bought and sold. A price had to be paid for this freedom, and for the lower classes this came in the form of greater restriction in the occupational sphere.

In no culture has a city evolved independently of agriculture, commerce, and industry. A market city could only live by importing its food supply from the outside, but this importation of food could only be continued by the exportation of manufactured goods to pay for its foodstuff. There was thus a new premium on production. Specialization, it was found, facilitated the manufacture of most goods. In the preindustrial cities this was a specialization in a particular product rather than specialization in a process. Still, even this type of specialization limited the individual's scope of economic activity. In the village and even in the stockade and agrarian city, he was not yet a specialist, confined to one craft. Only with the emergence of the market city did specialized work become for the first time an all day, year-round occupation.

A number of factors made the life of the specialist in the city bearable. There was a certain creativity in the work, and since the craftsmen produced the entire project, a certain pride and satisfaction followed its completion. What also made life bearable, if not pleasant, was the wide range of associations the resident enjoyed within the city. He was a member of a family, guild, and church, as well as a commune.

In many ways the most important representative of corporate life was the guild, which provided two bases for fellowship: common work and common religion. The merchant guild was a general body organizing and controlling the economic life of the town as an entity. The craft guild, on the other hand, was an association of masters in their own field to regulate production and establish norms of workmanship. Together they not only governed the town but controlled admission to almost every occupation connected with manufacture, trade, or even service. Just as the Church provided spiritual assistance from

41

baptism to extreme unction, the guilds provided material welfare and assistance from the cradle to the grave, and often built their own schools and asylums. It was largely through their efforts that the market town succeeded, as had no former urban culture, in providing for its sick, aged, suffering, and poor.

In the sixteenth and seventeenth centuries the city had to face the phenomenon of the resurgence of the village. By this time the disparity between city and countryside, politically speaking, had been largely removed. This new parity was abetted by the fact that security was gradually established in the provinces by the power of the consolidated nation state. Improved water transport and the introduction of better roads also served to reduce the remoteness of the countryside.

Merchant capitalists were quick to take advantage of this situation by farming out their work to the countryside. By so doing they could pay subsistence wages instead of the going town rates. At the same time they would escape the regulations of the guilds concerning the quantity and quality of production. It was under such a system that child labor became a major problem. To make matters worse, spinners and weavers lost ownership of the means of production and had to rent their implements. Moreover, scattered over the countryside the cottage workers could not readily communicate with each other or decide upon a common policy. Unorganized in guilds, they could not claim nor receive the protection of these town institutions. Since they owned neither the raw materials which they worked nor the finished product, they had lost their status as independent workers well before the Industrial Revolution.

The towns' economy suffered not only from the exodus of manufacturers but also from changing patterns of trade. The Atlantic Revolution, which created a global market and stimulated trade and manufacture, worked to the advantage of first Portugal and Spain, later England, France, and the Low Countries. The cities of Italy and Germany which had resisted incorporation were unable to profit from this commercial revolution. To make matters worse, military factors combined with the economic to weaken the autonomous cities. The old adage that gunpowder brought about the ruin of feudalism is not true. Rather it worked to undermine the autonomy of the free cities by forcing them to build heavier and more permanent fortifications, making expansion difficult and land within the cities far more valuable. It led to unfortunate patterns of housing, the absence of recreational areas, and destined a large part of their populations to substandard housing.

The cities also found themselves in conflict with the increasing power of the national monarchies. In fact, where monarchy consolidated first as in England, southern Italy, and Austria, the cities were kept in a state of subordination. Where cities resisted such incorporation as in Italy and Germany, they found themselves vulnerable to attack from the large and powerful nation states and their freedom much curtailed. The loss of municipal freedom tended to remove one of the most important distinctions between Oriental and Western cities—the luxury of self-government. By the end of the eighteenth century, developments in England and western Europe were setting the stage for the Industrial Revolution which would also work to transform the market city. Within a short time its dominance would fall to the industrial city. In order to understand the character and significance of the newcomer, one should be familiar with its predecessor.

Preindustrial cities, whether of the past or present, share one common denominator—they are not products of the Industrial Revolution. Consequently they rely on animate rather than inanimate sources of power. Present day preindustrial cities in Africa and Asia seem to share many features of life in Europe before industrialization. They are not identical, however, because these cities of the Third World can draw upon the services of the industrial community even though they are not a

EARLY URBANIZATION AND THE DAWN OF CIVILIZATION

part of it. As a result many of the preindustrial cities of Asia and Africa have been able to reach a far greater size than most preindustrial European cities.

The preindustrial cities of Europe were small for a number of reasons. The wall surrounding the city obviously limited its size as did defense considerations. However, there were other limiting factors. The manufacturing capacity of such centers was limited, and hence so was their ability to purchase food and support a large population. Agriculture remained relatively backward and not mechanized and therefore could not support huge population centers. The poor system of transportation whch prevailed meant that available food could not be drawn from remote regions. Inefficient methods of food preservation and storage also made it impossible to draw upon the resources of rich though remote areas.

The form and arrangement of the preindustrial city was in part determined by its economic and social structure. Since most streets served as passageways for people and animals used in transport, they did not need to be wide. Indeed space considerations served to assure that they be narrow. Such narrow, winding passageways served to provide shelter from the wind, rain, and in southern climates, the sun. This protective function should not be overlooked because many activities and services were performed on the streets, which were a second home to the poor of the city. Generally occupational groups resided apart from one another, providing some rationality for manufacturing and marketing.

The center of a preindustrial city was usually dominated by religious and political structures, even though the market may have been nearby. The core area was also the home of the ruling elite. Disadvantaged members of the community fanned out toward the periphery while the poor lived in the suburbs. In part, this pattern was a reflection of the poor transportation facilities.

The wealthy chose to live in the center of the city because they did not wish to be inconvenienced by a long, uncomfortable, and potentially dangerous trip. Another reason the center was preferred as a place of residence was that it represented the most secure area of the city.

The political class, which usually consisted of no more than ten percent of the social order, was composed of individuals holding positions in government, religion, or the guilds. They monopolized the most prestigious occupations, especially those involving mental rather than manual work. The most physically taxing, as well as the least remunerative work, fell to those at the bottom of the social ladder. Those at the top employed their prestigious posts, their money, conspicuous consumption, as well as their extended family relationships to maintain their supremacy.

In Naples as late as the nineteenth century the chasm between the classes remained wide. The ruling class, which flocked to the capital from every part of the kingdom and the peninsula, displayed countless features characteristic of a pre-industrial elite. They enjoyed extended family relations and showed an almost fanatical determination to protect the good name of their clan. Equally extreme was their attachment to pomp and ceremony, their ostentation in dress, and their affected speech and mannerisms. They flaunted their possessions in order to reassert and reinforce their upper class status. Perhaps most important of all, they showed an utter contempt for manual labor. *Dolce far niente* was the ideal of more than one aristocratic Neapolitan family. Their inactivity was relieved by the numerous balls, nightly soirees, the opportunity for amorous dalliances, drives through the countryside as well as the more fashionable streets of the city, and on some evenings conversations and card playing in one's box at the opera.

Far more numerous and in some ways more interesting and

45

important than the ruling elite were the milling thousands who inhabited the narrow streets and tenements of the port city, the forerunners of the modern slum dweller, the *lazzaroni*. Most likely deriving their name from the lepers, whose patron saint was Saint Lazarus, the *lazzaroni* were considered by some contemporaries to be the essence of all that was thieving, lazy, and corrupt. While it was fashionable for the upper classes to despise work and to live by their wit rather than the sweat of their brow, this was considered criminal when adopted by the lower classes.

Actually the *lazzaroni* displayed characteristics common to the lower classes among most preindustrial cities, but they seemed to carry these to an extreme. Thus they lived a good part of their lives in the street; they even slept and made love there. Not overly concerned about making money, this lower class element was determined to enjoy the leisure and the magnificent panorama which nature had endowed them with. In truth they did not require much. A plate of spaghetti and some bread, quenched with iced lemonade in the summer or hot coffee in the winter, seemed to keep them satisfied. Even their critics concurred that the Neopolitan poor were generally sober and were not inflamed by strong spirits as in the northern countries where the Industrial Revolution first took hold. They thrived on ice water and lemonade and the camaraderie of the streets of their beloved capital, which they made the most sung-about city in the entire world.

The preindustrial urban world, typified by cities such as Naples, was not without problems, and had to confront congestion, poverty, and even pollution. But the proportion of these problems was enlarged by the economic revolution at the end of the eighteenth and the beginning of the nineteenth century. One historian of the modern industrial city has observed that centers of this type were the result of three factors: the centralized nation state, the introduction of a new productive system, and a system of vastly improved communications and transportation. In the period from the sixteenth to the eighteenth century, the impact of the nation states was already being felt by the cities of Europe. The other two forces were soon to emerge and radically transform urban life.

PART II

INDUSTRIALIZATION AND URBANIZATION: THE EMERGENCE OF THE MODERN CITY

5. the age of iron and steam: an overview of industrialization

Frank J. Coppa

Despite the upheavals of the English, American, and French Revolutions, Europe following the Congress of Vienna, 1815, more closely resembled the continent at the time of the Peace of Utrecht, 1713, than it did Europe on the eve of the First World War. In the opening decades of the nineteenth century, the vast majority of people still earned their living from the soil and more than seventy-five percent of all Europeans lived in villages or isolated homesteads. Only in England and the Netherlands did the proportion of the population residing in towns and cities much exceed ten percent. Worldwide only three or four percent of the estimated population was to be found in towns of more than 5 thousand inhabitants.

The world of 1815 was one of candlelight and little night activity, of stagecoaches and sailing ships, of dirt lanes and gravel roads, of structured social classes and little mobility. Life in this environment was neither prosperous nor protracted. On the average, life expectancy was but twenty-five years, not much better than the century before.

Following the Revolutionary and Napoleonic Wars, most European cities remained market and political towns, the home of governmental bureaucracies and religious administrations, small shops, and handicraft industries. In their narrow, winding streets, craftsmen turned out wares as they had for centuries. Poorly lit by torches, candles, and oil lamps, both life and work patterns in such cities were determined by the availability of sunlight. Since rainstorms served as their only brooms, many of these cities were filthy; sanitary conditions were deplorable. This, in part, helps to explain the low life expectancy. Although most urban areas had experienced a steady growth, they did not as yet assume a modern aspect as regards either social stratification or economic development. Alexander of Russia returned in 1815 to a Saint Petersburg dominated by imperial palaces and magnificent churches. The Rome restored to the Papacy was plagued by tens of thousands of beggars, and even the Paris of Louis XVIII retained its medieval character.

Yet by 1914 urban patterns and life styles had drastically changed. A majority of western Europeans now lived in cities and worked in factories, shops, and offices. Europe's population residing in large cities of 100 thousand or more jumped from less than three percent in 1800 to more than twelve percent at the turn of the century and would reach twenty percent in 1950. Concurrently, there was a spectacular increase in the life expectancy, which doubled in the course of the nineteenth century. Furthermore, illiteracy, which had been almost universal among the lower classes, rapidly declined in Western Europe as almost all of its children were given the opportunity to attend publicly supported elementary schools. What brought about these dramatic, often startling changes?

The revolutionary changes that occurred in the first half of the nineteenth century and dominated the century to the close cannot be understood by a mere catalog of wars, revolutions, or even laws; reference must be made to Europe's economic life. After centuries of comparatively slow development, the island kingdom of Britain experienced a series of rapid agrarian and industrial changes which both to contemporaries and subsequent generations appeared revolutionary. One might well term a revolution any fundamental change which affects a large number of people, altering their mode of life and thought. Some have seen the entire history of the continent in the nineteenth century as the unfolding of two great revolutions: the political revolution in France and the revolution in agriculture and industry that emerged first in Britain and later in Western Europe. The French Revolution contributed to the evolution of liberalism and popular sovereignty; and it determined the nature of political conflicts and ideologies of the succeeding age. Revolution in the industrial arts and technology was required to fashion the social and economic features of the modern, urban world.

Observing that change was continuous, some historians consider the word "revolution" to be inappropriately applied to the evolution of the economy. Nonetheless, the term "Industrial Revolution" has a long, if controversial history. First employed by Frenchmen in the early nineteenth century to draw comparisons with their own revolution, it was given wider currency by the lectures of Arnold Toynbee published in 1884. By that time British reformers used the phrase in their search for the origins of contemporary problems. Since then it has remained standard usage for most economists. In order to evaluate the appropriateness of the term "revolution" to describe economic changes, one must assess the quality of life before and after industrialization and attempt to measure the magnitude of the transformation.

One economic historian, W. W. Rostow, has outlined the stages of economic growth and divided the process of industrialization into three broad phases. First noted was a preliminary period of 100 or so years, which makes possible the transition from a predominantly agrarian to a primarily manufacturing economy. This is followed by the crucial "take-off" phase, during which the rate of investment rises from five to ten percent and fundamental advances in production occur. Finally there ensues a period of industrial expansion which exploits the potentials of the new manufacturing techniques. The English economy in the mid-eighteenth century was in a transitional period. Although poor, it produced some surplus; and while relatively stagnant, it was not completely static.

Despite the fact that the country was still rural and agricultural, a number of towns were already important and the role of industry and commerce was far from negligible. In effect, Britain displayed those features that Rostow has deemed essential for "take-off," and this occurred between 1783 and 1802.

The economic consequences of industrialization in England are measurable. In part, these can be seen in the growth of national income per head, which roughly quadrupled in the nineteenth century. Likewise, the statistics of particular industries, in almost every case, show a sharp and continuous upturn after 1782. The number of blast furnaces increased ninefold from 1760 to 1805, as did the production of pig iron. In the two decades from 1780 to 1800 the number of cotton spindles doubled, and by 1830 the cotton industry employed some 500 thousand people, more than half of whom were to be found in factories located in urban areas. Industrialization changed both the way of earning a living and the way of life of the English. The proportion of the English population engaged in agriculture declined from forty-five percent in 1780 to twenty-four percent in 1830. By this time industrial production contributed about thirty-four percent of the national income and foreign trade, another ten percent. Both were vital to the well-being of the economy.

Britain, in the nineteenth century, was turned into the workshop of the world. Hand, animal, wind, and water power were superseded by the steam engine. This substitution was largely responsible for the establishment of factories, since steam could not be easily employed under the domestic system. At the same time metals, particularly iron and steel, replaced wood in the construction and engineering business. Coal, meanwhile, took the place of wood for heating homes and was essential for the generation of steam energy.

These changes were reflected in the English population. In 1700 it was some 5 million and by 1750 some 6 million— the increase in this fifty year period was not quite a million or between seventeen and eighteen percent. By 1800 the population was some 9 million, an increase of fifty-two percent in the second half of the eighteenth century. In England where the population would now increase about thirty percent each generation, the cities grew even more rapidly. For centuries English towns had been evenly spread over the countryside, their setting and size, with some few exceptions, determined by agriculture. In the middle of the eighteenth century the proportion of people living in cities of 5,000 or over was about fifteen percent. By 1800 no less than twenty-six percent of the population lived in such towns.

The growth of larger English towns was equally spectacular. At the opening of the eighteenth century there were only fourteen cities whose population exceeded 20 thousand, but by mid-century there were fifty-four. The industrial towns of Birmingham, Bradford, Bristol, Leeds, Liverpool, Manchester, and Sheffield, in addition to London, whose population passed the two million mark, had more than 100 thousand inhabitants. Manchester, which barely had 10 thousand inhabitants in 1750, reached 100 thousand in 1800 and by the mid-nineteenth century had 400 thousand!

It is not surprising that England, the first country to industrialize, became the most urbanized country in the world. No other state reached the degree of urbanization she had in 1800, until 1850. By 1860, fifty-five percent of the English population lived in areas classified as urban. By 1900 this had

55

INDUSTRIALIZATION AND URBANIZATION

jumped to seventy-two percent. This distribution of population clearly reflected changes in the economy, with population concentrating in the port cities, the London complex, or in the industrial cities of the coal fields.

Expansion of the English economy and the subsequent urbanization were in no small measure dependent upon the increase in the use of coal. England already used a proportionately large amount of coal at the beginning of the eighteenth century, and this consumption increased by leaps and bounds. The steam engine was evolved largely to solve the technical problems of draining the coal mines and hauling the heavy loads of coal. Coal was the fuel that enabled the iron industry to expand, and iron was the basic engineering material of industrialization and increasingly the vital structural material of the new urban centers. Coal also played an important role in the manufacture of bricks, the material that enabled construction to keep pace with the extraordinary urban expansion of the age. Considering the many uses for coal as a source of power and an essential element in countless urban related projects, it is not surprising that its production increased fivefold between 1800 and 1850.

Coal, which played a major role in industrialization, the population explosion, and urbanization, was ably assisted by the potato. Students of economic growth have long pointed to the importance of agriculture in the modernization of an economy. Professor Rostow, in elaborating his theory of stages of economic growth, has considered revolutionary changes in agricultural productivity essential for a successful "take-off." According to this view it is upon agriculture that a preindustrial economy had to depend for additional food, markets, and capital that allowed industrialization to proceed. Toynbee, too, saw the relationship between the reform of agriculture and the industrialization of England. Small wonder that an entire literature has evolved which considers an agricultural revolution no less

56

than a prerequisite for the modernization of transport, industry, and urban centers.

Certainly it is known that the Industrial Revolution in England was associated with an agricultural revolution. Prior to this development the best land was tilled in the open field manner. Under this system the arable land of each village was divided into three great strips, and then subdivided so that each farmer would get some land in each field. One strip was sown broadcast with a bread crop, for example wheat. Another was sown with a drink crop such as barley, while the third was left fallow to regain its fertility. The open field system was not productive, and it is not difficult to understand why. Since the same course of crops was necessary, no proper rotation was possible. Furthermore, much time was lost by laborers in traveling to dispersed pieces of land, and perpetual quarrels arose about rights and boundaries. Finally, there was the obvious wastefulness of leaving one third the land idle each year.

In England the agricultural revolution involved changes in agronomy and in proprietary arrangements. Specifically it meant the extension of arable land over heath and pasture land which had been held in common. Such enclosure of the commons had been going on for centuries before 1760, but with nothing like the rapidity which occurred afterwards. Enclosure of the land made possible farming on a large scale, in consolidated units in place of medieval fields cultivated in discontinuous strips. Unquestionably it was responsible for the dramatic increase in agricultural productivity, but at the price of transforming the village community of largely self-subsistent peasants into isolated agricultural laborers dependent upon the vicissitudes of the national economy.

Although the agricultural revolution was economically justifiable, its social effects were disastrous. Thousands of peasants suffered complete ruin, as the small farmer, cottager, and squatter were driven from the soil, their homes pulled down, and the land

57

INDUSTRIALIZATION AND URBANIZATION

they worked enclosed to form part of some larger estate. It was estimated that at the conclusion of the seventeenth century there was some 180 thousand small freeholders in England, but by the end of the eighteenth century this yeomanry had all but disappeared. The poet, playwright, and novelist Oliver Goldsmith decried this development in his poem, "The Deserted Village." In his view the yeomanry had two bleak prospects before them: industrial slavery in the cities or emigration to foreign shores. He considered both solutions unattractive. His lines suggested that in the city the peasant would find himself a pawn, surrounded by an affluence in which he could not share. Abroad, he would be uprooted, without values or tradition upon which he could rely. Critical of the growth of the cities at the expense of the countryside, Goldsmith warned,

> But a bold peasantry, their country's pride
> When once destroyed, can never be supplied.

Despite its unfortunate results, the agricultural revolution contributed to the industrial and urban revolution in three ways. First, it created a market for the industrial centers, by providing an increased surplus income which the urban and rural poor could spare from their subsistence needs to spend on manufactured goods. Second, it helped to create and feed the labor needed for industry. The extension of the arable land and the elimination of smaller producers not only encouraged the move to the cities, providing a labor force for the developing industries, but also assured the wherewithal to feed this teeming urban population. Without this increased food supply, the currency used to import cotton and wool for the textile industry would have gone to purchase food for the urban proletariat. Finally, it provided a substantial part of the capital required to finance industrialization both by investing in new industrial enterprises and by carrying the greater part of the tax burden of the state.

Some writers deem the agricultural revolution so important

that they attribute England's primacy in industrialization to her earlier agricultural reforms. No doubt these played a part, but a number of other factors were also important. England's capital accumulation was quickened by her island location and good ports which enabled her to develop the fishing industry and a flourishing overseas trade. She found a ready market for her goods because her land was compact and free from the tolls which burdened continental countries. The English market was made accessible by her location, by her rivers and canals, as well as turnpikes.

In her drive toward industrialization, England was blessed by a number of fortunate factors. She had coal, iron ore, and other minerals necessary for this economic transformation, and all were easily accessible. Long established craft industries provided the skilled labor needed for the factories, and she escaped the devastation of war to which the continental countries were subjected. Finally, England witnessed a number of innovations which changed technology and the organization of industry.

The most critical of the bottlenecks limiting the expansion of the British economy on the eve of the Industrial Revolution were two: the shortage of wood and the shortage of power. These limitations were overcome by converting Britain from a wood and water basis to one dependent upon coal and iron. This transformation which changed the nature of the island's economy and its cities was largely the work of two outstanding figures: James Watt who invented the steam engine and Henry Cort whose new furnace made possible a malleable form of iron.

The steam engine, first constructed in 1775, and improved thereafter, had a wide range of uses. Applied to industrial machinery it freed factories from dependence on water and air power and made it possible for large scale concerns to settle where the fuel and labor force were to be found. Until the nineteenth century industry more or less remained decentralized in small workshops. The use of Watt's steam engine as a prime mover modified this, as it did the quality of urban life.

INDUSTRIALIZATION AND URBANIZATION

When applied to the railway, the steam engine brought the unhealthy environment of the mine, once restricted to its original site, to practically every urban area. Smoke, noise, and dirt were jostled along with products and profits into the heart of almost every city. The railway age was made possible by the other crucial invention, Henry Cort's puddling process which brought into being a cheap and workable iron. The introduction of the puddling process permitted the iron industry to escape from dependence on the diminishing supply of native timber (it did not require the use of charcoal) and made it possible for the English to exploit their relatively abundant resources of coal and iron.

In conjunction with steam power, the availability of an inexpensive but durable iron supply helped to generate not only the machine system, the railway age, but the urban revolution as well. Quite clearly the main elements procreating the new urban complex were the mine, the factory, and the railroad. The economic foundation of the industrial centers rested upon the extensive exploitation of the country's coal and iron mines, a remarkable improvement in the quantity and quality of iron produced, and the use of a steady, stable source of power—Watt's steam engine.

Industrialization and the consequent urbanization developed first in England, reaching Belgium and France after 1815, Germany in the mid-century, and Italy and Russia toward the end of the century. Initially it appears surprising that large scale modern industry did not develop on the continent as readily as in Britain. France had a number of advantages that might have sparked early industrialization. In the eighteenth century her population was larger than that of Britain and she had a potentially larger labor force and a bigger home market. She was a wealthy country with both a rich agriculture and a flourishing overseas trade. The reputation of her craftsmen was unexcelled and her scientists took the lead in applying scientific knowledge to the solution of industrial problems. Furthermore, the French state had a long tradition of actively promoting manufacture and trade.

60

Frank J. Coppa

Germany, too, appeared to enjoy a number of advantages. She had high standards of industrial skills, and the techniques of her miners were copied the world over. In addition, she was richly endowed by nature with coal resources in the Ruhr, the Saar, and upper Silesia, while several of her fairs, including those of Leipzig and Frankfurt, attracted an international clientele. Equally important was her central position in Europe, which assured that large quantities of goods were transported on the Rhine and her other navigable rivers.

Unfortunately both in France and Germany these advantages were counterbalanced by forces hindering industrialization or at least retarding its development. In both countries internal custom barriers and troublesome road and river tolls shackled commerce and industrial expansion. In France the peasants were not pushed off the land as in England, so urbanization and industrialization proceeded much less rapidly. In Germany the lack of national unification until 1870 restricted the size of the market, although this was in part mitigated by the formation of the *Zollverein*. Eventually France and Germany industrialized and were to be subject to the problems as well as the profits of modernization.

During the Second Empire, 1852-1870, under the leadership of Napoleon III, the French economy passed from an artisan to an industrial basis. While the value of industrial production virtually doubled and the number of shops using steam power quadrupled, the urban population grew from one fourth to one third the total. Louis Napoleon took a special interest in industrialization and urbanization, which he believed to be the way of the future. This explains his concern for the country's cities, particularly Paris. Ably assisted by the Alsatian Prefect, G.E. Haussmann, Paris with its narrow streets and poorly lit tenements was converted into the city of lights, broad boulevards, and spacious squares whose population virtually doubled.

All the continents of the world, except Africa, grew enormously in population after 1700, but it was industrialized Europe that grew the most. As a result of industrialization the proportion of Europeans in the world reached an all time high from the revolutions of 1848 to the outbreak of the Second World War, when roughly one quarter of the world's population lived in Europe. While Asia increased threefold in population from the mid-seventeenth to the mid-twentieth century, Europe increased fivefold in the same period or more than sevenfold if its descendants who migrated to other continents are included.

Where did this increased population go? Within inner-Europe, the Europe of iron and steam, the tendency was for the population to concentrate in urban centers. The crux of this urban revolution lies not only in the migration of country people to the towns, but also in the growth of big cities at the expense of smaller towns. Increasingly the large city set the pace of modern society. Thus inner-Europe, which includes Belgium, Britain, France, northern Italy, and the western portions of Germany, contained not only most of the continent's capital, the heaviest concentration of heavy industry, the thickest railway network, but also the most important urban centers and the highest standard of living. Outer-Europe, which includes most of Ireland, the Italian and Iberian peninsulas, and eastern Europe, was overwhelmingly rural and agricultural and found itself politically and economically dependent upon the industrialized, urbanized West.

Beyond this region lay a third zone, the immense reaches of Asia and Africa. The long arm of western Europe flexed its powerful muscles in this area through its control of mines and oil wells, its exportation of technicians and capital, its virtual monopoly of modern technology, and the most efficient weapons of destruction science had devised. It dominated the world because its guns, its boats, and, perhaps most important, its wealth and economy triumphed from one end of the globe to the other. The people of the third world, with the exception of European-

62

ized, industrialized, urbanized Japan, were economically back-ward by European standards. They paid for their backwardness by falling prey to Western imperialism. By the eve of the First World War, Britain, France, and Germany alone accounted for seven-tenths of the world's productive capacity and for more than eighty percent of the world's foreign investments.

The western Europeans, having industrialized and set their market in order, turned to the rest of the world. In the three decades before the World War they partitioned most of the remaining world among themselves. The foreign territory owned by Britain was one hundred and forty times greater than the home country, Belgium's eighty times greater, and Holland's sixty times greater. Many attributed this to industrialization. Europe, which contained less than seven percent of the world's surface, controlled the greater part of its area and resources and had the highest standard of living. Small wonder that the under-developed, colonial world looked—and continues to look—to industrialization for liberation.

The United Nations has sympathized with the quest for modernization. It seems to believe that not only prosperity but peace can be achieved through industrialization. Industrializa-tion, however, is a double-edged sword, and a price has to be paid for the prosperity it promises.

6. industrialization and urbanization: European style

Frank J. Coppa

That the road to prosperity is paved by industrialization and urbanization is almost a dogma of the modern world. Undeniably, there is a striking difference in the standard of living of "developed" and "underdeveloped" countries. The productivity and prosperity of industrialized, urbanized Europeans have been the envy of all people who have sought to emulate and duplicate their achievement. But in their frenzied race toward modernization, "backward" regions have overlooked the unfortunate aspects of Europe's economic evolution. To properly evaluate the impact of industrialization and urbanization one must consider its detrimental results as well as its obvious accomplishments. The European and especially the English industrial experience is therefore of interest.

For Arnold Toynbee, who brought the term "Industrial Revolution" into general use, the essence of that development was not the increase in production, which was important, but the substitution of competition for regulation in the economic sphere. In part, he reached this conclusion because the first Industrial Revolution, which occurred in Britain, was not the product of government action. Instead individual initiative and the free air of England combined to unleash an outburst of energy which eventually transformed the entire world. Freedom from regulation proved to be a double-edged sword, which brought profits and prosperity to some while condemning others to grinding poverty. Examining the steady rise of paupers, whose numbers dramatically increased from 1760 to 1818, Toynbee concluded that the Industrial Revolution proved that free competition might produce wealth without producing well-being.

Looking at the rapid and haphazard development of new towns and the transformation of others, some complained that capitalism's emphasis on speculation and profit tended to dismantle the whole structure of urban life, placing it upon the sands of money and profit. Greed and gain, they lamented, had replaced the older town ideals of community and cooperation. From the beginning, there were those who did not share this pessimistic opinion and looked upon the changes wrought by industrialization as a new dawn for the people of England and the Continent. What is clear is that Europe owes to industrialization the emergence of two great systems of thought: economic science and socialism, while the world owes to it a concern for the study of town life and the first attempts to understand urban development.

Among the first figures to identify with the new freedom was Adam Smith, the father and founder of the new school of classical economics. There had been precursors; Quesnay and the physiocrats had coined the term *laissez-faire.* Even earlier in the seventeenth century Father Bandini of Siena emerged as one of the first proponents of economic liberty. Smith, whose *Inquiry into the Nature and Causes of the Wealth of Nations* appeared in 1776, is the best known publicist of free trade. The instinct to trade and the motivation of self-interest, according to Smith, were behind the drive to increase production. They were hampered rather than helped by regulations; hence he applauded industrial freedom. He acknowledged that each individual sought his own good, but by some mysterious hand this was converted into a

65

work promoting the welfare of society. Within such a system the government had but three functions: to protect the society from outside violence, provide an exact administration of internal justice, and initiate and maintain certain public works which it was not in the interest of the single individual to undertake. Free enterprise, it was believed, provided the possibility of un-limited progress.

This dream was marred by the persistence of poverty and drew the attention of Thomas Malthus, who examined the more dismal side of economics. He directed his attention not to the causes of wealth but to those of poverty. At the close of the eighteenth century in his essay on the *Principles of Population*, he traced the roots of poverty to the growth of population. The food supply, this harbinger of doom announced, grew arithmetically, while the population grew geometrically. It followed that the only remedy for unemployment and underemployment was the limita-tion of workers.

Malthus saw two general checks to population: the positive and the preventive. The positive one was peculiar to man and flowed from the superiority of his mind. Some men would under-stand that large families led to economic distress and would not abandon the single life for poverty. The preventive checks to population were varied. Under this heading he included all un-wholesome occupations, exposure to the elements, the poor nurs-ing of children, excesses of all sorts, a whole train of common diseases, war, and the ultimate check on population—famine.

Although nature seemed to veto the perfectability of man, Malthus, the clergyman, applauded it. In his view man's original sins were laziness and inertia. Providence had arranged the dis-proportion between population and food to awaken man from his stupor and savagery, and develop his mind. Consequently there was no more evil in the world than was necessary.

David Ricardo built upon the work of Malthus. He observed that as industry developed and population increased, poorer lands were put to the plough, benefiting those who had good land. They received a premium which they did not merit, and they sought to preserve it by means of a tariff which kept the price of grains artificially high. Ricardo claimed that it was in the interest of manufacturers and workers alike to resist the pressure of land-owners for such protection, for their interests were identical. In reality the situations of employers and employees often differed drastically. While a number of manufacturers were making for-tunes, many of their workers remained at the subsistence level. For this reason there were those who questioned the value not only of *laissez-faire* economics but of industrialization and urbanization as well.

The impact of the Industrial Revolution on the generations that experienced it is still being debated. One group contends that the trials and tribulations of the working class during this process had been unduly exaggerated. They deny the assertion that coun-try life was naturally better than that in the towns, and, they deride the romantic view of rural existence expressed in poetry and painting. At the same time they call into question the assump-tion that working for oneself is always better than being in some-one else's employ. They applaud rather than decry the break-up of the old social relationships, hailing this as an act of libera-tion, introducing mobility into a traditional, often stifling society. Finally, they point to the incontestable fact that the wages and standard of living of urban workers eventually rose and far sur-passed that of their brothers in the countryside.

The critics of industrialization, on the other hand, charge that in the nineteenth century it produced the most degraded urban environment Europe had ever seen: a world beset by poverty and fouled by pollution. The truth, undoubtedly, lies between these extremes. Unquestionably the Industrial Revolution increased the well-being of some classes and individuals at the same time that it weighed heavily upon others. Even the most optimistic champions of this economic transformation will admit that there

67

INDUSTRIALIZATION AND URBANIZATION

were abuses in the new factories, mines, and cities. Furthermore, it cannot be denied that with industrialization the factory increasingly set the pace of life in urban centers. Most elements of town life were subordinate to it. Factory employment not only dominated the schedule of most residents, but more often than not occupied the best sites in the city. [Men, women, and even children were subservient to the new steam "monster.]"

True enough, child labor was not introduced by the Industrial Revolution, nor was it the monopoly of the towns. It had long existed on the farm and formed an integral part of the domestic system of production. When factories were built in the countryside, mill owners entered into contract with the poor-law authorities to supply them with pauper children. To the cotton masters these unfortunate children were often regarded as much their property as the machines they tended. When steam superseded water power, free labor children and their parents took the place of the pauper apprentices. These new recruits were driven into the mills by the enclosure system and the development of machine industry which rendered their own skills superfluous.

Children and adults of both sexes were employed in the factories. Six or seven was the average age at which they started work, though some were forced into the mills as early as three. Sometimes parents were compelled to bring their children with them, for they were denied a job unless they were accompanied by the children, who were paid far less. Ironically, the wages of the parents were thus forced down by their own offspring. The lot of both was deplorable, for the work day ranged from twelve to nineteen hours a day in the busy times. Discipline was harsh and the children were beaten to keep them awake. On occasion they were tied to the machines as well as locked in the mill. Accidents were numerous, for the tasks were monotonous and moving machinery was not enclosed.

The industries of the town as well as the growth of urban centers increased the demand for coal and intensified the abuses which existed in the mining of this mineral. As late as 1842 it was a widespread practice to employ women and children below ground where they had the difficult task of hauling coal in the narrow shafts. Conditions underground were lamentable, for supervision was scant and women and children were subject to the animal passions of desperate men. As a result many lives were lost, bodies maimed, and vices of all sorts perpetrated.

The controversy still rages as to whether conditions in the town mills were any worse than they had been in the cottages of the countryside. Undeniably under the domestic system whole families toiled long hours. However in their cottages they were not subject to the whip and whim of an unknown overseer, were not punished for taking a drink, or driven by the pace of the machines. Most important of all, they were psychologically comforted by the thought that beyond their door was the greenery and fresh air of their garden.

The use of Watt's engine as a prime mover in industry altered this. It changed the scale of industry, making feasible a far heavier concentration of both industries and workers in the towns. It thus removed the worker from his rural base, which had provided him with a supplementary source of food and a sense of independence. At the same time it placed a severe strain upon family unity. Within the industrial city there developed a value system that recognized achievement much more than birth. Consequently the family had less to offer one of its members for submission to its authority.

To make matters worse, outside the stifling atmosphere of the factory was the foul condition of the town. Victorian cities were notable for their absence of amenities, the pollution of the environment, and the inability of their ruling classes to conceive of them as centers for people rather than for production. Small wonder that there were few parks and even less time to enjoy what few recreational facilities were available.

Government, both national and municipal, refused to assume

INDUSTRIALIZATION AND URBANIZATION

responsibility for even the most pressing urban problems. The towns, like so much else, were left to the mercy of individual enterprise and the conscience of those who enjoyed power. This trust was abused. The need for housing provided the speculator with a wonderful opportunity, because there were few laws to curb his cupidity. Thus the greatest number of houses were built upon the space available. This is why so many tenements were built not only in a string, but back to back, providing pitifully little ventilation and rooms into which the sun never shone. Houseowners, in turn, also took advantage of the shortage, renting every available space, including cellars, halls, and courtyards. In Liverpool, one-sixth of the population lived in cellars, and London and New York were not far behind.

Conditions in these industrial towns were not conducive to good health. Since the houses were so close, there was little sunlight or fresh air. The air was never clean in the closed courts, where putrid matter and stagnant ditches were always present. The streets of all save the great thoroughfares were unpaved, and drainage and sewage were primitive, if at all present. Throwing refuse into the streets and alleys was the regular method of disposal. Often chamber pots were emptied in this fashion from the higher stories, to the detriment of the dignity of the passer-by.

The privies, whose stench was foul beyond description, were usually in the basements, which they shared with working class families and the pigs which were also housed there. The pigs, acting as scavengers in the streets through which they roamed, were often the only sanitation force available. There were tasks they could not perform, for even dead bodies were left to decay and further poison the air.

Dirt, congestion, and lack of ventilation brought pests, disease, and untimely death. The health hazards in these cities can readily be imagined. Rats carried bubonic plague, flies spread various diseases, bedbugs tormented the little time one had for sleep, and the dark, damp rooms proved an ideal breeding ground for bacteria. The shortage of water and the infrequent use of soap contributed to this dismal situation. A disease, once contracted, spread not only to the ten or twelve members who occupied a room but to one's neighbors who were but a few feet away. The weather itself conspired to make life difficult. There was the horror of the hot days, when the stench became unbearable; the terror of the rainy days, because they caused the pestilence ditches to overflow; and finally the inadequate heat in the cold of the winter.

Small wonder that in the slums of Liverpool one infectious disease or another was always present. In Manchester the average age at death for workers was seventeen, while the upper classes, who enjoyed far better conditions, lived twice as long. So bad was the situation that the annual death rate from typhus alone in Britain was double that of the fatalities of all the allied armies at Waterloo.

Eventually the *laissez-faire* approach, which left many of England's cities a patchwork of private properties with little coordination, came under attack. The economic liberalism which had permitted the abuses in industry and the degeneration of town life had to confront a number of enemies. Among these were: far-sighted mill owners, Conservative and Whig statesmen, trade-union leaders, socialists, enlightened economic theorists, and a number of literary figures who sympathized with the plight of the urban poor.

Thomas Carlyle deliberately forged a vigorous and vehement style in order to shock his readers from their moral stupor and awaken them to the dangers of materialism and the money worship of the age. In his *Heroes and Hero Worship*, 1841, he invoked a leader who could help modern man escape from the anarchy of competition and the cancerous lack of concern for one's fellow-man. Elizabeth Barrett Browning, in her poem, "The Cry of the Children," poured out her heart in protest against the abuses of child labor and called for an end to the exploitation of the young:

71

INDUSTRIALIZATION AND URBANIZATION

> *Do ye hear the children weeping, O my brothers,*
> *   Ere the sorrow comes with years?*
> *They are leaning their young heads against their mothers,*
> *   And that cannot stop their tears.*
> *The young lambs are bleating in the meadows:*
> *   The young birds are chirping in the nest*
> *The young fawns are playing with the shadows;*
> *   The young flowers are blowing toward the west–*
> *But the young, young children, O my brothers,*
> *   They are weeping bitterly!*
> *They are weeping in the playtime of the others,*
> *   In the country of the free.*

Charles Dickens, who enjoyed a wider popularity than any of his peers, strenuously and systematically fought the abuses of the Victorian Age. In *Hard Times* he struck out against the immorality of the *laissez-faire* system which meant survival of the strongest at the expense of the weakest. In *The Old Curiosity Shop* he condemned child labor; in *Dombey and Son*, the self-centered, self-righteous attitude of the industrialist-capitalist classes; in *Bleak House*, the inequities of the law; and in *Oliver Twist*, the workhouse system.

Arthur Clough suggested in his poem, "The Latest Decalogue," that Victorian materialism had replaced the Ten Commandments. Describing the new morality, he commented,

> Do not adultry commit;
> Advantage rarely comes of it.
> Thou shalt not steal; an empty feat
> When it's so lucrative to cheat.

Theorists provided a scientific foundation to supplement and support the moral condemnation of economic liberalism undertaken by these literary figures. In his *Principles of Political Economy*, 1848, John Stuart Mill drew a distinction between the laws of production and those of distribution. He recognized that competition was not always the most satisfactory principle for the organization of society; while useful in production this was not so in the distribution of wealth. Even earlier the economist and historian de Sismondi had launched an attack upon some of the basic tenets of economic liberalism. In his strikingly modern view, the root cause of economic crisis was underconsumption on the part of the working classes.

At the same time the Utopian Socialists, repelled by conditions in the towns and factories, proposed alternatives. They were called "utopian" after Sir Thomas More's work; they were socialists because they believed in the collective control of the means of production. At a time when life in urban centers seemed to separate and alienate men they stressed the need for community and communal living. Although the Utopians differed in their solutions, they shared certain common beliefs. They all regarded the existing order as unjust. In their view the individual was not a commodity but something special; they sought an environment that would permit man to realize his humanity.

One of the first socialists was also one of the first cotton lords, Robert Owen of Manchester. Disturbed by the conditions of mill hands, he created a model factory in which he paid higher wages for shorter hours. He also proposed a form of relief which we would today term collective farming. The unemployed, Owen asserted, could form villages of from 500 to 1,000 settlers and work together to meet their needs. Critics called these planned communities "Owen's parallelograms of paupers." Charles Fourier was much more anti-industrial and anti-urban than Owen. Having no use for large scale industry, he called for men to live and work in small communities based on agriculture. Members would engage in a variety of occupations, shifting periodically to avoid boredom and fatigue. The dirty work in the commune, he contended, would be done by children who would enjoy it. A radical feminist, he called for complete equality of the sexes in his communities.

INDUSTRIALIZATION AND URBANIZATION

Saint Simon also criticized the existing economic and social structure, but his solution differed from that of Fourier. Convinced that "Politics is the science of production," he chose the slogan: "All for and through industry." Recognizing the supreme importance of industrial development, he did not wish to see it discontinued, only regulated. The state, his followers asserted, had to see that the well-being of society took precedence over that of the individual. It could also play a positive role by encouraging public works which would at once stimulate the economy and create wealth for the community. Karl Marx, who termed his socialism "scientific" to differentiate it from that of his predecessors, placed little faith in the state. He saw it as the instrument of class oppression and thus a force to restrict rather than reinforce. Only the destruction of the state and the class system, Marx proclaimed, would bring liberation to the working classes of the cities.

Despite this barrage of criticism, much of it well-earned, the industrial city eventually did provide a better life for most Europeans. The concentration of people in urban areas made it possible for them to agitate for reforms and higher wages. The trade unions which arose provided many of the services of the old guilds, in some cases more. Strict housing codes and the lighting of streets, first with gas then electricity, made the city a much more decent place to live. Health and welfare measures contributed to the improvement of the urban environment. Public health codes, as well as the general acceptance of immunization and inoculation, reduced the chances of epidemics. Thus by 1900 typhus and cholera were virtually eliminated from Europe. Death from smallpox, scarlet fever, and other infectious diseases became increasingly less common.

The standard of living of the industrial urban worker rose, so that he enjoyed a better life. Inspection of factories and disability insurance combined to mitigate the physical and economic risks of factory work. Statistics show that from 1860 to 1900, real wages rose from seventy to ninety percent in Britain, France, Belgium, and Germany. If the nineteenth century did nothing else, it would deserve credit for removing the dread of famine from the people of Western Europe. Throughout most of its territory, laborers could afford to eat meat regularly and increased their consumption of citrus fruits, sugar, and cocoa. Coffee and tea, once luxuries, became standard drinks for all classes. The cost of bread decreased markedly. Until the beginning of the nineteenth century, half or more of a working family budget might go for bread alone. By 1831 only one quarter of such budgets went for bread, and by the mid-twentieth century, bread only accounted for three percent of a French worker's budget and one percent of that of a New Yorker.

The large proportion of expenses which food and other necessities formerly took up was increasingly devoted to consumer goods and even creature comforts. Shoes, clothing, and furniture were all produced in amazing quantities at prices working-class people could afford. To understand the magnitude of the change, one need only recall that before industrialization a mirror six square feet cost relatively as much as a Cadillac today and was more rarely seen. Following industrialization, mirrors and even automobiles became common commodities. As a result workers assumed ownership of items which their relatives in the pre-industrial world could never have hoped to own.

At the same time there was a reduction in the work week and work day. Prior to the First World War, the ten hour day was standard and likewise the notion of the Sunday day of rest. After World War II, the eight hour day, the two-day weekend, and the coffee break were commonplace in Ameria and increasingly seen in Europe as well. For the first time in history the working class faced the promise and problem of leisure. There were Sunday outings to the countryside by train, the bicycle, and finally the

75

automobile, as well as a great interest in spectator and participatory sports. Novels and newspapers became popular, and workers could frequent the theater and later the movies.

Leisure opened new possibilities for learning, for most of the best universities and finest research facilities were found in urban areas. The urban dweller also found at his disposal museums, zoos, and the other centers of culture that adorned European civilization. Small wonder that the city acted as a magnet for millions; the migrants were convinced that the good and full life could be found only in these centers.

In 1900 if Europeans considered their civilization to be better than that of 1800, and far better than life in the rest of the world, this was in no small measure due to industrialization and urbanization. In point of fact, they assured Europeans and their descendants of the highest standard of living in the world. This prosperity was no panacea and did not automatically bring peace of mind to the people blessed by it. Rather it served to stimulate the level of expectation, ushering in new urban problems in its train.

7. industrialization and the American city

Theodore P. Kovaleff

In preindustrial America, urban life was the exception rather than the rule. While there were some cities before the Industrial Revolution, it was only after that event that there was any substantial growth in their number or their size. George Washington's America was less than ten percent urban. Until nearly 1840, each of the major cities in the United States was involved in commerce, and many of the citizens of the city earned their livelihood from it or in one of several service industries.

The average American household located in a rural area was remarkably self-sufficient. According to Alexander Hamilton's *Report on Manufactures*, it was a scene of manufacturing, much of which took place during the slack winter season. However, lack of space in the city plus the fact that commerce was not as seasonal explain why urban residents did not try to produce their own necessities. This led to the growth of the service and supply industries in the cities. As a result of the Napoleonic wars, part of the profits from the maritime commerce was invested in industry, especially textiles. Thus money and inventions helped change the pattern of American life from agricultural to industrial pursuits.

Industrialization and urbanization were almost Siamese twins. To a greater or lesser extent, industry depends on people and the people or workers usually lived near the industry. Hence, if a plant were not already located in an urban area, it would soon find itself in one on the mere strength of the fact that the workers had clustered on the spot and satellite services had then developed to take care of their needs.

Frederick Jackson Turner wrote that the frontier "explains American history." While his thesis was probably an overstatement, the existence of the frontier did exert an influence on the country. America was a labor-deficient area, and the frontier had something to do with it. There were never enough people available to work in the cities. Consequently, by the sheer mechanism of supply and demand, the American worker was able to earn a great deal more than his European counterpart. This meant he had more money to spend. However, expensive labor and the difficulties inherent in its recruiting led factory owners to adopt a great deal of labor- and money-saving machinery.

There have been many different answers to the question, "When did the Industrial Revolution take place in the United States?" Charles and Mary Beard viewed the Civil War, or Second American Revolution as they called it, as being responsible for much industrial development. This perspective has influenced many other historians, but there appears to be a great deal of evidence suggesting that the high but regular rate of growth, which Walt Whitman Rostow calls the "take off phase," probably came earlier than 1860. Robert Gallman has measured output in a complicated way, and he concludes that between 1838 and 1899 output increased eleven-fold. How this industrial expansion affected the cities is illustrated by their fantastic growth. Chicago, which did not even exist in 1820, had a population of over one million before the end of the century. Overall the increases are not as precipitous, but they are very impressive.

Improvements in transportation played a major role in the economic development of many cities. Before the existence

Theodore P. Kovaleff

YEAR	Total Population	% Increase over Preceding Census	Urban Population	% Increase over Preceding Population	% of Total Population	
					Urban	Rural
1820	9,638,453	33.1	693,255	31.9	7.2	92.8
1830	12,866,020	33.5	1,127,247	62.6	8.8	91.2
1840	17,069,453	32.7	1,845,055	63.7	10.8	89.2
1850	23,191,876	35.9	3,543,716	92.1	15.3	84.7
1860	31,443,321	35.6	6,216,518	75.4	19.8	80.2
1870	38,558,371	22.6	9,902,361	59.3	25.7	74.3
1880	50,155,783	30.1	14,129,735	42.7	28.2	71.8
1890	62,947,714	25.5	22,106,265	56.5	35.1	64.9

INDUSTRIALIZATION AND URBANIZATION

of cheap transportation, an area could be isolated and remain economically self-sufficient. Protected as if by a tariff barrier against goods from afar by the high costs of bringing them in, a local industry was able to dominate the area. Roads were so poor that it was almost unthinkable to haul freight by any other means than water. It was cheaper to ship goods from Pittsburgh to Philadelphia via the Ohio and Mississippi rivers, tranship the cargo to an ocean-going vessel, sail around the tip of Florida, and up the Atlantic coast to Philadelphia than it was to take them overland less than 300 miles. The building of canals and railroads changed all this. In place of local or at most regional markets, the transportation innovations brought about the development of a national market.

The use of the railroad was a fantastic boon to the city. While in this age of space travel there is a tendency to derogate the railroad, without it, even today, it would be difficult for a city to exist. In the nineteenth century, without competition from airplane or highway, the railroad quickly became essential. Cities grew up at the junction of rail lines; the importance of the railroad to the area, and its relation to the city, is illustrated by the original American name of Atlanta, Georgia. That city, which almost immediately was a transportation hub, was first called Terminus.

In addition to stimulating trade, the railroad was responsible for the growth of many other industries. Apart from the obvious ones, such as the locomotive and coach or freight car builders, the sector which benefited most was the iron and steel industry. Although the first railroad tracks were of wood, or iron-covered wood, these quickly wore out and soon more durable models of iron or steel were substituted; steel was also extensively used in the construction of bridges.

Key to the Industrial Revolution was use of an energy source to supplement man's own physical strength. In America both water and steam power were harnessed. Compared to the other countries which industrialized during the nineteenth

80

century, America was especially well-equipped for the use of waterpower technology. The Eastern seaboard has a range of mountains which runs roughly north-south not far from the coast. Between the mountains and the sea, there is usually a relatively high area, and then a drop to near sea level. Any river which flows over the drop will necessarily speed up, and this will provide power. At this fall line, as it is called, factories were built and cities developed. Glens Falls, New York; Fall River, Chicopee, and Springfield, Massachusetts, all evolved in this manner. In time, as steam technology became more efficient and as the disadvantages of water power became more apparent, steam and later electricity gradually replaced water as the power source. But by then the industry was in these cities, the workers were there, and usually both remained.

Technology altered the physiognomy of the city itself. Originally its boundaries were determined by the distance a person could travel on foot. Rich and poor lived relatively close to each other, for all had to walk to their place of work. The development first of the omnibus, and subsequently the invention of the railroad and steam ferry, opened more land for settlement and began a process of population dispersion which has continued to this day.

In the area of architecture, technology also played an important role. Until the development of new construction techniques and materials, a tall building was impractical to construct because of the massive walls and foundations necessary to support the weight of the upper levels. Additionally, until the invention of the elevator, the height of a building was limited by the stamina of the persons who had to climb the stairs. Finally, until the change from a "walking city" to one with public transportation, high-rise architecture was not needed; there were not enough people available in one place to justify the construction of so large a project.

Industrialization was, therefore, a major factor in changing

81

INDUSTRIALIZATION AND URBANIZATION

America from a rural to an urban nation. Old cities which had existed for their commercial functions began to emphasize more and more their manufacturing activities, and new cities sprang up in hitherto unsettled areas, all because of the opportunities provided by technological advances of the industrialization of America.

It is impossible to see in operation in any one city all the factors previously discussed, but the story of Pittsburgh does incorporate several. First chartered as a city in 1816, Pittsburgh gave little hint that in the future she would be a major industrial site. In 1817, the city council made a study of the state of business in the city. It found that there were more blacksmith shops than any other business, but none was large; the shoe and boot industry employed the most people; copper and tin workers made the most money; and the largest single factory in terms of number of hired hands made glass products.

Yet the city fathers showed a foresight which enabled their municipality to prosper and grow. Their vision is best exemplified by the construction of bridges across the Allegheny and Monongahela Rivers facilitating intercourse with the towns of Allegheny and Birmingham on the opposite shores. In time the expanding city of Pittsburgh annexed these and other districts.

Due to her location at the confluence of the Allegheny and Monongahela Rivers and the proximity of some of the most productive coal fields in the country, the iron and later the steel industry prospered in Pittsburgh. The first manufacture of iron took place in 1806, and by 1825 it had become the leading product of the city. By the turn of the century, over fifty percent (dollar value) of all United States iron and steel was made in Pittsburgh. Another key to her growth was the existence of large amounts of the type of sand used in glassmaking. Although the first glassworks was actually founded before the nineteenth century, for several decades it did not play an important role in the municipal economy. Then, with the tapping of the nearby natural gas fields and the utilization of their product in glass manufacture, the city became pre-eminent in the manufacture of glass.

The inventive genius of George Westinghouse is partly responsible for Pittsburgh becoming a city of sophisticated industry. In 1868 he was granted a patent on his invention of the airbrake, and he immediately formed a company for its manufacture; little over a decade later he organized the Westinghouse Machine Company, which manufactured various types of engines and turbine equipment; in 1882, he founded the Union Switch and Signal Company to produce the other items of railroad equipment he had invented; four years later he started the Westinghouse Electric and Manufacturing Company to develop and exploit the uses of alternating current. Despite the usual problems that beset an inventor and also the obstacles placed in his way by the "electrical establishment" which was committed to the use of direct current, Westinghouse emerged victorious; and Pittsburgh reaped the benefits of his industry.

Transportation also played a major role in the growth of the city. In the preindustrial period the area had been the scene of many shipyards, some of which produced flatboats built for one sail down the river to New Orleans, only to be dismantled for their lumber; others produced ocean going vessels which sailed down the rivers and thence to Europe. The necessity of a tie with the eastern seaboard led first to the construction of a canal link with Philadelphia. Although the builders dreamed of a canal like the Erie, with few locks, less problems, and more profits, their hopes were unfounded. In late 1852, however, Philadelphia and Pittsburgh were joined by the Pennsylvania Railroad, constructed in part thanks to the guarantee of its bonds by the Pittsburgh city fathers.

The growth and industrialization of Pittsburgh could not fail to have had a major effect on the quality of life of the area. In any fast-growing city at that time, housing was bound to be built in a careless manner and was usually of wood. There was, then, the

83

omnipresent danger of fire, and Pittsburgh suffered several major conflagrations in the nineteenth century.

Additionally, as early as 1800, there was another aspect of the city which attracted the attention of visitors—smog. Almost every house had two or three stoves which burned either wood or coal. As time passed, the various industries to which the citizens of the city pointed with pride all gave forth smoke that contributed to the prevailing pall. The water supply was another problem. The residents had drawn water from one of the rivers, but that had proved troublesome and sometimes even dangerous; so as early as 1824 an ordinance was passed providing for the construction of a municipal waterworks. The scheme was undercapitalized and it was not until mid-century that an adequate system was in operation; but even then there was no attempt made to purify the water.

Compounding the problems was the lack of a sewer system. Moving in to take advantage of all the jobs afforded by burgeoning industry were many immigrants who lived in densely populated areas and in unbelievable squalor. Epidemics were almost endemic; indeed, during 1854, people outside of the city refused to accept paper money from Pittsburgh because they feared it might be contaminated.

With industrial progress came labor difficulties. Whereas previously the business establishments had been small, and relations between employer and employee had usually been amicable, as the companies grew their labor problems multiplied. This was especially true in the iron and steel industries. The Homestead steel strike of 1892 was one of the most violent labor confrontations in all of American history. Although for a period of time the workers controlled almost all of the city, and while they used cannons, burning oil and dynamite, they were unable to persuade management, represented by Henry Clay Frick, to accede to their demands. After much bloodshed, including the attempted assassination of Frick, the matter was settled, and it was not until the 1930s that the steel industry was unionized.

84

Theodore P. Kovaleff

Perhaps no city has been more aided and hindered by its geographical location. First, helped by its situation at the confluence of two important rivers and by nature's gifts of coal and natural gas, Pittsburgh flourished. But as it grew, its limitations became more obvious, for rivers, even though spanned by bridges, can also imprison; and the city could only expand eastward. This created difficulties especially in the spheres of transportation and housing, but by the mid-twentieth century, a group of people, both Republican and Democrat, united to form a civic team, the Allegheny Conference on Community Development. Aiming to build a city and environs that were attractive to people as well as industry, the area became a model of urban planning and renewal so that by Pittsburgh's bicentennial in 1958, it was being studied by urban planners throughout the nation.

Industrialization, such as occurred in Pittsburgh, stimulated the growth of the metropolitan areas, and their growth paralleled that of the United States. Indeed, urban America was responsible for much of the nation's expansion. Thus the city is the foundation for the position of the United States as a superpower in the world today.

8. cities in Africa: the transition from traditional to industrial urban centers

Daniel R. Smith

Africa is the least urbanized of the continents, with only sixteen percent of the population living in cities of 20,000 persons or more. Several factors account for this relatively low rate of urbanization. Modern economic systems and technological innovations were not introduced on the continent until after the great colonial scramble of the 1880s. Thus industrialization, always a prime cause of city growth, appeared rather late in Africa.

Even after formal division by the European powers, entrepreneurs were hesitant to invest in the region. The physical geography of Africa with its high coastal plateaus, unnavigable rivers, and dense rain forests discouraged exploitation of the continent's natural resources. A shortage of manpower in many areas and a general lack of skilled indigenous personnel further discouraged industrial investment and consequently impeded urban growth. Resolutions by colonial administrations to develop Africa despite these impediments were thwarted by two global wars and a world-wide recession.

Thus, it has only been in the past fifty years that a major trend towards the growth of urban industrial areas has appeared on the continent. Not until 1927 did Cairo earn the distinction of becoming the first city on the African continent with a population of one million.

In the past few decades the growth of cities in Africa has moved forward at an unprecedented speed. Indeed, the size of many of the principal urban areas has doubled and tripled in the years following World War II. For example, during the period from 1945 to 1970 the population of Algiers increased from 461,000 to 973,000. In the same period Dakar expanded from a city of 125,000 to its present population of over 600,000. Similarly Dar es Salaam grew from 69,000 in 1945 to over 300,000 in 1970. Comparable rates of growth have occurred in virtually all of the major cities on the continent. The Urban Land Institute has estimated that if the current pace is maintained, the urban population of Africa, which was 28 million in 1965, will have increased to 48 million by 1975 and to 129 million by the year 2000.

Thus in a thirty-five year period the percentage of the total population living in urban areas will have increased from eight to twenty-five percent. The present trend toward rapid industrialization has had a radical effect on the traditional African concept of "city." As a result, the type of urban settlement common in preindustrial days has been replaced by the modern production-oriented metropolis.

The major cities of preindustrial Africa were primarily trade centers and administrative headquarters, concentrated along the coast or near navigable bodies of water. The livelihood of the inhabitants centered around trade occupations.

There were a significant number of craftsmen in the preindustrial cities who were attracted to the urban areas by the size of the markets and the ready availability of raw materials. However, production by native craftsmen was limited by several factors. There was virtually no use of animal, water, or wind power during the precolonial period. Since all work had to utilize human muscle, the production of goods was a slow, exhausting process. Transportation and communication facilities were almost nonexistent. Goods were relatively expensive and consumption limited. Most Africans outside the urban centers lived at the subsistence level and consequently there were few visitors to the city except for professional traders. At the same time, there was neither manpower nor capital available to stimulate the economy. Thus, the number of craftsmen tended to remain constant.

Goods were produced through a guild system which Africans developed before the advent of the colonial powers and which was quite similar to the European craft guilds of the Middle Ages. Workmen generally set their own standards of quality. Wooden household goods, tin utensils, weapons, farm implements and a certain amount of jewelry and ceremonial garb for the affluent were the primary goods produced. Traditionally, specific families possessed a monopoly of a given craft. The use of the apprentice system was widespread. A youth would usually begin training in the shop of his family elders as soon as he was old enough to perform even the most simple tasks. He would be elevated to the rank of journeyman, often upon reaching puberty, and would generally be initiated to his new rank through traditional family ceremonies. He would then become a master craftsman shortly after the birth of his first child.

Certain ethnic groups commonly monopolized specific crafts. Craftsmen of the same trade would often occupy a specific quarter within the city. Because of limited travel, traditional cities were quite homogeneous in composition and were often dominated by a specific tribal group.

Thus, the preindustrial African city tended to be a relatively small settlement, with limited production of goods through the craft system. Being totally dependent upon trade, the fortune of the cities followed that of the government. Indeed, the very survival of preindustrial urban centers was dependent upon the ability of the state to provide enough stability and control, and to encourage the exchange of goods.

European industrialization did not affect the structure of African cities or alter traditional society until after 1885, when the scramble for colonies on the continent began in earnest. At the

Congress of Berlin in that year, the major European powers agreed to establish clearly defined boundaries for African colonies, to use the principle of "effective occupation" to determine what nation had a right to claim any particular territory, and to settle all colonial disputes through international arbitration.

These agreements were an incentive to industrial investors, who could now be sure that the area in which they were risking capital was indeed the domain of their mother country. At the same time effective occupation held forth the promise of governmental assistance in controlling and utilizing the indigenous population. Finally, the principle of international arbitration reduced the risk of colonial warfare, which would be disastrous to industrial investments.

With the advent of European industrialization the structure and function of the African city was altered radically. European railroads soon reached all the major urban areas and port facilities. As a result, bazaars and market places were flooded with inexpensive, mass-produced goods. The influx of large quantities of European commodities quickly undermined the traditional craft guilds of the African cities. Local workmen could not produce goods as quickly or as inexpensively as could the European manufacturer. Consequently, the demand for native products declined rapidly. The traditional craftsmen soon found their business limited to luxury items and trinkets for the small white community and jewelry and ceremonial garb for the educated black elite.

In the past two decades, the rapid growth of the tourist industry has increased the demand for indigenous goods. Nonetheless as a result of urbanization, the traditional craftsman has lost the significant role he played in precolonial society. He has been reduced to a producer of luxury and curio items, while the tools and household goods he once made are now mass produced. Many of the craftsmen have abandoned their trade and now employ themselves in semiskilled occupations such as metal

89

repair, plumbing, and lumbering where they can at least partially utilize their talents. Others earn their livelihood producing accessories for manufactured goods, such as camera cases and jewelry boxes.

The decline in the role of traditional craftsmen has lowered the quality of their handiwork. Carefully planned apprenticeship programs have virtually disappeared. Family tradition as well as tribal and ethnic origins are no longer significant in the selection of new trainees. The choice of sites for major cities also changed with industrialization. Europeans, adhering to the theories of mercantilism, sought to establish cities near natural resource supplies to facilitate the extraction, processing, and preparation of raw materials for shipment to the mother country.

Urban areas with good port facilities were sought to export these raw materials and to return manufactured goods to the colony for sale to the indigenous population. Some preindustrial cities of the coastal regions, although greatly altered, thrived and expanded rapidly with the advent of European industrialization. Interior cities by contrast, especially those located far from natural resource supplies, soon faded into insignificance. Thus urban centers such as Timbuktu and Gao deteriorated to the status of decayed villages.

At the same time, industrialization led to the development of cities in areas which had previously never had significant urban settlements. This was especially true of southern and central Africa. Salisbury, Bulawayo, Leopoldville, and Elizabethville all developed as a result of the mineral wealth found in the vicinity.

During the colonial period blacks played a rather insignificant role in the development of urban areas. They were generally restricted to menial tasks and unskilled occupations in the industrial labor market. Few Africans even achieved the rank of foreman or manager in the urban industries. At the same time, although blacks comprised the bulk of the unskilled labor force, the percentage of the total African population living in urban areas never exceeded ten percent in any colony south of the Sahara. The cities were in reality the domain of the white and Asian settlers.

Pay scales for blacks were always lower than those of white workers. This forced Africans to reside in the poorest neighborhoods, and slums soon developed. Not until the late 1940s did educational facilities become available to most urban blacks. Low pay, inadequate housing, and lack of educational and business opportunity all joined to keep the indigenous population on the lowest rung of the socioeconomic ladder.

Conditions for natives in the urban areas of the southern colonies such as Rhodesia and Nyasaland were even worse. White communities were able to avoid the presence of an impoverished African majority by establishing rigid pass laws prohibiting blacks from traveling in urban areas unless on their way to or from work. Blacks engaged in industry were settled in special quarters, well apart from the white-dominated central city. Thus, the African was able to serve the urban community without sufficiently enjoying the social, economic, educational, and health benefits of city life.

Independence has produced several significant changes in the industrial centers of Africa. Most black-controlled governments have undergone intensive programs of "Africanization" to place blacks in positions of authority as managers, foremen, and corporation executives. Increased educational opportunity has swelled the ranks of the skilled and literate African labor force. Programs of nationalization and socialization, especially in the East African nations, have shaken the European and Asian control of industrial facilities.

The present trend in African urban growth is toward the rapid expansion of existing major cities rather than toward the development of new urban centers. This is due in large measure to the lure that the city offers to rural blacks, who annually abandon the

91

countryside in increasingly large numbers. Such migrants are attracted to the largest, well-established urban centers and generally will not settle in the smaller cities. The result is an imbalance in the size of major urban centers.

Often the largest city within a given nation contains four to eight times the population of the second largest city. The major city generally accounts for over fifty percent of the total urban population of the nation (but normally less than ten percent of the total national population). Because of this trend, few significant new urban areas have developed since the 1950s. Exceptions to this rule include Marsa Breya, the oil refining center of Libya, and Nouakchott, the new capital of Mauritania.

Today, despite the relatively small total urban population, cities play a vital role in the lives of the independent nations. The major city is usually the intellectual, artistic, and social capital of the country. As the residence of most of the nations' black elite, it is generally also the center of political activities and the seat of the government. In addition, the major city is generally the financial, transportation, and communication center of each independent nation. Most of a nation's major banking concerns have their headquarters in the principal city. The capital is usually the focal point of the national highway system and contains the chief airport and railroad terminals. It is usually the broadcasting center of the national radio and television network.

In the case of the seaboard nations, the capital city is normally also the main port of the trade. A principal city usually contains from sixty to ninety percent of the nation's skilled labor force. This is all the more significant given the fact that the urban population is generally less than ten percent of the total national population. Thus Dakar, which contains fifteen percent of the population of Senegal, is the residence of seventy-five percent of those employed in commerce and eighty percent of those employed in manufacturing.

In addition, cities contain the greater percentage of a nation's electrical facilities and a disproportionate percentage of the health

92

services and facilities. Small wonder that urban areas such as Dar es Salaam, Conakry, Bangia, Nairobi, and Lome enjoy an influence over national affairs which is far out of proportion to the percentage of population they actually represent. Often urban areas are the only areas within a given nation which exhibit concrete evidence of significant modernization. It is no surprise that the industrial cities of Africa were the focal points and headquarters of virtually all the independence movements of the 1950s and 1960s.

For most Africans the move from the rural community to the city is the first step toward individual autonomy, a break from traditional tribal, clan, and familial bonds. In crowded urban areas it is virtually impossible for the extended family to survive. Thus, the modern nuclear family has become the basic social unit for industrialized Africa. Loyalty to the tribal group and to more distant relatives quickly vanishes in the diversified occupational pursuits and social activities of the city.

Excessive migration to the cities has proven to be a serious problem for urbanized Africa. As an ever-growing number of young Africans receive an elementary education, they flock to the cities in search of employment. However, because of a lack of investment capital and a general lack of stability, most African nations have expanded their educational systems much more rapidly than their industries. This causes a flooded job market and an ever-increasing number of unemployed educated and semi-educated persons. Excessive migration also produces severe housing shortages. This problem, coupled with the necessity of caring for the unemployed and providing additional health services and police protection for the overcrowded areas, seriously taxes city budgets.

The fact that the unemployed are incapable of paying taxes further complicates the situation. The result is the expenditure of city revenue on basic protective and health services with little or no allocation of funds for industrial development. As African cities grow in size, they fail to provide housing, transportation and communication facilities, police protection, and employment opportunities in proportion to their expansion.

Unemployment rates vary from area to area, but anywhere from twenty to eighty percent of the black labor force is normally unemployed in any given African city. So great has the problem become that some cities have resorted to radical legislation in an attempt to alleviate the situation. In 1968, for example, Kenshasa issued an ordinance requiring all unemployed persons to return to their place of origin within thirty days. Similarly, in 1964 Kenya tried to force unemployed urban residents to return to agricultural pursuits. The following year, Tanzania attempted a similar program. Although all such efforts have been generally unsuccessful, they reflect the dire need of most black nations to alleviate urban unemployment.

The steady influx of a large number of migrant workers has created further problems for African cities. The overwhelming majority of the migrants are males between the ages of fifteen to forty. Consequently, an imbalance of sexes has occurred in most of the urban areas on the continent. This further contributes to city development problems by increasing crime rates and reducing opportunity to develop stable, married family units. This problem is especially acute in southern Africa, where legislation often prohibits migrant workers from bringing their families with them to urban centers.

All in all, the future of the modern African city is far from promising. Urban areas are the center of the cultural, social, political, and economic activities for the newly independent nations. Yet, unemployment, low pay scales, inadequate housing, and poor health facilities present serious problems which must be solved if the cities, as the pacesetters for the nation, are to advance. The traditional role of the city as trade center and home of the small craftsman faded with the advent of industrialization. Only if industrial growth is able to expand sufficiently to employ the great awakening indigenous population, can Africa hope to solve the present crisis within her cities.

94

PART III

THE IMPACT OF URBANIZATION IN THE UNITED STATES: AN AMERICAN REVOLUTION IN THE MAKING

A. problems of the asphalt environment

9. transportation and the transformation of urban life

Jacob Sodden

Oscar Handlin once said that improved transportation led to the destruction of distance. It is now possible to encompass larger areas within the scope of urban life. Combined with the diverse pursuits of our daily lives this has produced the larger, dynamic, differentiated, and complex social organism, the modern city. Throughout history an intimate relation has prevailed between modes of transportation and the location, growth, position, and role of cities in our society. Toward the end of the nineteenth century, however, cities were no longer small, compact geographic entities. We expanded the area of the cities and in that way embellished our life style and were able to enjoy many more amenities, pleasures, and activities through a modern application of the division of labor and differentiation in the ways we utilize space within urban communites.

The common carrier, introduced in mid-nineteenth century, achieved the breakthrough for the city. By "common carrier" I refer to the horse-drawn omnibus, electric street car, subway, motor bus, and commuter train. Regardless of the type of technology, the common carrier made it possible for the humblest urban resident to travel from one part of a large city to another. Among other things this provided him with options regarding the location of his home and place of work and where he shopped and pursued his recreation. This ability to move around encouraged, or at least did not restrict, the ever increasing distances between these points within the larger city. Thus, there developed the complexities of the contemporary city. However, this enthusiastic exercise of options, coupled with specialized land use, permitted the expansion of cities to reach the point where the liabilities of growth now negate the benefits derived from it.

Unfortunately, because of the ability of most people to own and operate automobiles, there has been a "regression" back to private transportation. Americans want to live in concentrated urban aggregations of human beings at the same time that each person insists on his right to choose the mode of transportation for getting around, usually the private automobile. This is regression if we concede that the common carrier prepared the nineteenth century city for its role in the industrial society and led to the twentieth century city. The cities which reached their zenith in the nineteenth century suffer most from traffic congestion, although newer cities such as Los Angeles which grew up in the automobile era are not immune either. Three examples will serve to illustrate the problems which have developed.

Lehman College, a division of City University in the Bronx, is progressively converting more and more space, both off and on the street, for parking facilities at a time when space in New York City is at a premium. The Community Planning Board within whose area the college is located was asked in 1971 to aid the college in procuring more parking space. As a member of the board, I first inquired why so much space had already been requisitioned for that purpose. The answer was that the land used for parking belonged to the college, and it asserted its prerogative to do as it pleased with it. This blatantly spurious legal fiction that the Board of Higher Education owned land which could not be touched by other city bodies was countered by the observation that while it was appropriate for the City of New York to provide free college education, it would also be a good idea to prohibit students from

100

using automobiles to travel to that free education. Several legislators to whom this idea was suggested considered it a political potato too hot to handle.

A second example of how the automobile helps create urban problems is reflected in the factors held significantly responsible for the Watts riots in Los Angeles during the mid-sixties. This black community was not among the worst in terms of residential facilities and amenities. However, blacks who lived there were deeply frustrated in part by the transportation problems in the area. Los Angeles has a poor and attenuated public transit system, which only added to the problem since many blacks in Watts could not afford to own an automobile. Even if there were jobs available, how could Watts residents get to them? The Pacific Electric interurban railway system, which flourished in the Los Angeles area up to the 1920s and which could have supplied it with a well-suited public transportation system, was dismantled in later decades to a point where the very rights-of-way were obliterated. The lack of public transportation had effectively isolated the residents of Watts from the rest of the city.

The third example which comes to mind relates to the great consternation experienced by New Yorkers when one of their football teams, the Giants, announced their plan to move to a new sports complex in New Jersey. Their abandonment of Yankee Stadium in the Bronx for, among other reasons, the lack of parking facilities was viewed as an act of treachery against old and loyal Giant fans. Actually, the logical resolution of this dilemma is not to keep the Giants in the Bronx, but to erase city and state lines and convert all of the New York area into one metropolitan entity; the ecological and geographic entity should become a political one as well. After all, the Giants are only following the many hundreds of thousands of New York residents who preceded them in leaving the city proper to move to suburban homes. Again the expanded use of private transportation had disrupted another segment of urban life.

New York, like most of our cities today, is spread out, dif-

101

A. Problems of the Asphalt Environment

fused over a larger geographic area. The problems with which we have to contend as a consequence of this diffusion are better understood and more amenable to solution if we recall how transportation helped create this urban sprawl. All of us are, of course, ready to affirm that we prefer the expanded city because land use differentiation makes possible a more elaborate and versatile life style. But the fact is that the city grew and was enlarged spatially and culturally without some kind of ultimate or even casual overall design which might have led to a happier, more convenient, and rationally sound integration between and among the differentiated land use patterns which presently prevail.

The critical features in the relationship between transportation and the contemporary city may best be pointed out by comparing two diagrams which depict the ecological, cultural, and geographic differences between the nineteenth and twentieth century city. The modern city possesses a metropolitan network of transportation in contrast with the nineteenth century city's urban network. Usually the expanded metropolitan network of transportation was superimposed on an existing urban network, which was designed to meet the needs of an earlier age. This means that traffic facilities and travel concepts built to accommodate transportation needs in the nineteenth century now constitute the basic foundation for an enlarged system which must satisfy the increasing mobility needs of the twentieth century city.

Although transportation was crucial to the urban centers of both centuries, they were based on different concepts. The primary feature of the travel network in the nineteenth century was the fixed route. This is only partly true today because the automobile, among other things, has made routes of travel infinitely more diffuse and flexible. In the accompanying chart, "a" represents the nineteenth century central city; the lines emanating from it are travel arteries which were usually rail lines. The little circles on the rail lines represent small towns, referred to as "satellite towns." Although dependent on the large city, these towns were pretty much independent of each other. For example, two towns five miles apart but on different rail lines were much less related to each other than two towns twenty miles apart but on the same lines of travel. In other words, the smaller cities were directed toward the central city but the land between the travel arteries was not absorbed into a solid, total urban network. As a matter of fact, the dividing line between urban and rural was quite pronounced and the areas between cities were rural in character.

In contrast to this, the modern city, with its metropolitan transportation network, is no longer a tight urban area but rather diffuse and all-encompassing, larger in circumference, and without empty spaces. This was due in large measure to the fact that private modes of transportation were now available to most people. When it became possible for most people to own automobiles and the suburbanization movement went into high gear, roads emanating from the central city were built, usually in the areas between the rail lines. New construction of all types, including residential, industrial, commercial, and office facilities, were built in the vacant area within the triangle formed by the two rail lines merging into the central city. Soon whole suburban communities came into existence in these marginal areas. This prompted the construction of circumferential highways to embrace a whole metropolitan area.

Today there is a belt system for New York City, a beltway for Baltimore and Washington, D.C., Route 128 for the Boston area, and similar systems for many other large cities in the United States. These circular roads intersected the existing rail lines which, of course, continue beyond the commuter zone. Thus the large central city and its satellite towns as depicted in Figure 1 became the metropolitan network of Figure 2. In it, the central city "a" expands to embrace a larger circle "b." Area "c," located between the rail lines and served by roads and highways, is the lower density area in which urban and rural characteristics

103

A. PROBLEMS OF THE ASPHALT ENVIRONMENT

intermingle. Nevertheless, this new metropolitan transportation network has the effect of making areas "a," "b," and "c" into one integral social and ecological unit composed of the old central city, the area into which it has expanded, the satellite towns swallowed up like small fish, and the most recently built up areas between the old travel arteries. The circle of dashes represents the circumferential roads intended to ease and speed movement from one point to another in the total area without the need to penetrate the core.

A look at a map of the metropolitan New York area and surrounding counties leads us to another interesting observation concerning the broadening out and filling in of marginal spaces in the new configurations of urban complexes. Progressive construction of bridges which link parts of the area to each other has taken place. The first important bridge built, the Brooklyn Bridge, links lower Manhattan to an adjacent part of Brooklyn. Then came in succession the Manhattan Bridge, the Williamsburgh Bridge, the Queensboro Bridge, the Tri-boro connecting Manhattan, the Bronx, and Queens, and then the Whitestone Bridge and Throgs Neck Bridge connecting the Bronx and Queens. The first four bridges were built with pedestrian and mass transit facilities, but the last three are only for motor vehicles and require the payment of a toll. Presently planned is the construction of another bridge connecting Oyster Bay in Nassau County with Rye in Westchester County, both points obviously out of New York City but within its expanding metropolitan area. The urban integration of broader areas is reflected in progressively outward construction of bridges and roadways. Some 75 or 100 years ago New York City was encompassed within a compact area; it is now much larger and diffuse, and the proposed Rye-Oyster Bay Bridge will simply close a gap in a series of concentric circles around the center of the city. These are more crucial to the urban area than are adequate travel arteries within the central city itself.

New York City is not unique. The bridge construction in this

104

area only brings into clearer view what is true of other metropolitan centers. The circumferential highways built for other cities, for example, Route 128 in greater Boston, are located well beyond the city's limits. This is to allow for future expansion of the circle of integration of urban conglomerates. The bridges in the New York area only closed the gaps in the transportation network of a broader and more diffuse pattern of land use. They were superimposed on and cross over the rail lines which emanate from the center of the city and which, in an earlier, premotor vehicle era, were sufficient to achieve the needed integration for a constellation of urban communities featuring the large city in the center and small communities only along rail lines. Until the construction of the Verrazano-Narrows Bridge, Staten Island, politically part of New York City, was far more oriented to New Jersey. Today Staten Island real estate is booming because the new travel facility has brought it into closer integration with the rest of New York City. Furthermore, it is interesting to note that the second level of that bridge was constructed much earlier than anticipated because of the rapidly increased flow of traffic.

A similar situation prevailed at the southern terminus of the New Jersey Turnpike, near Wilmington, Delaware. Much sooner than original projections indicated, a sister span was built for the Delaware Memorial Bridge, linking New Jersey to Delaware on the main route from New York City to Washington, D.C. The role of travel arteries in the changing pattern of land use is thus illustrated on an even grander scale. The Megalopolis in the northeastern part of the United States, from southern New Hampshire and Boston to northern Virginia and Washington, D.C., may be viewed as one great integrated metropolitan area incorporating New York, Philadelphia, Baltimore, and Washington, as well as New Haven, Providence, and Boston into a continuous metropolitan region. All of this developed because of progressive improvement in modes of transportation.

An engaging but effective way of illustrating these emerg-

A. PROBLEMS OF THE ASPHALT ENVIRONMENT

ing patterns for large cities is to recall that Ebbets Field in the center of Brooklyn and the Polo Grounds in Manhattan were demolished and replaced with Shea Stadium in Queens, a relatively marginal part of New York City. The new stadium is surrounded by a giant parking lot and a network of parkways and highways. Even more revealing is the fact that the Minnesota Twins play in Bloomington, a suburb between the Twin Cities, and the Washington Senators were shifted to a location between two great cities in Texas rather than within any one particular large city. This is also reflected in the trend toward naming big league ball teams by state designation rather than by city—the Texas Rangers, California Angels, and so forth. Improvements in methods of transportation have made it possible for metropolitan areas to grow larger and larger, as cities run together to become urban conglomerates or conurbations. It is therefore not unreasonable to contemplate the shift of the New York football Giants to New Jersey at a point on the other side of George Washington Bridge. In reality this is merely a relocation within the same metropolitan community. Some decades ago, the Newark Bears and the Jersey City Giants were important minor league baseball teams. Today neither team exists. The decline of minor league baseball in New Jersey was due to an expanding transportation network which allowed fans to travel longer distances in shorter time to watch the big league teams in New York City. The scope of the integrated and interdependent metropolitan area is growing ever larger.

It is no longer bizarre but rather commonplace for New Yorkers to commute to Miami or Palm Beach for a weekend. Today these resorts are recreational backyards for people who live in the metropolitan conglomerate we call Megalopolis. Long ago, improved transportation turned the Adirondack Mountains of upstate New York and the ski slopes of Vermont into recreational facilities for urbanites. According to some, this has had the effect of reducing weekend vacationing within the city.

Although these areas are still geographically classified rural, they are urban culturally and economically because the local residents derive their livelihood by catering to the leisure pursuits of city people. Were it not for the fact that urban dwellers could travel several hundred miles with ease, this kind of differentiated but integrated land use could not have unfolded. These are manifestations of the wide-ranging effects of the forces of urbanization which on a more local level produce a blurring of the urban-rural dichotomy. Years ago one could recognize the relatively abrupt end of the urban community and the beginning of rural areas as one moved out of the city. Today, urbanization has reached out beyond the city and urban areas fade away slowly into a marginal area which contains intermingled aspects of both urban and rural, a condition we have come to call "rurbanization." The latter is the suburban areas which in the United States surround all large cities and necessitate their redesignation as metropolitan regions.

Having described some of the advantageous features of the recently emerged patterns of land use in American cities, I will round out the picture by touching upon some liabilities and disadvantages which have resulted as well. Among the things which have happened and trouble us deeply as a result of increased mobility and the concomitant growth and spatial expansion of cities is the polarization of races. Blacks overwhelmingly live in the central city and whites, especially the affluent, live on the periphery or in the suburban communities. As a matter of fact, improved highway networks make it possible to bypass the inner city completely, thus rendering invisible black poverty in the slums. Whites are detached from the problems of the black community which is both out of sight and mind. Black and white communities are isolated from each other although in reality they are mutually dependent, for both are segments of a single, large urban unity.

To conduct transportation planning has become more difficult. We have the traditional kinds of movement from the outer part of the city to the central business district where people work. However, other patterns have developed. There is much reverse commuting, people living in the central city and travelling to the outer portions of the city or beyond to go to work. For example, many blacks who live in Harlem are employed in the large Ford Motor Company assembly plant in Mahwah, New Jersey. Cross-commuting is a pattern in which those who reside on one point of the circumference of a large city travel to another point either in a wide, high-mileage arc or through the heart of the city with its frustrating and time-consuming traffic congestion. What were once constructed as leisurely, pleasure parkways are now commuter arteries. The trip to work by conveyance in today's expanded city sometimes takes the same amount of time as the one by foot in the compact city, but it adds pollution to the environment and reduces muscle tone in the human body.

The new traffic systems and travel patterns also tend to make the inner city obsolete. This should not be permitted to happen. The city has been the center of culture as well as the generator of intellectual, scientific, and technological advance. But the automobile is hungry for land. Many millions of dollars are needed to construct a mile of highway within the built-up parts of a city. A tremendous amount of land is needed for parking and the construction of highway and turnpike rights-of-way and interchanges. Other city arteries have been turned into ugly commercial strips by the automobile, and most service stations are eyesores. The motor vehicle culture has taken a considerable amount of land off the tax rolls, placing an extra burden on other sources of income for urban communities. This is true at a time when the less affluent are left in the city while those capable of paying higher taxes often reside in communities outside the city proper. Estimates indicate that one traffic lane of public transportation (rail) can transport from 20,000 to 40,000 persons per hour; a lane of highway can only transport 2,400 persons by automobile. This is far too generous a contribution to make to the automobile in congested urban areas.

It is unfortunate also that many urban and semi-urban areas are so deficient in public transportation that people are almost completely dependent upon the automobile. The poor are severely penalized because they have to spend a far greater share of their meager income on the ownership and operation of cars than they should. A recent estimate has put the cost of operating an auto at about fifteen cents per mile. Some urban dwellers can indulge in this luxury; many should not. In spite of this, the urban land use and population group distribution patterns within the present-day urban community leave no alternative.

Today people are travelling by private conveyance in more directions for a wide variety of reasons. The contemporary city is both a product and causative factor of this increased flow. Urbanization and spatial mobility are inextricably bound together and what affects one will probably affect the other. Better organization and management of human energy and creativity can improve the quality of urban life.

A. PROBLEMS OF THE ASPHALT ENVIRONMENT

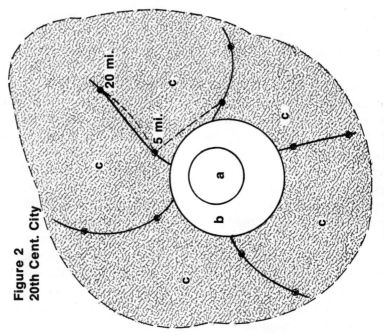

Figure 2
20th Cent. City

Metropolitan Network

20 mi.
5 mi.

Figure 1
19th Cent. City

20 mi.
5 mi.

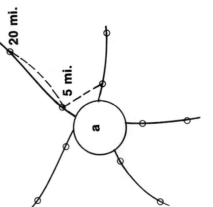

Urban Network

10. the modern plague: urban pollution

Richard Stalter

Pollution is an undesirable change in the physical, chemical, or biological characteristics of the earth's air, land, or water that may harmfully affect human life and/or that of all organisms, our industrial processes, living condition, or our natural resources. Pollutants include things that are used by man and increase as people multiply. They increase because the demands that people make on the environment increase as technology advances. Rates of pollution are higher in urban areas than in rural regions and are higher in more industrial states than agrarian or underdeveloped ones.

When human populations were small and man lacked the technology that he has at present, the amounts of litter and garbage were comparatively small. Today, with a population in excess of three billion, the world's pile of refuse increases at the rate of approximately one and a half million tons per day. This vast amount of material is even more significant when it is viewed by the city dweller. The concentration of great numbers of people in the cities exacerbates the problem. The average city dweller produces approximately 1,500 pounds of garbage a year.

Much of this material passes into the air in the form of solid pollutants, amounting to a total of 140 million tons annually. We

A. Problems of the Asphalt Environment

become cognizant of this waste when it coats our clothing and cars or causes difficulty in our breathing. But air pollution is not new. The walled cities of Europe had problems with wood smoke 700 years ago. The advent of coal as fuel in the early thirteenth century was the harbinger of the smog era. By the middle of that century the problem had become so intolerable that Parliament issued a death penalty to reinforce laws prohibiting burning coal in London. Other cities during this period had similar problems.

Perhaps the most publicized recent smog problem occurred in 1952 when an estimated 4,000 people lost their lives due to dense smog which covered London for four days. During fifteen days of heavy smog in 1963 the normal death rate in New York City increased by 650. It is estimated that fifty million Americans live in cities which have a major smog problem.

To understand the effects and causes of smog, one must examine atmospheric circulation. Air masses are not evenly dispersed over the earth's surface. Rather, the air's composition, gaseous pollutants, and movement depend on the nature of the ecosystems included within each specific area, defined as an "air-shed." The prevailing winds for most of the United States during most of the year are from west to east. There are some seasonal variations, especially for the southernmost parts of the country. This prevailing movement of air masses replenishes the air-sheds of the country with fresh air but occasionally special meteorological conditions prevent this.

The most common of these conditions is temperature inversion, which consists of a layer of warm air overriding a layer of cold air. The warm air acts as a trap for the exhaust of autos and factories, while being caught and concentrated in the layer of colder air. Topography (such as conditions that exist near Los Angeles) and slow moving high pressure systems in the troposphere may cause conditions that produce temperature inversions. The result is smog, the visible material trapped in the air below an inversion layer.

112

The composition of smog reflects the life processes of the city. An incomplete list of some of these substances would include sulfur dioxide, nitrogen oxides, carbon monoxide, aldehydes, organic acids, and various hydrocarbons. In addition, secondary pollutants may form from the primary emissions. These compounds are just as toxic as their predecessors and exist as certain acids and aldehydes. Dr. A. J. Haagen Smit has described the various photochemical reactions that produce these toxic substances. According to him, automobiles are the primary cause of most organic vapors, carbon monoxide, and carbon dioxide. Other contributors include heavy industry, refineries, public dumps, and home incinerators. These are much more serious in heavily populated urban areas.

The increased amount of smog over cities produces another interesting phenomenon, the greenhouse effect. The burning of fossil fuels such as gasoline, oil, and coal release large amounts of carbon dioxide, carbon monoxide, sulfur dioxide, and other gases. Many city dwellers know of the shroud that hangs over homes and apartments that is caused by these processes. The high concentration of these gasses absorb heat (longer wave length radiation) which would normally be reflected off into the stratosphere. The accretion of heat energy from this longer wave length radiation tends to raise the temperature of the lowest atmospheric layers. To corroborate this phenomenon, the suburban dweller can check his thermometer with the morning temperature in the city. The difference in temperature between the core of the city and a suburban area twenty miles away may be more than twenty degrees under certain conditions.

However, recent evidence suggests that on a world wide basis the opposite effect may be produced. The increase in the amount of dust and gasses in the earth's atmosphere may reduce the amount of solar radiation reaching the surface of the earth and may also initiate cloud condensation. This would tend to cool the surface of the earth. Aynsley (1969) postulates that an

113

increase of only five percent in the cloud cover over the world would drop temperatures to the point that the earth would be plunged into a new ice age.

Another type of pollution that threatens the quality of the city's environment is noise pollution. Noise is measured in decibels, a relative unit of measurement based on the log of the ratio of sound intensity to a reference level arbitrarily established as a sound pressure of 0.0002 microbars. This arbitrary measurement can barely be heard by man. A sound of ten, twenty, or fifty decibels represents ten, twenty and fifty times the threshold intensity respectively. Noise on a busy city street corner may range from 70 to 100db (decibels) while noise under a jet airplane at takeoff may be as high as 160 db. Noise higher than 120 db causes physical discomfort, while noise at 180 db is lethal.

The most difficult problem in noise control may lie in evaluating types and effects of noise. A sonic boom, for example, may be more disruptive to a class of students than continuous noise. Perhaps the performance and emotional stability of students in school near airports might be compared to similar students in quieter situations. Another area of research might be the incidence of violent crimes as related to the amount of noise in a particular area. If the body is constantly bombarded with noise, the concentration of adreneline in the individual's system might be higher than in a quieter situation, and make the individual more prone to commit crimes.

Apart from its effect on people directly, a sonic boom may break windows or even crack walls of buildings. Consideration of the SST and the concomitant effect of the sonic boom and noise in general may have partially resulted in the project's demise in the United States.

The automobile also creates problems in urban areas. It is one of the greatest consumers of natural resources in our country, indeed some sixty percent of all the rubber and twenty percent of the steel in the country are used in manufacturing cars. The automobile accounts for sixty percent of all of the air pollution in the United States. In cities the automobile may cause eighty percent of the pollution, and at certain times of the day (commuter "rush hour") it may produce over ninety percent of all the carbon monoxide in the air and more than sixty percent of all the unburned hydrocarbons.

The large number of cars (now over 100 million) has resulted in the need for more roads, and by 1980 over four million miles of road will be paved in the United States. New roads do not always alleviate the problems they were supposed to solve. The Long Island Expressway, for example, was planned to handle the traffic of the "future." Many individuals who travel this road to and from New York City have ample experience that the planners grossly underestimated the number of cars that would use the facility. The traffic problem of other major cities is equally bleak.

Garbage or solid waste is one of the largest and toughest problems of the public works department. Each day approximately 800 million pounds of garbage are produced in America. Garbage consists of metals (tin cans and aluminum cans), glass, paper products (cardboard boxes and food packages), leaves, sticks, and other organic yard debris, abandoned cars and trucks, food processing wastes, lumber, metal scraps, soot from factories, masonry, paints, concrete products, stone (from building demolition), and many other products. The collection and subsequent disposal of these wastes is costly. It has been estimated that the cost of garbage disposal services is in excess of one and a half billion dollars. It is quite probable that the figure may double or triple by 1980.

The problem of garbage disposal is especially serious in large cities where population density is high and land for disposal of wastes is limited. One of the chief ways that wastes are disposed of is by means of the sanitary landfill, consisting of layers of garbage mixed with layers of soil. In certain areas the sanitary landfill may be used to form fill for levees (where flooding is a

115

problem). In Evanston, Illinois, a mound of soil and refuse was covered with dirt and seeded; now it is the site of a winter toboggan and sled run.

Unfortunately, the affluence of American society creates a large waste disposal problem with a corresponding apathy for corrective measures. Saving old bottles or aluminum cans is "not worth the effort." Making compost heaps of grass clippings, weeds, and leaves, which would alleviate a tremendous amount of organic matter from dumps, is harder than buying fertilizer at the store. It is only recently that we have begun to think of positive uses for the discarded byproducts of an abundant economy. For instance, we are now investigating the possibility of using certain waste material to power generators in urban areas.

Prior to the Industrial Revolution the amount of waste in lakes and rivers reached only local significance. In primitive societies human excrement was often thrown into the streets and during times of heavy rains was washed into the nearby streams and lakes. The advent of the indoor toilet in the early nineteenth century did not really change the situation, since the sewage was then collected and dumped untreated into the nearest waterway. Even today in the United States approximately twenty percent of the sewage produced is dumped into watercourses in this manner.

Pollution of coastal waters is a serious problem since cities traditionally pipe their waste out into the ocean. The situation has become so serious that many bathing areas near cities are now either closed or so polluted that their use is seriously limited. Unfortunately the usual "solution" to this problem is to dump sewage further out in the ocean!

One of the major pollutants in urban areas is detergents. In the 1950s many detergents consisted of complex molecules that were not readily broken down by stream and water bacteria. The primary culprit was alkyl benzene sulfonate, which was widely used in most synthetic detergents. The result was layers of foam and scum in many urban areas where these detergents were used.

116

Later, detergents were placed on the market that were readily degraded by bacteria. One important part of these detergents was phosphorus, a substance usually found in limited quantities in aquatic ecosystems. The dumping of large amounts of these detergents into the nation's waterways resulted in a population explosion of algae and bacteria. The rapid growth of these microorganisms often depleted the oxygen areas and caused fishkills. Another unpleasant side effect was the population explosion of certain algae that rendered ponds and lakes aesthetically unattractive. In the early 1970s ecology-minded businessmen placed low phosphate detergents (or their substitutes) on the market. The use of these detergents may partially solve the "detergent pollution" problem of our urban aquatic ecosystems.

Other problems of water pollution include radioactive isotopes, mercury, heavy metals, and lead pollution. Mercury pollution has caused swordfish to be withdrawn from United States markets. Mercury compounds have been used to suppress seed-borne diseases, to provide protection against fungal attack during seed germination, in pulp industries (paper production), chlorine factories, and even in the manufacture of certain acrylic paints. Control of mercury pollution in industrial waste water is difficult. Like DDT and other compounds, mercury may become magnified at each trophic level of a particular ecosystem. Efforts are now being made to monitor the levels of mercury and other toxic compounds and to keep their levels as low as possible.

Many other man made products are nondegradable pollutants, such as tin and aluminum cans, plastics and cellophane, nylon, and poisons such as DDT, mercurial salts, and long-chain phenolic compounds. The solid wastes at best will accumulate in the ecosystem unless recycled where possible by man. The poisons mentioned above not only accumulate but may also become biologically magnified as they move along food chains. The solid wastes are a much greater problem in and near urban environments. The other substances are a problem throughout urban

117

and rural ecosystems. Substances such as DDT can be found in penguins in antarctic ecosystems where no DDT has ever been used. The answer to the question of how DDT could enter the bodies of penguins is related to their food habits and how DDT moves along and becomes magnified in food chains.

The health of the city dweller usually is affected to a much greater degree by air pollution than his rural neighbor. Carbon monoxide, a gas produced by the incomplete burning of fuel (especially prevalent in automobile exhaust), may cause nausea, headaches, and dizziness. Carbon monoxide is absorbed into the blood much more readily than oxygen. Increased amounts of this gas in the blood impairs mental processes and might be a major factor in the cause of accidents in the city. Sulfur oxides irritate the upper respiratory tract and will also damage trees, destroy pigments, corrode metals, and harm textiles. Nitrogen oxides irritate the eyes and nose. These gasses stunt plant growth and corrode metals. Hydrocarbons, which are produced from burning a multiplicity of compounds, may cause cancer. Under proper laboratory conditions certain hydrocarbons have retarded the growth of plants and have caused abnormal bud and leaf development. The particulate matter in the atmosphere may corrode metals, cause grime on buildings, and aggravate lung illness and obscure vision.

It is important to note that the aforementioned pollutants are both specific and general. The concentration of these substances and synergistic effects (that is, two or more substances working together to increase the deleterious effect of each pollutant) cause a great amount of human suffering. A final point to ponder is the effect that pollutants may have on the genetic material of man. Pollutants (exclusive of radioactive wastes) may produce some mutations. Since most mutations are harmful, the cost to future generations in terms of treating these genetic disorders should be considered when efforts are made to produce a healthy environment.

118

11. ecology and urban areas

Richard Stalter

The scope and diversity of the subject matter that may be included in the concept of ecology are so great that they cannot be adequately dealt with in a short essay. The term "ecology" is derived from the Greek word *oikos* meaning "home of" and *logos* which may be translated as "the study of." "Home" implies both the presence of organisms and also conditions linking them to their environment. Thus, a simple definition of ecology will suffice: the study of organisms in relation to their environment. Much of the basic subject matter of ecology has long been part of general scientific knowledge. This knowledge has been added to by specialists in other fields of biology such as botany and physiology, and areas in science outside of biology including geology, climatology, and geography.

As a specialized field of science, ecology is relatively new. Most individuals were unaware that the field existed until a few years ago. Actually the name first appeared in 1869 as "oecology" and did not immediately gain wide recognition and acceptance. Most of the advancements in the field have occurred during this century.

Although ecologists may concern themselves with organisms, populations communities, or even larger or smaller levels of organization, the basic unit of ecology is the ecosystem. An ecosystem includes all of the living organisms in a given area that interact with the physical environment so that there exists an exchange of materials between living and nonliving parts within the system. A vacant field or a rotting log in the city park can be studied as an ecosystem. An ecosystem may be more or less sharply set off from surrounding ecosystems, as a lake is set off from the surrounding dry land, or one ecosystem may grade gradually into another. Moreover, the grading or separation of ecosystems may depend upon the criteria used by the examiner, so that distinctions between a pond and the surrounding forest may be very small if one concentrates his study at the edge of these two ecosystems.

One concept of ecology which is related directly to urban life is the role of energy in ecological systems. "Energy" is defined as the ability to do work. The behavior of energy is described by the following laws of thermodynamics. The first law of thermodynamics states that energy may be transformed from one type to another but is not created or destroyed. For example, chemical energy can be transformed into heat energy. The second law of thermodynamics states that no process involving an energy transformation will spontaneously occur unless there is a degradation of the energy from a concentrated form into a dispersed form. An example is the dispersion of heat from a hot object such as a radiator into the cooler air of a room.

The second law of thermodynamics is related to the stability principle. According to this concept, any natural enclosed system with energy flowing through it tends to change until a stable adjustment with self-regulating mechanisms is developed. These self-regulating mechanisms are needed to bring about a return to constancy should a system change from the stable state to the unstable state because of a momentary outside influence. The myriad of activities occurring in urban areas constantly test the self-regulating mechanisms of ecosystems within the city or near them.

120

Richard Stalter

The city violates most of the natural laws of energy and is maintained by exploiting the environment. Fossil fuels that may have taken thousands or millions of years to form are burned each day to run man's machines and heat his homes and offices. Moreover, the city produces a vast amount of waste that greatly taxes the ability of decomposer organisms to break down these substances into simpler forms that can be used again by the living components of the aquatic and terrestrial ecosystems that surround the city. Many of the waste products of the city are not broken down since the decomposer organisms lack the special enzyme systems needed to break down these waste products. Also, the city's industries may produce toxic substances such as mercury or lead which may accumulate in one trophic level (portion of the food chain) or may become magnified in each succeeding trophic level.

The city and its inhabitants alter the environment and the ecosystems that surround them by producing an undesirable change in the physical, chemical, or biological characteristics of the surrounding air, land, or water. These deleterious changes may affect human life as well as that of other organisms. In addition our industrial processes, living conditions, and our natural resources are affected. A single word connotes all of the above— pollution. As technology advances people make greater demands on the environment. It is obvious that rates of pollution are higher for more industrialized areas of the world and are highest near the urban sites of these countries. As areas become more urbanized, the rate of pollution increases and greater stress is placed upon the urban ecosystems.

The city may disrupt (pollute) the ecosystems in and near itself in several ways. In the manufacturing of substances, wastes may be dumped into the waters or into the air. Two examples are mercurial salts and long chain phenolic compounds which do not degrade readily in the natural environment. These nondegradable pollutants not only accumulate but are often biologically magnified as they move along food chains. Frequently they combine with other compounds in the environment to produce additional toxins. These compounds kill or retard the growth of living organisms in and near the city's ecosystems.

In addition to the nonbiodegradable substances are the biodegradable pollutants. These substances include domestic sewage which can be decomposed by natural processes. In the process of degradation, however, the microorganisms may utilize all of the oxygen in the water to break down the excess organic material. The other life in the streams, rivers, lakes, or oceans need oxygen and may die if amounts of oxygen are reduced or are depleted.

The city's need for power is much greater than similar sized rural areas. In addition to the burning of fossil fuels to run generators, atomic energy is also being used to generate power, and the increased use of atomic power has generated two new problems of pollution, thermal pollution and radioactive pollution. Thermal pollution places a great deal of stress on aquatic ecosystems and the nature of life near thermally polluted areas may be drastically altered. For example, the phytoplankton component of the ecosystem may be changed if the microscopic plants cannot live at the elevated water temperatures and thus the entire food chain may be altered since the heterotrophic organisms (everything from zooplankton to insects and fish) ultimately draw their nourishment from the producers of the ecosystem. In addition, the warmer water may exclude certain heterotrophic species from the area.

Radioactive wastes are also a problem since many radioactive substances are readily picked up by organisms and are magnified at each step of the food chain. Even a small amount of radioactive material may cause mutations that over a long period of time may lead to the demise of organisms, or if the material is greatly concentrated will kill the organism almost immediately. Higher forms of life, such as mammals, are much more susceptible to radioactive material than lower forms of life, such as insects. If man eats organisms that are even slightly contaminated by radioactive material, his progeny may be affected. It is important to note that mutation rates would probably be small. However, when millions or even billions of individuals are considered, even a very small increase in the number of genetic defects would be costly.

The need for housing space has resulted in the filling in of marshlands which are among the most productive areas of the world. Since salt marshes are located within the boundaries of the major cities on the east coast, let us examine in some detail the effects of urbanization on the rich estuaries and marshes in the eastern United States.

When the United States was first settled, people chose coastal areas or large rivers since these areas served as excellent ports that would link them with their parent countries. The major cities of colonial America: Boston, New York, Philadelphia, and Charleston all had excellent port facilities. As these cities grew, the marshes bore the brunt of their expansion. (*Life and Death of a Salt March* by the Teals outlines the utilization of the marshes in Boston by the colonists even before 1700.) Today each of these cities, with the exception of Philadelphia which is not a salt water port, has destroyed a large portion of its salt marshes and has polluted its estuaries. The importance of marshes and estuaries can be demonstrated in the following ways.

A comparison of the productivity of various ecosystems will demonstrate the importance of a salt marsh. Both the open ocean and desert produce about the same amount of organic matter, approximately one third of a ton of organic matter per acre per year. Farms in most temperate regions produce between one and a half to five tons of plant material per acre per year, though some extremely productive farms produce slightly higher amounts of plant material. Estuaries and salt marshes, however, produce from five to ten tons of material per acre each year.

Their high productivity results from their constant tidal replenishing with nutrients. The same tides usually cleanse the area of wastes that are dumped into the area, but if pollution is severe, this cleansing may not be accomplished since much of the same volume of water that floods the marsh at one tide may reflood the marsh again and again, because of the peculiar flushing dynamics of estuaries.

To emphasize the importance of marshes and estuaries, let us examine the myriad life forms that exist in the marshes and estuaries or depend upon these ecosystems for their complete or partial life cycles. Many fish that spend much of their time in the ocean spawn in estuarine environments and/or spend a portion of their lives in the estuarine environment. Shellfish and shrimp are other commercially valuable estuarine species.

In addition to the obvious value as a producer of food, the marshes serve man in still another way. During severe storms the marshes mitigate the savage effect of the pounding surf. The marshes are covered by shallow water during the time of storms and the waves that arrive in this area will break and their tremendous energy dissipate before they can do serious damage to land. The only damage to the marsh would be the deposit of sand washed from other areas, that is, barrier beaches and the erosion of portions of the mud bank at the lowest tide level. After the storm the marsh will quickly rebuild itself. The plants will spread vegetatively by rhizomes or by seed into the damaged areas. The plants will trap mud and other debris and gradually the damage to the marsh will be repaired.

In spite of the important functions of salt marshes, man has unwisely destroyed the marshes with dredging spoils and has used marshlands for houses or industrial buildings. These areas may be completely destroyed during severe storms since they are usually not very high above sea level and the action of large waves may completely destroy breakwaters and the houses and buildings behind them. Even if the salt marshes were not the nursery grounds for shellfish and fish, it would be far wiser and cheaper to allow the land to remain untouched.

Unfortunately it is difficult to educate people when viewing marshes as marshes or land when covered with dredged material worth $100,000 per acre or more in urban areas. The vast brackish marshes in the New Jersey meadowland have been ravaged by those who use the area as a garbage dump. Undeveloped land such as the New Jersey meadowland has always been viewed as worthless since man could not build his homes or industrial buildings on these sites.

Thus, to summarize, most ecosystems near urban areas have a profound effect upon more than just the life within the area or ecosystem considered. Destruction of natural habitat may hasten the forces of erosion which will cause costly repairs or cause the necessity of the construction of breakwaters to protect built up portions of our low-lying urban areas. In addition, a severe storm may cause extensive damage to the above site in terms of damage to buildings and to human life. For example, if the city of Charleston, South Carolina is hit by a strong hurricane at flood tide much of the city may be destroyed. Charlestonians to date have had the good fortune to have been missed by most hurricanes or have been hit by the storms at low tide.

The above example points up the need for city planners to acquaint themselves with ecological concepts when they are planning massive projects in marshlands or in low lying areas. First, marshes should not be used as building sites, garbage dumps, or areas where dredging spoils are dumped. Land that is near tidal creeks or marshes should be set aside as park land, or better still, as sanctuaries since severe storms may destroy anything that is built on old marshes. Individuals who plan to build in new areas should be educated to the pitfalls that might destroy their buildings if they were to construct in these flood and storm vulnerable areas.

The marshes should not be used as garbage dumps or for

125

sewage disposal. These practices may destroy the plants in the marsh. Death of the plants will lead to erosion of the marshland. As the marshes erode, much of the silt may accumulate in ship channels and will greatly increase the cost of harbor maintenance. If the sewage does not kill the plants and animals in the marsh, it will render commercially valuable shellfish unfit to eat. Tons of commercially valuable oysters go unharvested in polluted waters in the harbors of many of our southern cities. In addition, the combination of sewage and decaying vegetation will produce noxious odors that will offend the city dweller's olfactory senses and the quality of life of the urban environment.

The cutting of trees and destruction of terrestrial habitats has similarly reduced the number of organisms that can be found in fields and forests. However, some animals have adapted themselves to the change of forest habitat to urban sprawl. For instance, rats may be favored by the city environment. Old buildings, open dumps, and poor refuse collection often result in increased rat population in the city. Setting poison or trapping the rats will only temporarily alleviate the problem of rat infestation if the other problems are not corrected. Given a certain amount of food and adequate shelter, a portion of the city may support a rat population of a particular size. If you remove most of the available food the rats will die or leave the area to find food elsewhere.

The activities of the city contribute to the alteration of ecosystems. Many of these activities such as manufacturing, heating, transportation, and building are obviously necessary to maintain the city and its inhabitants. Urban life is here to stay but cities need not completely and irreversibly alter the environment. To solve some of the problems of the city and to improve the quality of the life of its people, the following suggestions are offered.

Measures should be provided to encourage and enhance mass transit. Most of the pollution in our country is caused by the exhaust of automobiles. The roads that connect the city to suburban areas are often not equipped to handle the number of vehicles that travel to and from the city during the business day. Moreover, once in the city, parking places are scarce or non-existent. These factors should encourage people to use buses, subways, and trains to commute to work.

People should be educated as to the desirability of recycling substances such as paper, glass, and aluminum. In addition, levels of air pollution, water pollution, and noise pollution can be reduced and in some cases eliminated. With proper education, individuals may be willing to vote for measures that would provide funds that may be used to clean up the environment and make the city a healthier place to live.

The enormity of many environmental problems might be reduced if models of the problems are considered and analyzed with the modern tools of technology such as computers. Mathematical models could be used to predict, for example, how many cars could be accommodated on a particular road at a particular time. The legal aspects of pollution laws must also be reconsidered. First, strong laws must be enacted and enforced to prevent further pollution. Second, individuals working for local, state, and federal agencies must become environmentally conscious and then perhaps they will come to consider the problem as a priority in the defense of mankind.

Finally, environmental research must be undertaken with massive funding. To determine the needs of research, planners must ascertain where the specific problems exist and develop technologies that will eliminate these problems. In addition monitoring systems may be needed to trace the movement of waste materials through ecosystems near the cities. If these steps are taken, the quality of life in the city will improve, and the ecosystems in the city and adjacent to cities may not be irreversibly altered.

12. the darker side of urban life: slums in the city

Ronald H. Bayor

Slums are found in many American cities and are clearly the most obvious example of the problems facing urban America. While most people are aware of the existence of these blighted sections, few understand the forces which have created slums. How do good areas of a city, represented by decent housing, adequate sanitation facilities, and low crime, disease, and mortality rates become slums in fairly short periods of time? The process has been one which has been repeated over and over again in a large number of cities. An effort will be made to observe slum formation in three different situations: in nineteenth century New York, in nineteenth century Boston, and in twentieth century New York. Also the similarities in slum living will be noted.

The first point, however, which should be considered is exactly what is a slum? It can be defined as an area of dilapidated housing with a high population density of low-income individuals. The area is also marked by high crime, disease, and mortality rates. The actual structures in slums can vary depending on the city under study. For example, New York's slum sections are usually made up of apartment houses four or five stories high while those of Philadelphia are mainly attached row houses two stories high. Slum housing could also consist of unattached shacks or shanties as found in Washington, D.C. and Chicago. All are different forms of housing, found in slum areas. The important fact is that although the look of the slum can vary, the forces which create them remain the same.

Nineteenth century New York represents a good example of these forces at work. The area in question is lower Manhattan, which, before the entry of immigrants about 1825, was an upper and middle class section, considered fashionable and convenient because it was near the business district. In 1830 the well-to-do population began to leave the area and move further north in Manhattan. Abandoned was the good housing and still clean and peaceful streets. The out migration of the prosperous class was the result of the expansion of the business district into the residential section and the influx of poor immigrants who needed to be near their places of employment.

The look of the area changed rapidly with the population shift. Some of the good housing was razed and replaced with commercial structures. The remaining residential buildings were allowed to deteriorate since it was expected that these dwellings would soon be torn down to make way for still more commercial developments. Rather than this occurring, the buildings began to house the poor immigrants. However, the structures were ill suited for the poor class. One immigrant family could not afford to buy or rent a dwelling which had housed one middle class family. Therefore large buildings, where only one upper or middle class family had lived before, were partitioned to house a number of immigrant families. The conversion of stately mansions into boardinghouses is an illustration of the subdivisions which accompanied the change in class populations. However, even this was not enough to meet the housing needs of the larger and poorer immigrant group.

The incessant demand for housing led to the construction of new dwellings crowded in among the old. What was once a spacious lawn became the site of a poorly built shanty. What was

129

once an alleyway became the site of a tenement. The area began to take on the crowded look of a slum. Builders and landlords, desirous of quick profits, built cheaply and charged high rents to this house-hungry population.

The factor of high rents for poor families was in itself a part of the slum formation process. It further impoverished these people by forcing them to pay more out of their income for rent than was economically wise. It also forced many to take in boarders to help pay the rent. The need to bring strangers into the home for monetary reasons, besides creating a social problem within the home, also increased density levels in each slum structure. Finally the crush of population and the demand for housing led to the conversion of cellars, attics, and stables into apartments. By 1850, 29,000 people were occupying cellar apartments in New York.

Overcrowding was therefore one of the prime forces in the creation of the slum. The average block density in lower Manhattan increased from 157.5 persons in 1820 to 272.5 persons in 1850. Overcrowding combined with deterioration of existing housing because of lack of repairs and cheaply constructed new housing quickly converted what was previously a good area into a slum. With a large, poor population living in close, inadequate quarters, the neighborhood saw a rise in disease, mortality, and crime rates. A slum had emerged.

The second example is that of Boston in the mid-nineteenth century during the period of Irish immigration. Here the forces which create the slum are remarkably similar to the process in New York. The Irish, when they arrived in Boston, began to congregate near the docks, workshops, and offices in the older sections of the city. The middle and upper classes which had inhabited the area began to flee leaving behind what was adequate housing for them. The entry of the Irish brought in a poorer and larger population with the subsequent demand for more housing. Overcrowding quickly developed and soon every middle and upper class dwelling was partitioned for its new inhabitants. A need for new housing produced cheaply constructed dwellings built in every conceivable empty lot. What was once an area of homes with spacious grounds became a congested slum with dilapidated houses packed closely together.

The increased demand for housing also fostered high rents as landlords had virtually a captive population unable to move elsewhere due to discrimination and the cost of commuting to work. High rents, as in New York, necessitated the taking in of boarders and produced the same results, overcrowding. Within a short time the area became noted for crime, disease, filth, and poverty. Another slum had emerged.

The slum creation examples cited thus far have been inner city areas in which immigrants first settled. Both sections also were near central business districts. In the illustration of slum formation from the twentieth century, the area was far from any central business district, was not a first settlement zone for immigrants, and was long considered to be an upper class suburb. Yet the same slum creation process was at work. The area is early twentieth century Harlem in New York.

Harlem was the last place, according to contemporary observers, that a slum would ever emerge. In the late nineteenth century it was strictly an upper middle and upper class section kept as a preserve for the rich who settled there to escape the immigrants of the inner city. Poor transportation facilities kept the population of the area low. Harlem remained a prosperous suburb even after the elevated railroad extended into the neighborhood in 1879 and population increased. The major types of dwellings were the luxury apartment houses complete with elevators and servant's quarters as well as privately owned brownstones. Rents were high enough to keep out all but the well-to-do. Harlem was a good, stable, wealthy community.

Due to forces introduced in the late 1890s, the area was to change drastically within twenty years. The first indication of

131

change came with the construction of subway lines into the Harlem area. The result of new, cheap transit lines was to encourage building in anticipation of a large influx of population. The houses constructed were still of a good type for the expectation was that other prosperous families would move into the neighborhood because of the improved transportation system. By 1904, most of the builders were beginning to realize that too many structures had been put up. The population of the area increased but not by the numbers hoped for. As landlords competed for tenants, rents fell. Faced with financial collapse, the owners opened the houses to anyone willing to pay. This included blacks who were moving up from the west side of Manhattan and anxious to secure decent housing. Previously there had been little black penetration of Harlem due to discriminatory practices. With the entry of a larger and poorer population, the housing, once maintained at a high level by the landlords, was slowly allowed to deteriorate. The slum was emerging.

As in the cases of nineteenth century New York and Boston, when the poorer class moved in, the middle and upper classes began to flee. Left behind were mansions, luxury apartment houses, and brownstones. Filling the void were blacks not only from New York but also from the South. The black population of Harlem increased from 91,000 in 1910 to 327,000 in 1930. The population increase created a demand for housing which sent rents up again, but this time it was a low-income group paying the rents. The result, in many cases, was that boarders were brought in to help pay the rent. Overcrowding followed.

The buildings also were not suitable for the poorer group. Apartments of six or seven rooms were perfect for a large, prosperous family but not for a small, working class one. The housing had simply been built for another class, but the blacks made an effort to adjust to what was unsuitable but at least decent housing. To make use of the large apartments and pay the rent, families often doubled up or the apartments were partitioned so that seven

132

rooms became seven apartments. Many brownstones and mansions were converted into boardinghouses which were clear indications of the deterioration of the neighborhood. What was needed was low cost but decent housing with apartments to fit the size of the families in the community. This was simply not available, and as a result overcrowding in each dwelling occurred.

The slum finally emerged when the area began to show the usual increases in the crime, disease, and mortality rates. Harlem at this point was an undesirable, deteriorating residential community where once had stood a seemingly durable wealthy neighborhood.

The same slum creation forces were at work in these three examples and would also fit other situations. Whether the area was a nineteenth century Boston inner city section or a twentieth century New York suburb, the decline of the neighborhood began with the out migration of the wealthier citizens upon the entry of the poorer population. After this class shift, overcrowding, high rents, lack of building maintenance, and increases in social problems all produced slums very quickly.

Not only was the slum formation process similar, but living conditions in these areas remained remarkably alike. Boston's slums in the nineteenth century were noted for their lack of sanitation and sewerage facilities. This was partly the result of overcrowding and partly the lack of interest by the city government in expanding and improving its services in poorer neighborhoods. The sections of the city which needed improvements were often the most neglected. Slums in general were well known for the garbage on the streets, rats, and overall filth. All this was a perfect breeding ground for disease and explains in part the high disease and mortality rates in slums.

The complaint expressed most often in all slum situations concerned housing. The crowding, lack of ventilation and light, and dearth of repairs were frequent grievances of slum dwellers. In the Boston slums, cellars were converted into apartments and

133

were described as having no light, poor ventilation and often filled with two to three feet of water due to faulty plumbing. The apartments both above and below ground also were not heated properly, another factor related to high disease rates. In such conditions it was virtually impossible to keep the residence clean. Walls were unpainted, roofs leaked, windows were few, and stairs were usually made of cheap wood and poorly constructed. It was no wonder that the slum dweller fled the area as soon as he had enough money and discriminatory housing barriers broke down. Housing, however, remained the predominant slum problem.

These conditions were ably described by Jacob Riis, a journalist, who wrote a number of books about slum life in New York in the late nineteenth and early twentieth centuries. In his book, *The Children of the Poor*, Riis described the horror of slum housing:

> I have in mind one . . . "flat" among many, a half underground hole in a South Fifth Avenue yard, reached by odd passageways through a tumbledown tenement that was always full of bad smells and scooting rats. Across the foul and slippery yard, down three steps made of charred timbers from some worse wreck, was this "flat," where five children slept with their elders. How many of those there were I never knew. There were three big family beds, and they nearly filled the room, leaving only patches of the mud floor visible. The walls were absolutely black with age and smoke. The plaster had fallen off in patches and there was green mold on the ceiling.

This description by Riis indicates that approximately sixty years after urban slums first appeared on a large scale little had yet been done to improve the life of the slum dweller. Of course, even more disturbing is the fact that similar conditions can be found in slum areas today.

134

There were some early city and state efforts to deal with the housing problem through the passage of tenement reform legislation. The major tenement house act in the state of New York was passed in 1901. This law required bathrooms and running water in each apartment, windows in every room, and fire protection measures such as solidly constructed stair-cases. Previous to this law, staircases, made of cheap wood, often served as death traps for tenants escaping the frequent fires that plagued the slum sections. To enforce the law in New York City, a separate Tenement House Department was established which was able to work along with the Building and the Health Departments to supervise the new and old tenements. The law was generally effective in relation to new housing, but it was difficult to renovate the old tenements. However, even with renovation and tenement laws, the old problems of high rents, poverty, and overcrowding remained. What was really needed, so contemporaries thought, was low cost but decent housing.

In Chicago, the most important tenement law was passed in 1902. This legislation provided that room sizes be increased, plumbing improved, windows put in, and the structure of the building made stronger. Housing built according to these regulations was referred to as "new law tenements." However, as in New York, many of the older dwellings remained which did not comply with the new regulations. Still many necessities were not covered by this legislation. It was not until 1910 that Chicago required a kitchen sink with running water in each apartment. Central heating requirements also came later. The new laws brought improvements but at a slow pace.

The attempt to provide good but low rental housing for the slum dweller through the construction of "model tenements" also was tried and failed. The first major effort in this direction was by Alfred T. White, a builder and philanthropist, who constructed tenements in Brooklyn in the 1870s and 1880s. His idea was that decent housing could be provided for low

135

income families while at the same time making an acceptable profit. His tenements were therefore well lighted and ventilated, had fireproof exterior staircases, sinks in every apartment as well as playgrounds. The buildings were well maintained, and boarders were prohibited to prevent overcrowding. The elimination of boarders was not an economic hardship for the tenants since rents were within what the lower income family could afford to pay. The idea was a good one, but due to the lack of interest of other builders it failed to produce a significant change in the housing situation. For the majority of builders, the goal was to maximize profits by building cheaply, charging high rents, and crowding as many people as possible into the tenement.

A different approach by private builders to construct decent housing was the Paul Laurence Dunbar Apartments in Harlem financed by John D. Rockefeller, Jr. The idea was to build a number of model apartment houses within a slum neighborhood in an effort to rehabilitate that area. The apartments were to be from two to five rooms in size. Boarders were forbidden. Nurseries were provided for working mothers and clubrooms for teenagers. Every room had adequate ventilation and light, and the building was well constructed. Seemingly everything that could be hoped for in slum area housing was provided. The building opened in 1928 just before the Depression, and this is what destroyed the plan. Since the Dunbar apartments were considered to be excellent housing, rentals were not low.

With the coming of the Depression, many tenants saw a decrease in their earnings and therefore were not able to pay high rents. The management was forced to lower the rents, do away with the restriction on boarders, and divide the larger apartments. The failure of this development is more significant when it is noted that the tenants were carefully chosen and represented an economically stable group. Rockefeller eventually sold the Dunbar apartments, and the private effort to create a neighborhood of decent housing within a slum failed.

At this point in the 1930s, the federal government stepped into the housing field with the creation of low rent projects. The financing of these projects was a turning point in slum redevelopment in the sense that the government had not felt itself responsible to provide housing for the poor before this. At the same time slum clearance was begun with the intent of totally rebuilding slum neighborhoods. Problems were evident in this approach also. More housing tended to be destroyed than was built creating a housing shortage in the slum area and raising rents higher. The projects have been criticized for becoming slums themselves. Although providing better housing, the life style of the slum remained and this is related to poverty indicating that more will be needed to eradicate slums than good housing. Finally, the projects have been castigated for being too institutional and thereby lacking the warmth and neighborly attitudes of the old communities.

Slums, now a fixture on the American urban scene, have thus far defied solution but that does not mean that the problem is insolvable. However, any answer will obviously have to deal not only with housing but also with poverty and discrimination. The immigrant experience of the nineteenth century reveals that these people were able to emerge from their slum patterns of living only after discriminatory housing, occupational, and educational barriers were removed and income rose. Coupled with the rehabilitation of poor housing, the slum problem can be handled.

13. urban political bosses: a transitional necessity in the modern American city

Philip C. Dolce

"Urban boss" and "political machine" are terms rapidly becoming part of American folklore. Though both terms have bad connotations, it can be questioned whether the boss and his machine following were totally evil and immoral. The roots of boss rule run deep in the American past but did not begin to reach fruition until the last half of the nineteenth century when the physical growth of American cities was enormous.

In 1880 only nineteen American cities had a population of 100,000 or more people. Just twenty years later the number of cities with this population nearly doubled. Urban centers such as Chicago, Detroit, Cleveland, and Milwaukee all doubled their population within a single decade. By 1900 the urban population in the United States had multiplied five times in just forty years. Along with physical growth, cities also experienced an enormous industrial and commercial expansion during this period.

Both the economic expansion and the population increase of American cities were in part due to the arrival of millions of new immigrants searching for a better way of life. American cities were soon filled with people who came from diverse national, religious, racial, ethnic, and cultural traditions. By 1910 the foreign born and the children of foreign born or mixed parentage became the largest segment of the urban population throughout the nation. The physical expansion of cities necessitated by population increases was rapid and unplanned. Suddenly, city, county, and state jurisdictions became confused causing a fragmentation of political power. As cities grew in size, they became more complex in operation. New services had to be created to serve rapidly expanding populations. Water and sewer systems had to be expanded, overhauled, or created. Streets had to be lighted, cleaned, and paved. Public utilities such as light, gas, and transportation had to be provided. New housing had to be built while schools for millions of children had to be created.

Municipal governments throughout the United States were relatively informal in operation and therefore, completely unprepared to respond to these rapidly changing conditions. The officials of many cities were usually prominent citizens who served without pay and devoted a few hours a day to their municipal duties. Most urban services were either nonexistent or provided on a voluntary basis. Roving bands of hogs, for instance, served in some cities as garbage collectors. Kitchen waste usually was allowed to run into the streets, few of which were paved. Volunteer fire departments were the norm in most urban centers while professional police departments were all but nonexistent. City government was usually decentralized, with inadequate home rule powers, and philosophically committed to a minimum interference in its citizens' lives. Thus, a gap was created in our political system by the changes resulting from swift industrialization and enormous urban growth. America's emerging cities seemed plunged into crisis and disorder.

Into the midst of uncertainty and change came the boss and the political machine. The boss and machine politicians offered organization and continuity while imposing order and direction

139

in American cities. They did this by unofficially centralizing political power and thereby allowing cities to function. In short, the political system of boss rule was necessary in the transition of America from a nineteenth century relatively simple agrarian society to a highly complex urban industrial society of the twentieth century. By 1890 virtually every sizable American city either had a political machine or was in the process of developing one.

What were these political machines like? To some individuals such as Lord James Bryce, the political machine was an organization held together by the evils of patronage and spoils. Others pointed out that the political machine was undemocratic, resembling a feudal system of unswerving loyalty and unquestioning obedience. No doubt there is a great deal of truth in this view. Edward Flynn, one of the strongest political bosses in New York City, stated about his organization: "It is not only a machine; it is an army. And in any organization, as in the army, there must be discipline." Some political machines did resemble an army or a large business corporation. Tammany Hall, at the height of its power, had 32,000 committeemen and the only place large enough to hold a meeting was Madison Square Garden. It also had thousands of municipal jobs at its disposal and a multi-million dollar payroll. In reality, the machine was an organization composed of diverse lower and middle class groups which combined to control city government.

The man who directed the fortunes of the political machine was called a boss. A boss was a professional city politican who succeeded in building up a reliable voting organization. He might serve as an elected official but usually his power was of an unofficial nature. Whether elected or not the boss had to be a good administrator who could get things done. Most bosses were born in poverty or were of working class origins. Tammany Hall, the most powerful political machine in America, was led by men who started life in lowly economic occupations. William Marcy

140

Philip C. Dolce

Tweed was a chairmaker's apprentice; John Kelly, a soapstone cutter; Richard Croker, an unskilled laborer; and Charles Murphy, a horsecar driver.

Men like these were excluded from the more conventional routes of personal advancement because they lacked status, education, and money. Politics enabled them to get ahead with the only asset they really had—raw talent. With drive, determination, and organizational ability, these men emerged as political bosses. Men such as these were basically a pragmatic lot who did not express any particular philosophy or ideology of government. Instead they came to regard politics as a business which they entered primarily for material reward rather than as a means of reforming the social order.

The urban political boss was in reality a businessman whose basic stock was influence and power. These immaterial commodities could produce a municipal franchise, change a restrictive city ordinance, or grant large favors. With such tremendous power at his disposal, the boss could set his own standards of service and justice for no laws or rules governed his actions. Some bosses were able to use their positions to make enormous personal fortunes. In cities such as Pittsburgh, Chicago, Philadelphia, and New York the boss was able to parlay his position into becoming a millionaire. Of course, not all bosses were quite so wealthy but few died in the poverty from which they sprang.

How did the boss gain such tremendous power? Was it because of the ignorance of illiterate immigrant voters or the fact that the better elements of society shunned politics? While both of these ideas were important, perhaps the most vital concept in understanding the reasons for the emergence of political bosses is contained in the word "service." The boss and his machine cohorts provided service to the city by fulfilling functions which were inadequately carried out by the official agencies of government. The boss centralized the decision–making process and accomplished things. When Lincoln Steffens asked Tammany

141

boss Richard Croker, "Why must there be a boss, when we've got a mayor and council?" Croker replied, "That's why. It's because there's a mayor and a council and judges and a hundred other men to deal with."

George Cox, the political boss of Cincinnati helped to impose order on a city which had become almost helpless as it grew into a complex urban center. He gave the city a stable centralized government, while expanding the fire department, and launching an extensive street paving program. He also supported the growth of the University of Cincinnati and expanded the city's park system. Other urban political bosses provided similar services and direction for their cities. In part, the boss' service to his city was a by-product of his willingness to help the business community and his immigrant constituency.

The boss rendered invaluable aid to the businessmen of his city. Sometimes this was done in a corrupt manner, by selling franchises and by illegally reducing taxes on certain property. However, the boss also rendered many legitimate services which were badly needed. As cities grew in importance, businessmen were forced more and more to depend on the efficiency of municipal government. Construction contractors needed building permits or zoning changes. Railroad companies needed permission to extend their lines into the city. Banks, which held mortgages on extensive property in the city, constantly demanded assurance that their urban investments were sound. Large department stores demanded a variety of efficient city services to attract customers while utility firms needed constant municipal cooperation in order to operate successfully.

City governments throughout the nation were unprepared to deal with these and other complex problems. Official authority was dispersed in a number of municipal boards or agencies. It was extremely difficult to coordinate the decision making process much less to get prompt action. The boss could act with speed and efficiency to produce results. He had no scruples about cutting red tape, taking short cuts, or manipulating city agencies.

142

His lack of ideology meant that he was not inhibited by the prevailing theory of limited government. The boss took responsibility and made decisions. He was willing to tax, spend, and build. In return he received the big payoff from grateful business leaders.

Probably the most notable service the boss provided was to the large immigrant communities within his urban domain. The boss was an entrepreneur dealing in votes and therefore he could not afford to show any racial or ethnic biases. By building up a coalition of support based on the votes of various ethnic and racial groups, he helped to blur the hostility which existed between these groups. Thus the boss unconsciously served a pacifying function which helped to hold these raw American cities together.

The boss and machine politics also served as a bridge between the Old World and the New for the immigrant. Most immigrants brought with them a concept of politics as a personal affair where governmental activity was vested in a strong leader. The boss fulfilled that image but in the process he introduced the immigrant to the democratic process of representative government. For many immigrants this was the first time they were allowed any role in governmental activities. Soon they became aware of the importance of their ballot and its potential power to obtain service.

The most important service the boss provided for the immigrant was in the material realm. In an age before social security, unemployment insurance, and other forms of organized social benefits, the boss and the machine provided an informal welfare service for the immigrant. In a time of need the boss was there to provide jobs for the unemployed, housing lists for the newly arrived, medical care for those who could not afford it, and food for the needy. The boss or a member of the machine would use his influence to intervene with public authorities if a tax bill was overdue or a son was in trouble with the police.

The boss lightened the dreariness of the slums by providing

143

entertainment for the immigrants. He provided parades, staged parties, and arranged excursions to the beach. In a less affluent age, before the widespread use of mass media, these simple pleasures were eagerly looked forward to. Some bosses, like Frank Hague of Jersey City and James Curley of Boston, energetically spent public funds to provide municipal facilities which the immigrant poor needed such as hospitals, parks, and public bathhouses.

It was not just the aid that was given but also the manner in which it was provided. The boss was seen as a good neighbor who knew the residents personally and lived in the area. He or a member of the machine were constantly available. In an impersonal, urban industrial society the boss and the machine humanized the political system. In contrast to this, official government agencies were usually cold, bureaucratic, and limited in their assistance to the public. They would look into the legal claim for services to a "client" who was assigned a number for proper identification. These bureaucrats even managed to standardize suffering into categories of help.

The political opponents of the boss and the machine were usually labeled reformers. Some, like Tom Johnson of Cleveland, honestly wanted to aid immigrant groups but unfortunately most were structural reformers. Their major aim was to change the structure of municipal government in order to obtain honest, efficient, and economical government even if it came at the expense of human needs. A good example of structural reform could be found in the administration of John P. Mitchel who was elected mayor of New York City in 1913. Mitchel was dedicated to the idea of efficient and economic government and tried to achieve it in part by cutting municipal appropriations to schools and charitable agencies. To the immigrant seeking survival and security, the reformers' abstract theories were of no help.

Reform administrations usually were hostile in attitude toward the immigrant. Attacks on vice and gambling always carried a negative judgment of immigrant morality. Civil service was a threat to the immigrant's ability to obtain government jobs. Constant emphasis on economy usually meant cuts in public services which newcomers more than any other group needed. In short, what the reformers failed to grasp was that the immigrant needed help not moral platitudes. While reformers preached self-help and limited government, the boss held political power by practicing paternalism and providing municipal service. Boston's mayor, James M. Curley summed it all up when he said, "Reform administrations suffer from a diarrhea of promises and a constipation of performance."

Although the boss was the traditional enemy of reformers, this did not mean he opposed all reform measures. Since the boss was usually a pragmatic fellow, he might support certain reform legislation if the people demanded it. This seems to be especially true in New York during the first two decades of the twentieth century. Tammany Hall members supported political reforms such as women's suffrage, the direct election of senators, and extended home rule powers for cities. They also helped enact socioeconomic reforms such as consumer protection laws, scholarship programs for the underprivileged, safety regulations in factories, and workingmen's compensation. Although many of these proposals originated in other quarters, their ultimate success required the support of Charles Murphy, the boss of Tammany Hall.

While boss rule and machine politics had beneficial effects on urban centers, the cost of political expediency is never small. Laws were flaunted, funds were embezzled, election returns were tampered with, and municipal franchises were sold as if they were private property. Scandals, bribery, and corruption usually were by-products of boss rule. Although no regulations or restraints governed the actions of the bosses, they never realized the potential of such enormous power. While the boss attempted to aid individuals personally, he never thought of politics as a means for fundamental social change or the permanent amelioration of slum conditions. He accepted the social and economic structure of American capitalism and worked within it. Lack of ideology and the drive for material reward limited the boss' scope of action.

With the exception of Richard Daley in Chicago, boss rule and machine politics are now relics of the past in most cities. By and large they were products of a particular age filling certain needs, some of which are no longer required. The rise of the welfare state diminished the need for boss rule. Government, business, and labor unions now provide social benefits such as social security, unemployment insurance, medical benefits, and pension plans. Therefore, the economic and social rewards that the bosses used to hand out are no longer necessary. The immigrant began to assimilate into American society and no longer had to rely on the boss. At the same time civil service regulations were cutting off the patronage power of the machine. In a prosperous age politics became more ideological and the boss always had greater success dealing with tangibles rather than ideas.

Now that the boss and the machine are almost gone the question could be asked, are our urban areas much improved by their absence? True, corruption and patronage have diminished but so has the continuity of leadership and the personal link citizens once had with government. Is image politics, directed by advertising agencies and television, any better than the politics of self-interest? Today where is the citizen's personal link with city government now that the clubhouse is gone? No one advocates a return to boss rule, but we must recognize that this system filled certain needs, some of which still exist today.

B. the city of the mind:
education, communications, and
the urban image

14. playing and watching in the Gilded Age: the beginnings of the modern era of sports in America

Richard Harmond

The rise of the city after the Civil War brought about immense changes in American social-cultural patterns. One of these changes, as we shall see in this essay, was the establishment of amateur and professional sports as a part of the American way of life.

During the late nineteenth century we started consciously to become a sports-minded and a recreation-oriented people. This represented an important shift in traditional thinking and behavior. On the eve of the Civil War, for example, knowledgeable contemporaries lamented the lack of exercise among town dwellers. "Neither men nor women," as one historian observed, "played games." If there were a "national game," it was probably horseracing. By the 1890s, though, millions of urban dwellers were riding about on safety bicycles and engaging in numerous other forms of physical activity. Moreover, several million Americans annually watched professional baseball—the national pastime—while huge crowds attended professional prize fights.

Obviously, a number of factors contributed to this remarkable transition. The decline of Puritan orthodoxy, with its negative attitude toward play and leisure, was one such factor. It was significant, too, that with a gradually improving standard of living and a shortening of the work week, following the urban and industrial revolution, Americans were in a position to support recreational activities. Nor should we forget that most of our sports and games were European imports. Above all, however, it was the emergence of a new urban industrial civilization which accounted for the American people's growing appetite for physical exercise and spectator sports.

The games and sports a people play reflect the way in which they think, work, and live. Thus, when most Americans were farmers they enjoyed the out-of-door activities characteristic of a rural way of life. A hard working and thrifty-minded people, most of our ancestors lacked the time, wealth, or inclination to engage in leisure amusements. Instead, these active and hardy agriculturalists found fun and excitement in such practical pursuits as hunting and fishing, as well as such play-work activities as house and barn raisings, corn husking contests, and quilting bees.

These rural pastimes were, as a student of the subject remarks, "pitifully inadequate and unsatisfying for factory workers and for the large numbers of people caught up in the meshes of the business and industrial world." So as the urban-industrial portion of the population grew (between 1860 and 1900 it climbed from about one-sixth to one-third of the total populace), there arose both a physical and psychological need for new kinds of activities and diversions.

In addition, physicians and others were deeply concerned about the effects which the spreading pattern of urban sedentary living was having on the population's physical condition. Throughout most of the nation's history, these authorities asserted, the average American had received all of the exercise he needed in his daily round of chores on the farm or in the shop. "Civilization itself was a gym," as a writer in *Outing* pointed out. However, as the nineteenth century progressed, and the wilderness was tamed and cities were established, greater numbers of people began to earn their livelihoods at less physically demanding tasks in factories, offices, and stores.

Life grew softer in other ways too. Trolley cars, for example, induced city dwellers to walk less, and elevators relieved them of the necessity of climbing stairs. Indeed, according to one alarmed observer, this easier scheme of living had produced a generation of people "prematurely aged," and possessing "easily prostrated physiques." The medical men of the 1870s, 1880s and 1890s concluded that exercise was essential to offset the physically debilitating effects of the sedentary life. Hence, they urged Americans to compensate for the missing muscular effort of their forefathers with various forms of created activity.

City residents responded enthusiastically to this call for a more active life. Some decided on roller-skating, a sport first introduced into the United States in the mid 1870s. Others took advantage of the newly established urban gymnasiums and public playgrounds. Still others enjoyed walking contests, or joined outing and hiking clubs, organizations that were especially popular in the 1880s and 1890s. Lawn tennis won its converts, as did skiing, golf, croquet, and polo.

The rising popularity of amateur athletics was manifest in other areas as well. The first intercollegiate track and field contests, for instance, took place in 1874, and thirteen years later the National Cross Country Association was formed to stimulate interest in cross-country racing. While baseball, as we shall see, was the most widely attended spectator sport of the time, the game was also played by zestful amateurs on city lots, as well as at the high school and college levels.

Moreover, two of the great sports of our own era, football and basketball, were introduced in the Gilded Age. The first recorded intercollegiate football game took place in 1869 between Princeton and Rutgers. Over the next generation the game evolved into recognizably modern form (minus, however, the

151

all-important forward pass), and by the 1890s football was well established in many of the eastern, southern, and mid-western colleges of the United States.

In the meantime, James A. Naismith, looking for an indoor, evening game that might be used to fill the winter gap between the football and baseball seasons, invented the game of basketball in 1891. It quickly gained acceptance with members of athletic clubs as well as in high schools and colleges. Since it required little in the way of space, basketball especially appealed to city people. A uniquely American game, basketball is our one important sport which does not have European origins.

No sport in this period, however, gave so much physical exercise to so many men and women as did cycling. In the 1880s when the high wheel bicycle—a machine difficult to master and dangerous to use—was the standard vehicle, cycling was an activity restricted to athletically inclined men. During the period 1885-90, the cumulative achievements of a group of largely European inventors resulted in a bicycle that was at once safe to ride and relatively easy to pedal. Its notable features included the tubular construction and ball bearings of the high wheel bicycle, along with two equal size wheels (thus eliminating headers, the bane of the high wheeler), chain gear drive, a diamond-shaped frame, and pneumatic tires. This, of course, was the safety bicycle, and it speedily caught on with the American people.

In 1890, at the dawn of the modern bicycle age, there were only about 150,000 riders in the United States. But the new safety bicycle began to prove so attractive to segments of the public that by 1893 there were close to a million riders in this country. By the summer of 1894 even society people had taken to the safety, and cycling became a "marked feature of the Newport season." Indeed, across the land adults of all ages and both sexes surrendered to the bicycle passion,

152

although it was in the urban-suburban complexes of the north-east and midwest that the largest body of riders was to be found. By 1896 there were probably four million riders in America. This was a striking figure when compared to the 150,000 or so cyclists of 1890.

People cycled because it was fun, and because the sport gave them firm and healthy bodies. This latter consideration was especially important to women. However, with the rise of the city, women found themselves increasingly confined to the home. They also found themselves restricted by Victorian prejudice from participation in energetic outdoor activities. By the closing decade of the nineteenth century some progress had been made against this "deep-rooted prejudice." Women, for instance, participated in such sports as tennis, croquet, and golf. These activities did not acquire anything resembling a mass appeal. Most women needed an easily learned, enjoyable, outdoor exercise which, at the same time, did not tax their strength nor seriously breach current standards of decorum. Cycling met these conditions. Not surprisingly, then, American women, who had been "starving for sunshine, fresh air," and some sport "to keep their bodies healthy and robust," took eagerly to the wheel. Thus began the widespread participation of women in outdoor athletics.

Aside from the need for physical exercise, there was another more subtle, but nonetheless important reason why so many millions of Americans took up cycling. They required psychic relief from the long, tedious day spent in the office, shop, factory, or home. In short, Americans of the Gilded Age desired a means of temporary escape from the tension-prone urban industrial environment they inhabited.

There were few who protested the opinion of a contemporary observer that "nervousness" was the characteristic malady of the American nation. It was not considered accidental, either, that this nervousness had appeared after several decades

153

of unprecedented technological change, or that the condition seemed to be such a marked feature of urban life. Economist David A. Wells, for instance, suggested that the replacement of the slow-moving letter by electrical communication had so accelerated the decision-making process of businessmen, that the increased mental and emotional pressure on them had led to an alarming rise in nervous and physical disorders. The Chicago *Tribune*, surveying a broader range of mechanical innovations, remarked that it was the American's "fate to live in an age when railways, telegraphs and fifty other inventions" had contributed "immeasurably to the wear and tear of the individual and separate units of society."

Approaching the matter from a slightly different view, a Harvard professor explained that his was an age of progress, but that the price had been high. This could be seen, he went on, in the big cities where civilization was most advanced, but where life also was most rapid and intense. These urban centers, he believed, were "like so many great furnaces," consuming their inhabitants "in order to keep the machinery of our complex social organism in motion."

There was no dearth of advice for the nerve-wracked Americans of the "great furnaces." Cycling restored one's "confidence and cheerfulness," advised a physician, and caused the future once again to look "bright and full of hope." Or, as the author of *Hygienic Bicycling* informed his readers, on wheels "all morbid thoughts take their flight." Devotees of the wheel also reminded overwrought insomniacs that bicycling was a "nerve calming medicine," and a "sweet restorer" and inducer of "nature's sweetest restorer—dreamless sleep." It may even be that for some cyclists, *scorching*— referred to by a disgusted Englishman as "cyclomania"—was a form of escape.

A physical relief from the tensions of society was one benefit. A number of cyclists, though, looked to Nature for

154

peace of mind. They mounted bicycles, fled the city's "maddening crowd," and headed for the country. Once there, miles from "so-called civilization," they refreshed themselves with the sights and smells of green fields, brightly-colored flowers, and stretches of shadowy woods.

Inasmuch as cyclists were able to ride away from their problems, the safety bicycle acted as a psychic palliative. This was no small achievement. However, around the turn of the century, when adult Americans began to discover the possibilities of the automobile, they promptly abandoned the bicycle. It seemed unlikely in the early years of this century that the silent steed would ever stage a comeback in the United States.

The urban resident more inclined to watch than to play found his safety-valve in spectator sports. This can be seen rather clearly in the cases of baseball and boxing. Like many American sports, baseball began as an aristocratic activity which was subsequently democratized, professionalized, and finally commercialized. In the pre-Civil War years baseball was a sport for amateur urban gentlemen. The war, though, democratized the game, for the soldiers at army camps discovered that playing baseball was an excellent way to release dammed up tensions. The men carried the game home with them in 1865 and soon intercity and regional rivalries sprang up. When, in the summer of 1869, the Cincinnati Red Stockings toured the land and won sixty-five contests and tied one, the professionalization of baseball followed rapidly. In 1876 the professional clubs of eight cities were brought together to form the National League. In the decade or so after that date, techniques and equipment were improved, and the game took on all the essential elements as we know them today.

Professional baseball enjoyed a high popularity in the Gilded Age. In 1890, for instance, some 2,200,000 fans paid to watch major league baseball. "The fascination of the game,"

155

B. The City of the Mind

commented *Harper's Weekly*, "has seized upon the American people, irrespective of age, sex or other condition."

For the urban fan—whether cheering for his favorite nine, groaning at a score by the opposition, or screeching at the umpire—attending a baseball game was one way to let off emotional steam. As Lewis Mumford suggests in his *Technics and Civilization*, the spectator at a professional contest,

> is now at one with a primitive undifferentiated group. His muscles contract or relax with the progress of the game, his breath comes quick or slow, his shouts heighten the excitement of the moment and increase his internal sense of drama; in moments of frenzy he pounds his neighbor's back or embraces him. The spectator feels himself contributing by his presence to the victory of his side, and sometimes, more by hostility to the enemy than encouragement to the friend, he does perhaps exercise a visible effect on the contest. It is a relief from the passive role of taking orders and automatically filling them, of conforming by means of a reduced 'I' to a magnified 'It' for in the sports arena the spectator has the illusion of being completely mobilized and utilized.

Attending a game was also a unifying experience, for loyalty to the home team helped to bridge socio-economic class barriers. And where city life tended to destroy the sense of belonging to a common social order, rooting for the home club helped to build up a feeling of community solidarity. Baseball, then, served an integrative function, countering somewhat the powerful disintegrative forces of urban-industrial life.

We should recall, too, that a large number of the players were sons of Irish immigrants. This gave the Irish-American community heroes like Michael Kelly, Hugh Duffy, Ed Delahanty, and Joe McGinnity with whom to identify. These were heroes who had "made it big" in America legitimately. Where working men might earn $600 to $700 a year in the 1890s, top professional baseball players earned $3,000 to $5,000 for six months' work. In this way, too, baseball acted as a safety-valve, as well as a source of inspiration for newly arrived immigrants.

Names such as Paddy Ryan, Jake Kilrain, "Gentleman" Jim Corbett, and, of course, John L. Sullivan indicate that boxing filled a similar role in the Gilded Age. But it was not only Irish-Americans who followed the exploits of Sullivan and other professional fighters of that era. Though "respectable" opinion tended to be ambiguous about the sport, professional boxing nearly rivaled baseball in popular interest. Since pugilism catered to a taste for violence, at least one historian believes its popularity represented a vicarious lashing out at the constraints and frustrations of urban industrial culture. Watching a boxing match, then, was one more way Americans of the Gilded Age attempted, psychologically, to cope with city life.

The games and sports of the Gilded Age were an important part of late nineteenth century, urban, American civilization. More than that, they reflected the nature of that civilization.

15. the social impact of urban life: liberation or alienation?

William A. Osborne

"How're you goin' to keep 'em down on the farm after they've seen Paree?"

These lyrics of World War I vintage speak volumes about the romance between the individual and the city which has long existed. The rapid industrialization and urbanization which occurred toward the end of the nineteenth century caused millions of people to try to adjust to life in America's teeming cities.

The change from a rural to urban setting involved more than mere geographical movement. Social, economic, and psychological adjustments had to be made if the individual was to thrive in his new environment. For instance, with industrialization a new economic relationship developed. The principal function of the farm family, which had been production, became consumption in the city. Even more significant was the advent of a steady flow of cash available to the family from a father's or mother's wages. This had a profound effect on the whole history of marriage and family life in modern times. The effect is best labeled "individualism."

The availability of funds served at first to widen the male's range over the whole area of the city, to purchase recreation in a saloon, a brothel, a theatre, a ball park, a restaurant, or a night club and to select who would be his companions. This new found freedom simply but inadvertently diminished his family ties. When one adds to this the development of labor unions and the consequent increase in wages, the augmentation of personal autonomy seems obvious. Henry Ford, with his contribution of mass produced automobiles, simply put "the icing on the cake."

These developments struck also at the patterns of courtship and sexual behavior. The "speakeasy" of the 1920s gave way to the "roadhouse" of the 1930s about the same time that the automobile liberated dating and courtship from adult surveillance. Whatever the results may have been in terms of sexual morality (or immorality), there can be little doubt that the new urban environment presented far more sexual opportunity and stimulation than could be contained by either family or church. For one thing, the city housed the "red light" district. The extramarital sexual experience, so commonly desired if *not* sought after, had a precarious existence in rural areas. But whatever the legal history of prostitution, it has shown the persistence and tenacity of crabgrass in the modern city. The fact that today it may be in a state of decline, giving way perhaps to other more "esthetic" forms, such as the call-girl and the singles bar, simply indicates that the institution persists in a new form.

Much the same can be said of the bar or the pub. In the pre-World War II era, it was more commonly called the saloon. In a general way both the brothel and the saloon served the individual in his quest for relaxation or relief from the boredom of the assembly line. Interesting things happened in saloons. One could always find out what was *really* going on in the neighborhood: whose marriage was on the rocks and whose was likely to be next and why. Then too, there was the jokester and the storyteller. Of course there was always the sympathetic bartender on whom one could unburden his latest woe or borrow "a fin 'til payday." Perhaps the best way to summarize the role of the bartender and the saloon—combining them into a single institution—is to call it a male brokerage for sex, politics, and sports. Here the man who wanted a prostitute could find an address. He could also find out the name of the politician with power and influence. And he could always find someone to rehash with him the goings on in Comiskey Park or Yankee Stadium. Invariably too there was a back room, where a man could win or lose a week's wages. By the 1930s the shuffleboard and pinball machine appeared for the benefit of the more timid gambler.

But the days of the saloon as an exclusive male haven, were numbered. As money became tight after the crash of '29, the single man and his date ventured in. The nickel beer, after all, offered a night of drinking for a half dollar or less. Soon a back or side door was broken through by the owner to accommodate the "lucrative" couple. And to make it respectable he nailed a sign over the new door: "Family Entrance." The saloon was giving way to the bar. World War II dealt the final blow. For it smacked of disloyalty to refuse entry to "the boys in uniform" just because of an accompanying female, to say nothing of it being poor business practice.

Yet the demise of the saloon as a male citadel does not alter the original function: service for the individual. Where formerly the city offered the opportunity to maximize oneself only to men, by the late 1960s it was offering—half-heartedly—the same opportunity to women. The bar now serves them too. But generally speaking, the women's liberation movement has not yet reached that point where a lone woman feels as free as a man to enter any bar any time. Women's individuality, in other words, can most comfortably be asserted only in the company of another.

In truth the city offered both men and women a more exciting version of the single life. Single people who lived in rural areas did not share the anonymity or wide range of options found in the metropolis. Rooms, boarding houses, and in recent decades apartment houses and resident hotels offer one not only a choice of interiors but more importantly, a choice of companionship. One can choose to live alone, with a sibling or other relative, a member of the same or opposite sex. The choices are not equally available, to say the obvious. But from the perspective of the centuries this is undoubtedly the first time that the city has offered to women, as well as men, on a mass scale, such a range of choices.

This revelation immediately raises several critical questions. Given such a massive dose of individual freedom, with millions of its citizens released from the constrictions of rural existence, what has been the effect on society? On the family? How has the individual fared? Can the present troubles of the city be traced to this liberation of the individual? Perhaps if we take a closer look at the nature of this "liberation" and how it developed, we may be able to gain some insights into these questions.

In a sense the process of liberation may be said to have commenced with the economic transformation. For it was the transfer of work from the countryside to the city that drew workers in the same direction. Furthermore, the city in becoming the economic center of the nation also became the locus of a wide variety of goods and services purchasable by wages— and this on a massive scale hitherto unknown. The relationship between consumer operations and the individual wage earner became, in other words, dialectical or mutually enhancing. Steady and growing wages, for example, presented a market for

B. The City of the Mind

the mass produced automobile, which, in turn enabled the wage earner to search a wider area for housing, employment, and recreation. The wallet, pocketbook, and later the checkbook and credit card carried the keys to greater individual mobility, if not freedom itself.

By World War I the United States was thoroughly an urbanized and industrialized society, which is to say that many Americans had been "liberated" from farming, had moved to the city and were enjoying all it had to offer. The family had been stripped of major functions—economic, educational, and recreational. And husbands and wives had assumed new but separate roles in the world of politics, business, unions, religion, and a variety of clubs and associations. All of which were geared incidentally to the interests of men or women or both but seldom to families.

Rapid social change is probably the best overall description for the new urban experience. The increase in literacy, years of schooling, the development of the mass media, particularly radio and popular journals—all these represented not merely new experience to which to accommodate but rather higher and broader levels of vision or awareness. The critical changes, in other words, although conceived by the marriage of wages and urban residence, were taking place in the mind. And here undoubtedly is the most promising area in which to probe for insight into the question of how the individual has fared in the urban environment. The mental health survey offers a ready made diagnosis.

Sociologists and psychiatrists have been taking such surveys now for several decades. That is, they have been taking local or nationwide samples, interviewing, or using medical diagnostic records, and then associating this data with age, sex, education, income, and other variables. Unfortunately, even were it possible to assemble here, all the available findings for the last seven or eight decades, it would still not be possible to put together

162

a "before and after" picture; that is, before and after urbanization. The basic reason is the change in diagnostic technique and terminology plus the fact that the more recent development of nationwide sampling has made it difficult to compare more recent data with that collected in older studies. However, even with this serious limitation the evidence presented in recent works is revealing.

An examination of the more representative and thorough studies of the mental health of the American population reveals a rather grim picture. Apparently economic modernization and individual liberation has been accompanied by an appalling mental disorganization. The National Institute for Mental Health completed a nationwide survey in 1967 which indicated that some sixty million people were classified as "borderline schizophrenic or as exhibiting other deviant mental behavior in this category." Roughly speaking this figure amounts to between twenty-five to thirty percent of the total population. The language is perhaps too alarming in the sense that it includes those with only one or two symptoms of schizophrenia, but not the illness itself. If the survey and its findings were unique then perhaps it could be challenged or discarded. But such is not the case.

A more classical (scientific) and strictly urban study was done by a team of sociologists and psychiatrists in the early 1960s. "The Midtown Manhattan Study," as it is commonly known, concentrated on that one area and after a rigorous sampling procedure classified the respondents according to severity of symptomatology. This chart from Srole, Langer et. al., *Mental Health in the Metropolis* illustrates the classification system as well as the findings.

Categories 2 and 3, it will be noticed, add up to fifty-eight percent of the sample. This is the silent but suffering majority who, while able to hold on to their jobs perhaps earn promotions and marry with varying degrees of success,

B. The City of the Mind

HOME SURVEY SAMPLE

	WELL	18.5%
No apparent	MILD SYMPTOMS	36.3
disability	MODERATE SYMPTOMS	21.8
in carrying	MARKED SYMPTOMS	13.2
out adult roles	SEVERE SYMPTOMS	7.5
	INCAPACITATED	2.7
		100%

N = 1660

nonetheless are noticeable to the trained eye as enduring one or several symptoms of disquietude. This might take the form of chronic or frequent overindulgence in food or alcohol, heavy dependence on drugs, and inability to maintain satisfying human relationships. Whatever the symptom or combination thereof, it is enough to deprive this majority of the quality of life enjoyed by the fortunate eighteen percent in the "Well" category.

From the statistical point of view one could not project these findings to the American population at large. However, the evidence of other studies, of similar and dissimilar technique, taken in different areas, warrant the conclusion that the midtown Manhattan sample is not unique. A replication study in any other large city would undoubtedly produce similar results.

Perhaps the most alarming of recent surveys is one made of children in 1969. It was found that twelve percent of this nationwide sample were classified as suffering "serious mental illness" and thirty-four percent were in a "moderately impaired" category. These children, in other words, are starting out impaired—perhaps inheriting or absorbing the "hang-ups," defects, or weaknesses of their parents surveyed earlier. The abbreviated reference to these mental health surveys—we should like to remind the reader—is not to prove the United States a sick nation or the urban experience a failure. The purpose is simply to add some scientific evidence to what is already a commonplace observation that something has gone awry.

What the ailment is no one really knows. Nor can we be sure how closely it is related to urbanization or urban life. One thing that scholars could do to make a more satisfying diagnosis possible would be to develop a more organic or ecological theory that would relate individual mental health to environmental factors rather than medical ones. In scores of urban centers depression, loneliness, alcoholism, and withdrawal are found as frequently as self-actualization and the maximization of the self. If these surveys are accurate and mental affliction has reached epidemic proportions in our urbanized society, then clearly liberation in the cities has been purchased at the cost of alienation and *anomie*.

16. the impact of television: the communication of social disintegration

Winston Kirby

Television, as we know it, was born in the cities. Many cite a favorite date or incident for the birth of TV. Some point to May 17, 1939, the date of the first baseball telecast, a remote from Baker Field in New York City with Princeton playing Columbia. Others may cite the A.T.&T. experimental telecast of 1927 in which Herbert Hoover, then Secretary of Commerce, appeared. The real purists may prefer the year 1884, when a German, Paul Nipkow, developed and patented a scanning disc for transmitting pictures by wireless. Nineteen forty-eight may be recalled as the year in which Milton Berle took control of TV viewing habits and converted urban behavior on Tuesday nights into a uniform experience. Tuesday nights were referred to as "Berle Nights." TV set sales soared and massive chunks of people were locked into a homogenized experience. Perhaps, from a pragmatic point of view this is a more realistic landmark for TV's birth.

However, I associate TV's birth with the New York World's Fair of 1939. In that year on April 20th, David Sarnoff whose contributions to communications were extraordinary, said "and now we add radio sight to sound. It is with a feeling of humbleness that I come to this moment of announcing the birth in this country of a new art so important in its implication that it is bound to affect all society.''

Later that year General Sarnoff wrote: "Television will bring to people in their homes, for the first time in history, a complete means of instantaneous participation in the sights and sounds of the entire outer world. It will be more realistic than a motion picture because it will project the present instead of the past.'' So in 1939 we perceive the forward leap of a new communications medium with viewers also acting as instant participants. General Sarnoff's phrase, "instantaneous participation in the sights and sounds of the entire outer world'' described the coming sharply altered life-style of all urban communities.

In the earlier days of TV the medium was only available in the cities. For years huge geographical areas had no access or at best highly limited access to TV. We could have attempted an essay entitled "TV and the Cities'' in the early fifties, but could not have explored one entitled "TV and the Country'' because of the absence of rural TV. Even today there are areas where TV reception outside of the cities is limited. Perhaps some social scientists will do a study of those who live in difficult reception areas and develop evaluations about their attitudes, behavior, and perceptions as contrasted to those in high-density urban areas.

In 1948 there were only thirty-six stations on the air. These were spread among nineteen cities. However, these nineteen cities represented about one third of the population of the United States. Nineteen forty-eight was also the year in which the Federal Communications Commission mandated a freeze on all new applications. I emphasize the word new as there were about seventy applications for construction permits approved prior to the freeze. The purpose of the freeze was really twofold: to review the whole question of frequency alloca-

167

tion with one eye heavily slanted towards U.H.F. and to decide what to do about color TV.

During the freeze, which lasted for four years, there was considerable agitation on the part of networks which felt that their limited coverage proscribed increased advertiser support. More closely related to our theme was the pressure emanating from population groups who believed they had been deprived of equal viewing opportunities. As noted earlier, only nineteen cities carried television in 1948. Pittsburgh had but one station and this was the tenth largest city in the country. Denver, the thirty-second largest city in the United States, had none. Other major cities without TV were Little Rock, Austin, Portland, Maine, and Portland, Oregon. However, in 1952 two thirds of the population could now view TV in sixty-three cities with 108 stations. One more statistic: in 1948 there were one million receivers in the land. By 1952 there were over seventeen million TV receivers. The population covered by TV had only doubled; whereas, the TV sets in the hands of the consumers had increased by seventeen times its 1948 figure.

All of this TV hunger so apparent more than twenty years ago and equally as apparent today cannot help but have had some effect on city life. Of course, TV has had significant effect throughout the country, but its roots lie in the cities and I propose its impact is disproportionately greater in the cities than outside.

The average family spends almost six hours a day viewing its TV set. These six hours have to either replace or share other activities. Unless you want to consider the possibility that the six hours were spent in no activity. However, even the last alternative though possibly a purely passive, meditative, or reflective way of life and conceivably most desirable, has been replaced by TV. Now what does this mean in terms of urban behavior?

168

Primarily it has created more segmental relationships among people than ever before. In an earlier nonurban environment people tended to know each other in a variety of ways. The person from whom you purchased your groceries was a possible visitor in your home. The dentist, who treated your teeth, was apt to be sitting next to you in church. Walking down the street was apt to be an opportunity to exchange greetings with others, as contrasted to today's faceless, nameless experience.

With the growth of modern urban centers, one began to know people segmentally rather than wholly because of the specialized relationship they had with one another. One has limited contacts with people with whom one works. One sees the grocer only in the social structure of seller to buyer. One goes to the dentist only to have his teeth examined. One has golfing friends, companions with whom one goes to ball games, and so on. Rarely is there a well-rounded relationship including work, play, church, and social experience.

Television has been an added force to further segmentalize relationships. As one moved from a rural to an urban environment, one moved from relationships on many levels with the same people to relationships of sliced or segmental interaction. However, there were in all socioeconomic areas in the pre-TV world more opportunities for frequent and varied though tenuous relationships with other people. The six hours of viewing per day has sharply reduced these opportunities.

Organizations which produce broadcast audience research do not always agree on rating figures, but there is a consensus on TV viewing differences between those who earn a small or middle income, as compared to those in larger income brackets. One difference is that families with middle and small incomes view TV more in the daytime, more in the early evenings, more in prime time, with a degree of equalization in viewing for all income groups in late evening only. Another statistic shows that

169

the larger the family, the greater the amount of viewing—no doubt a function of less disposable income.

In recent years the difference between the day and night populations of inner cities is considerable since white city workers withdraw at the end of the working day. The actual physical separation obviously proscribes comingling and interaction outside of the working experience. Television has been a force to further widen the cleavage between the inner cities and the suburbs. We shall go one step further and point out that television has widened the gap even between one suburbanite and another. The dependency and joy that people placed in one another for communications and shared experience has diminished. This has contributed to the development of segmental and relatively anonymous relationships.

Let us explore the concept of homogeneous cultural experiences, partially a function of our six-hour TV day. Up to the advent of TV, the experiences of individuals and their families were generally individual experiences. To be explicit, one family member might be reading, drinking, speaking with a friend, attending a club activity, listening to the radio with part of his sensorium capacity and studying with another. There was a sense of doing something that was particularly yours, or, as they say today, "doing your own thing." In the early days of TV, long prior to its reaching the population saturation point for set ownership, there was group viewing in the homes of those who owned TV sets. Yet, the viewing of TV was only a part of the social experience. Since videotape had yet to dominate the medium there was a sense of uncertainty about each program in which the viewer felt as if he too was a participant. The possibility of human and mechanical error gave TV an extra dimension. I speak of that period in the late '40's and early '50's with Studio One; The Goodyear Playhouse; Kukla, Fran and Ollie; Garroway at Large, and the early Ed Sullivan programs. TV was live and for me more exciting but not so monopolistic of one's time.

Videotape was an influential force in weakening viewer empathy with reality. In fact the influence of tape has often dulled man's sensitivity to the grizzly events he sees on news shows. These events, of course, are real and not the illusions of a pre-taped episodic experience. Today's viewer is fairly sophisticated. He knows that what he sees on the tube is often pre-taped. The live drama is rarely there to activate his responses. Today it is primarily through sports that the TV viewer is able to partially empathize with the world beyond his home. However, the continuing impact of pre-taped television has impaired man's sensitivity to reality when presented on the tube.

As TV set sales increased to virtually 100 percent saturation of every household in the country, the group experience which included TV as part of the overall life experience was weakened. Man became more passive in initiating his own social, intellectual, and recreational experiences. The question of how to spend one's time is now too easily resolved by selecting your evening's activities, and your day's as well, from TV program selections offered in your community. Of course, during prime time the networks are the arbiters of your evening's experience—not the local station.

Gordon Childe, an Australian archaeologist, used a number of different criteria to define a city. They are population density; great art, writing, and numbers, that is, symbolic or digital communication; exact and predictive sciences; full-time specialists; concentration of surplus products; a society based on residence rather than kinship; monumental public buildings; foreign trade made possible by surplus; and a class-structured society based on the unequal distribution of property.

Louis Wirth, the distinguished sociologist, vis-à-vis Childe focuses on the idea of a city being large, dense, and having a fairly permanent settlement of heterogeneous individuals. We note elements of agreement between Wirth and Childe in their approach to urban characteristics—particularly in specialization, seg-

171

mentalization, and the subordination of kinship patterns of associations and friends to those based on residency. I extrapolate that with the development of TV the characteristics that make urban life attractive (for example, its specialization and its pursuit of excellence) have been sharply eroded. TV is not a Machiavellian villain; it is only an instrument of technology which has become too powerful. If you accept my point that we are becoming homogenized and passive then we are losing the very excitement and the pursuit of excellence that makes metropolitan area living so dynamic. For example, urban language, in fact all language today, seems less interesting and more uniform. The New York *Times* recently quoted an advertising executive who in referring to his commercial said:

> We've created a natural language for TV; we've given the man in the street ammunition to be a comedian. That's the psychological reason for the success. The characters in the commercials are personable, vulnerable people—the average man can identify with them, he can use their lines and be sure of getting a laugh. We've made the average man a kind of hero.

The agency man is correct in that recently one could rarely go through a day without encountering the lines of a commercial dealing with indigestion. There is truth and also some arrogance in the agency statement that "we've created a natural language." Its misfortune lies in the widespread acceptance of a graceless aphorism. This acceptance tends to reinforce the commonplace rather than offer more interesting language alternatives.

Any discussion about TV and the cities should include some current theoretical thinking about mass communications which generally embraces four major theories. The individual differences theory offers the idea that not only do human beings differ biologically, psychologically, and attitudinally but more importantly that personality differences, developed from one's environment, provide the material for each to view the world in a different manner from his neighbor. To amplify this, one might say that TV enables persons to respond to the world around them with individual perceptions despite the sameness of viewing habits.

Another prevailing theory about mass communications purports that people who belong to groups with similar characteristics such as sex, occupation, age, education, income and, so forth, respond to stimuli in a similar manner. This is referred to as the social categories theory.

Another theory, that of social relationships, holds that relationships among people bring about a flow of communications in which the person who receives information from the mass media acts as an influencing agent in communicating attitudes and information to those less exposed to mass media. This is referred to as the "two-step flow" of communication and also co-opted "opinion leaders" into our language. If we accept this postulation for all media, think how forceful it is for TV in particular.

The fourth theory is that of cultural norms, which reaffirms my position most strongly with respect to TV's influence. The cultural norms theory states that TV, in fact all mass media, creates the belief that cultural norms exist for most of us to which we should subscribe or feel unfulfilled if we do not. This is like the self-fulfilling prophecy in that if we believe a situation to be real, we respond to that situation just as if it were real. Now think of the impact of this theory when one sees a so-called family program produced for a general audience and notes that it equates happiness with the accumulation of things. These things can include a color TV set, the car the neighbors have that you do not, and the splendidly furnished apartment or house the so-called average family possesses. Unhappiness is the reverse of the aforementioned or to put it another way—"How can one be happy if you lack certain possessions?" In an urban environment, more

173

B. The City of the Mind

widely separated from nature's pleasures, the cultural norms theory has particularly great impact.

Although students of mass communications tend to believe that TV is an instrument that reinforces beliefs rather than shapes new attitudes, they generally concede some flexibility in their conclusions. They acknowledge that for some viewers, whose attitudes and convictions may not be too firm, it is possible to develop new convictions and norms strongly influenced by TV. Understand that this group does not reinforce its beliefs; it accepts new ones. Should this group only represent a modest percentage of our population its total effect can be staggering. If only one percent of our population is malleable we are talking about two million people that can be influenced by television programing. Again, I strongly suggest that TV's impact on the cities has helped to homogenize us and has also contributed to our intellectual passivity. It has, of course, given us great entertainment, great drama, and great documentaries—but at what cost to ourselves? When I speak of passivity, I refer to our loss of maturity and our loss of self-sufficiency. Social and personal acts of violence are too often the acts of frustration, envy, and hatred— but rarely if ever the articulation of a self-directed man.

One cannot and should not talk about the cities without taking note of their changing racial pattern. Therefore any discussion of television's impact on the cities must of necessity see how the variegated ethnic composition has been interrelated with TV. In 1960 sixty-nine and a half percent of all whites and seventy-two and two-fifths percent of all nonwhites lived in urban areas. At the turn of this century the reverse racial dominance existed with forty-three percent of the whites living in cities and twenty-two percent of the nonwhites. The nonwhites were then a minor segment of the urban population.

Now our largest metropolitan areas, the twelve largest to be precise, contain about thirty-three percent of all the American blacks. I refer specifically to the central cities of our largest metropolitan areas. They are New York, Los Angeles, Chicago, Philadelphia, Detroit, San Francisco, Boston, Pittsburgh, St. Louis, Washington, Cleveland, and Baltimore. These same areas receive a major segment of the dollars spent for TV advertising. More importantly, commercials which offer travel, automobiles, and other luxury items are seen by central city viewers with greater frequency than the peripheral city communities in which a smaller percentage of nonwhites live.

Nonwhites often cannot afford these items but nevertheless are bombarded with the need to have them in order to be part of the mainstream. Obviously the advertiser promoting luxury items is less interested in the central city. He is interested in the area surrounding it. Consider for example, what New York is from an advertiser's point of view. It is Bergen, Nassau, Fairfield, and other similar affluent, out-of-city counties which comprise a larger segment of TV households than those based in the central city.

Paradoxically, studies show that blacks view TV heavily during the day as well as at night. Their ratings, that is the program ratings for blacks, generally exceed those for whites. Yet, there are few commercial network TV programs specifically directed to blacks and no major TV stations owned by blacks. Some might question whether TV stations should single out any racial or ethnic group for programing direction. I respond by saying definitely yes at this point in time. As a general rule I do not believe in quotas. However, when television programs are almost completely characterized by middle or upper class socio-economic living patterns they assist in creating even wider gulfs of frustration among the more disadvantaged in the cities.

Perhaps the events that took place in Chicago during the Democratic Convention of 1968 offer empirical evidence of the great, the very great, interrelationship between television and the cities. In August of 1968 thousands of people converged on Chicago to act out their frustrations and to express their concerns

175

B. The City of the Mind

about so many problems that seemed to trouble this nation. They were Vietnam repudiators, remnants from the June Poor People's March in Washington, D.C., the turned-off, the turned-on, the backers of Eugene McCarthy, the stragglers from the mainstream and so on.

Several hundred television personnel were on hand to record the convention and note the demonstrators. You all recall the outcome—demonstrators and police met head-on in a frightfully bloody confrontation. Hundreds were injured including reporters. How much of this violence might have been mitigated if TV was not on hand is a fair question. This question is raised to point out that there is interaction—and I believe strong interaction between humanity and TV. By interaction I mean the viewer wants to be seen as well as see. Since most of this country's population resides in the city the interaction is greater in the urban setting.

Although my presentation may appear to be critical of TV, it is not without appreciation of the medium's many benefits. The aged and the infirm have received information, entertainment, and companionship. The loneliness of many has been ameliorated by the availability of the tube. Newcomers to our land have had splendid opportunities to perceive the culture of this country in a less painful fashion than their predecessors. Again, I state this point with caution since so much of our normative culture has been misrepresented on TV. The norm has often been the wishful thinking of the script writer rather than the sociologist's more studied definition of the mainstream.

The availability of sports events at the moment they occur has imparted a sense of national participation and excitement almost without precedent. The less frequent but important cultural events embracing theater, music, and literate personalities have made these dimensions of culture available to those who pursue it. Let us also pay tribute to TV's efforts in adult education. Also, let us be grateful for the laughter and adventure it offers to most of us.

176

Futhermore, recent studies have shown that significant numbers of people within our urban centers live in fear. This is particularly true among the less privileged. Their sources of fear include assault, rape, robbery, and homocide. Television has offered some surcease to the shut-in urban resident.

Marshall McLuhan (and one cannot easily discuss TV without some reference to him) makes the distinction between hot and cool media. A hot medium is one which offers much detail and considerable information. I believe Mr. McLuhan would refer to a photograph as hot and a cartoon as cool. Television, according to Mr. McLuhan, is a cool medium demanding considerable involvement; that is, the viewer must work hard to complete the TV image. An extension of this involvement has created in the viewer an intense desire to involve himself in every aspect of his environment not just an isolated fragment such as the institution of neighborhood and community. I refer particularly to the younger viewer who has been bred on TV. He sees the world in its totality, via the tube, not just his neighborhood. By even further extension, the product of the TV age does not identify with his city or apparently any city. He is a product of this, his planet, or as McLuhan says, the global village.

In summary then, man has moved from an oral, to a literate, and now to an electronic age. Its effect on him as a man of the cities has accentuated the segmental relationship aspect of his life. Television has accentuated the cultural norms theory of defining our norms. It has also made man more homogenized and culturally passive. Unfortunately our cities have felt this impact more sharply for that is where TV is most concentrated.

17. urban education: a study in institutional accommodation

Vincent Falzone

In the 1830s, the renowned Horace Mann formulated a clear definition of the role of education in American life. In his view, education was to serve as "the great equalizer of the condition of men . . . the balance wheel of the social machinery." Especially in urban America, education was often looked upon as the means by which sons and daughters of immigrants could climb to higher rungs on the social, cultural, political, and economic ladder.

Yet the uniquely heterogeneous nature of the American city has proven to be a formidable hindrance to the achievement of that goal. In order to function effectively the urban school systems have an obligation to accommodate themselves to the differing ethnic, religious, and racial backgrounds of their students. As each distinct group arrives with its peculiar needs, diverse from the rest of the population, new problems confront the school administrators. They are often engulfed in an incessant struggle to adapt their institutions to the special needs of the newcomers.

In the past, the problems which faced city educators have been especially complex. With respect to nineteenth century Irish and German Catholic immigrants, the issue was religious accommodation. So too, the language difficulties of these German children and that of recent Puerto Rican migrants mandated the development of bilingualism in certain city school districts. Finally, racial accommodation became necessary as a result of the twentieth century influx of black children into the previously white urban areas. All of these difficulties are peculiarly urban in character since most rural and suburban areas tend to be more homogeneous in ideas, color, and class.

New York City had provided two excellent illustrations of the problems which confronted the urban school systems. In the 1840s, a religious controversy arose over the teaching of the Bible in the city's public schools. In this case, failure of the educational authorities to adapt their school curriculum to the needs of the ever-increasing Catholic school population helped lead to the creation of a nationwide parochial school system. On the other hand, in the twentieth century, the continuing racial controversy between black and white city dwellers has not yet been resolved. Efforts at reconciliation and accommodation continue in order to prevent the establishment of racially segregated school systems.

The urban religious controversy was deeply symptomatic of the ingrained anti-Catholicism prevalent among nativist Protestant Americans. Hatred of Catholics and foreigners has been a steadily growing force in American life since the settlement of the American colonies. The descendants of the Puritans and Anglicans, Englishmen retained a lingering bitterness against the Catholic Church which had, after all, done battle with Henry VIII and his daughter, Elizabeth. This hostility was evident in the colonial and early national periods of our history manifesting itself openly in the reaction to the Quebec Act of 1774 and later in the Alien and Seditions laws of 1798.

Quite naturally therefore, Americans were alarmed by the increased numbers of German and Irish immigrants who sought a new life on our shores. The preponderant number of Catholics among the new arrivals, particularly those who congregated in the increasingly populous American cities, prompted nativist Americans to fear a transfer of papal power from Rome to America.

179

Thus by the 1830s and 1840s, Protestants came to believe that increased vigilance was required to protect Americans from this foreign threat.

In this atmosphere of religious intolerance in 1840, the real battle between New York City Catholics and Protestants over education erupted. New York schools at this time were under the control of the Public School Society, a semipublic organization formed to care for the instruction of children financially unable to attend religious or private schools. The society shared in the common school fund, a New York State appropriation administered locally by New York City's Common Council.

New York City's Catholics were particularly offended by the religious intolerance evidenced by the Public School Society. As a part of its allegedly nonsectarian curriculum, the society insisted that its schools include a regular program of prayers, hymns, and religious instructions, all of which conformed to the Protestant tradition. Naturally, the Protestant King James Bible was an integral part of that curriculum.

In May 1840, Catholic bishops formally registered their opposition to this alleged violation of the hallowed principle of separation of church and state. They strenuously denounced the enforced instruction of Catholics in the Protestant religious tradition. Particularly, they rejected outright the private interpretation of the scriptures which was an integral part of the Protestant creed. The hierarchy asserted that only their church, and not the individual, was to interpret the scriptures for Catholic children. Thus, to achieve this end, they advocated a separate system of Catholic education.

The leaders of the Catholic drive for separate educational facilities were the immigrant Archbishop of New York, John Hughes, and New York Governor, William Seward. Hughes, who had emigrated from Ireland in 1817, welded Catholics in his diocese and elsewhere into a potent force determined to protect themselves from the thrusts of nativism. Seward was a member of the Whig party, the spiritual descendant of the nativist-

180

inclined Federalist party. Yet, unlike other Whigs, Seward consistently demonstrated his sympathy for the plight of the alien and foreign born. Catholic children, he felt, should be free from exposure to Protestant religious practices. Also, the large influx of Germans into New York City convinced him that they should be taught in German rather than English-speaking schools.

Thus, the battle lines were drawn. Throughout 1840, Hughes and other Catholics tried unsuccessfully to force the Common Council to allot a portion of its fund for the establishment of Catholic parochial schools. Then in 1841, the Catholics flexed their political muscles in the November state election campaign. They showed that in New York City, Catholics held the balance of power in the Democratic party. Only those Tammany Democrats who had received Catholic endorsements won seats in the assembly. Thus the Democrats, who prevailed statewide by large majorities, did not wish to risk alienating this important segment of their urban political coalition.

Seward then took up the Catholic crusade. Motivated as he was by his commitment to toleration and diversity, he also saw the political desirability of weaning away Catholics from their traditional Democratic moorings. In 1842, he recommended and steered through the legislature a bill which called for the abolition of the Public School Society. In its place, the bill created an elected board of school commissioners. The board was to have the power to administer and control the educational system and to allot the funds among public and private schools alike.

Thereafter, the combined efforts of Seward and Hughes convinced other bishops to take up the fight for separate schools. Consequently, in 1884, the American Catholic hierarchy officially mandated parochial school education for all Catholic children. Thus the failure of nativist New Yorkers to adapt themselves to the religious convictions of the newly arrived Catholic city dwellers helped result in separate rather than integrated school systems.

In the twentieth century, black school children in urban

181

areas throughout this country found themselves in a situation painfully similar to that of Catholic students in the 1840s. Fortunately, separate black and white urban school systems have not yet resulted. Unless the current, but long delayed efforts at integration and cooperation continue unabated, separate schools remain a distinct possibility.

Twentieth century black Americans began migrating to the city in such great numbers that the problem of black education has become increasingly an urban one. After World War I, the flood of immigrants from abroad was sharply curtailed from a high of 1,200,000 in 1914 to a mere 110,000 by 1918.

To compensate for the loss of immigrant labor, northern and southern business interests began to actively recruit blacks from the rural South. The movement to the cities slowed to a trickle during the Depression decade of the 1930s, but it has continued with great intensity since World War II. Indeed, in an era when many whites have been moving from the inner cities to the suburbs, the black population more than ever has become heavily concentrated in the American urban centers.

Yet, predictably, the urban school systems have only slowly begun to adapt themselves to the large predominance of blacks under their jurisdiction. Charles Silberman in his memorable work, *Crisis in Black and White*, has addressed himself to the New York City educational crisis. He cited several surveys in the 1960s which concluded that by the eighth grade, the academic performance level of Harlem black students had fallen about two and one-half years behind the white grade level.

Among the various factors which contributed to this educational lag, three are especially noteworthy. In the first place, perhaps too many white teachers believe emotionally, if not intellectually, in the cultural inferiority of their black students. It is indeed difficult to avoid communicating such a strongly held feeling to their students. Second, the quality of teaching offered to black youngsters is probably inadequate because of the under-standable reluctance of many good teachers to venture into the urban jungle. Finally, the dialect which the black child is exposed to at home often differs enough that the white man's English of the classroom is like a foreign language.

Clearly then, these factors illustrate the special problems faced by black children in pursuit of a meaningful education. Yet these difficulties are not insurmountable. Blacks can be stimulated to learn more about a world in which all races, colors, and creeds are shown to have played an integral part.

An important obstacle in the path of black assimilation into the urban educational mainstream has been the previous tend-ency of school textbooks to ignore the black American. In other words, school texts have not been successful in building an effec-tive bridge between the blacks' own lives and the community in general. Too many textbooks have been filled with slanted views of American life. Often the so-called American was portrayed as being Caucasian, Anglo-Saxon, white collar, and middle class. Thus the child of the black ghetto whose appearance and environ-ment did not conform to the text characters could easily derive from these differences a deeply rooted inferiority.

Any treatment of urban education would be incomplete with-out a discussion of desegregation in the city schools. In 1954, in its momentous *Brown vs. Board of Education* decision, the Supreme Court declared: "In the field of public education, the doctrine of separate but equal has no place. Separate educational facilities are inherently unequal." Yet, today tensions over school deseg-regation are running higher in the Northern cities than in the South. Many students of urban problems are battling to assimilate children of all races and creeds into the city's school system. They have become increasingly frustrated when confronted with northern desegregation or the rapid increase in the number of schools with predominantly black student bodies. For example,

183

B. The City of the Mind

Silberman noted that between 1957 and 1963, the number of New York elementary schools containing ninety percent or more non-white students more than doubled, despite the 1955 commitment of New York's Board of Education to desegregation as a major policy goal.

In a real sense, urban *de facto* segregation is more evident in the schools than in the population at large. This is primarily because the black population of the cities is younger than the white population. Proportionately, more blacks than whites are in the child-bearing ages. Also they are less inclined to use effective methods of birth control. Washington, D.C. for example, has a black community amounting to about seventy percent of the population. Yet well over eighty-five percent of the children in her public schools are black. Clearly, efforts at massive desegregation in the nation's capital are doomed to failure.

In most other American cities, however, attempts have been made to achieve desegregation by means of school busing. But manifest signs of discontent with the policy are evident, particularly in the Northern white suburban areas. These parents understandably object to the busing of their children to inferior urban schools.

The real question then is not the desirability of busing, but rather the importance of integrated education to blacks and whites alike. Both races would be the beneficiaries of a heterogeneous urban school system. Education, to contribute to this desired result, should do more than merely develop the powers of the intellect. It should inculcate in the young a firm belief in the brotherhood of man in order to prepare them for the real world outside the classroom. It has not always done so.

The American city has often failed to adapt its institutions to changing urban realities. Intolerance and exclusivity rather than tolerance and diversity guided New York City's public school officials of the 1840s, a fact which helped lead to the development of a separate Catholic school system. In the twentieth century,

184

public school education has not succeeded in its efforts to assimilate black Americans into the heterogeneous urban school systems. But these efforts must continue. Only when racial accommodation is successful can education play its role as the urban panacea.

18. anti-urbanism in America

Philip C. Dolce

In the ancient world the word "city" was synonymous with "civilized life." The city was the locus of nearly all man's technological, cultural, and ideological innovations. Yet despite this, man throughout the ages has felt that there was something inherently wrong with urban life. This was certainly true in the United States where the central city was usually viewed with suspicion.

It has been said that the United States was born in the country and moved to the city. This nation was urbanized in a relatively short space of time. In 1860 less than a quarter of the American people lived in a city or a town. By 1890 a third of the population resided in urban areas and twenty years later almost half the entire population was located in cities. The drastic transformation of our society only increased the hostile reaction cities engendered in the American mind.

Anti-urbanism, a term which usually refers to large corporate cities, is a highly controversial theme in American history. Some scholars have questioned its validity on a number of grounds. For instance, at the same time southerners and westerners were attacking northern cities as corrupt and evil, they were attempting to build up their own urban centers in order to gain greater economic influence in national affairs. The inconsistent and sectional nature of such condemnations seemed to cast doubt on their validity as true indications of anti-urban sentiment. Anti-urbanism also has been used as a political ploy in certain areas of the country where politicians appeal to rustic images in order to gain votes. Agrarian hostility to the city has been interpreted by some as merely a reflection of the declining fortunes of rural America unable to face the economic challenge of the cities.

Some historians also have pointed out that anti-urbanism may only be a masculine viewpoint. Men might have been free on the frontier or farm, but women were not because of the emphasis placed on physical strength in these areas. In urban centers women first found the economic opportunity to compete with men on equal terms. Finally, some authorities have concluded that anti-urbanism is really only a selective judgment process in which an individual forms a negative opinion on a few factors in the urban environment but is really not hostile to all elements of city life.

While all of these ideas have some validity it would be foolhardy to dismiss anti-urbanism as inconsequential. Indirectly, most of these arguments attest to the longevity and popularity of this theme while attacking its inconsistent nature. However, any widespread sentiment which originates from diverse sources over a long period of time and is rekindled by different historical circumstances can hardly be expected to be consistent. The growing sentiment against British rule prior to the American Revolution as expressed by James Otis, John Dickinson, Sam Adams, James Wilson, Benjamin Franklin, Thomas Jefferson, and others is not only inconsistent but often contradictory. Yet it would be silly, on the basis of this evidence to conclude that there was really no widespread feeling of opposition to British rule in America.

It is also intriguing that the preponderant argument against anti-urbanism is usually economic in nature. However, eco-

B. The City of the Mind

nomics may only prove that people recognized the necessity of large urban centers but still disliked them intensely. Finally, it is true that anti-urbanism is selective in nature, but this should be of small comfort to urbanologists. A city is a highly complex structure, with so many different facets, that it is hard enough to grasp its meaning completely much less dislike it all. Since the city cannot be comprehended as a whole it is represented symbolically in a variety of images. Robert Park, the eminent urban sociologist, believed that the city was really a state of mind rather than a concrete reality. Therefore, if one has a predominately negative image of the city he can be classified as being anti-urban. This is true even if the image is false or narrow in scope. Just because the bases of racism and anti-Semitism are distorted, illogical, and false does not mean that we can conclude that racism and anti-Semitism do not exist.

It seems that the usual image of the city whether formed by rational construction, aesthetic reaction, trained perception, or random feeling is frequently hostile in nature. A good example of this is when Mayor John V. Lindsay labeled New York "Fun City." Confronted with an overwhelmingly hostile reaction, the Mayor was unable to substantiate his statement. The negative reaction was due to the fact that this label did not fit the image many people had of New York City. Also, when two persons, one a British aristocrat and the other a suburbanite, wrote letters to the New York *Times* commenting favorably on the cultural aspects of New York, a number of responses were received by the newspaper angrily pointing out the alternative image of the city as one of filth, drugs, violence, and hopelessness.

Not just the ordinary citizen holds negative views of the large central city. Poets, playwrights, statesmen, and intellectuals also have shared deep reservations about urban life. Morton and Lucia White in their book *The Intellectual Versus the City* have pointed out that distaste rather than enthusiasm has been the usual reaction of most of our creative thinkers toward the city. Thomas

Jefferson was extremely hostile to large urban areas. He said, "The mobs of great cities add just so much to the support of pure government as sores do to the strength of a human body." In 1800, during a yellow fever epidemic, Jefferson supplied his most bitter observation on the large American city. He wrote, "When great evils happen I am in the habit of looking out for what good may arise from them. . . . The yellow fever will discourage the growth of great cities in our nation, and I view great cities as pestilential to the morals, the health, and the liberties of man."

Later, Jefferson came to the realization that the nation had an economic need for cities, but this did not change his negative view of large urban areas. One reason Jefferson along with many other founders of our republic distrusted large urban centers was that they did not believe that big cities could ever provide a hospitable environment for the democratic government which they had created.

This negative image of large cities was shared by many of our leading literary figures. Ralph Waldo Emerson felt that life in the city was "artificial and curtailed." Henry James believed that the city lacked order, structure, and history. He spoke of it as "a heaped industrial battlefield." Henry Thoreau made his feelings about cities absolutely clear when he refused an invitation to the Saturday Club of Boston. He said the only room he was willing to visit in the city was the men's room. Other intellectuals also shared deep reservations about large cities including such individuals as Louis Sullivan, Frank Lloyd Wright, and John Dewey. While most of these creative men, with the exception of Thoreau, found some use for cities, their essentially negative views about urban life were not formulated without adequate reflection or long experience.

The process of urbanization was painful for most urban dwellers during the early part of the Industrial Revolution. High density living, poor shelter, and inadequate sanitation helped to create almost inhuman living and working conditions in our large

189

cities. For example, the Tenth Ward in New York City increased its population density from 432 persons per acre in 1880 to 747 persons per acre in 1898 making it possibly the most crowded district in the world. The city was basically an unhealthy place to live. The high rate of mortality especially among the young and the danger of fatal epidemics constantly reminded urban residents of the environmental dangers of the city.

The city also was viewed as an artificial creation which separated man from nature. Permanent residence in large urban areas was thought to be dangerous to the human condition. Novelist Harold Frederic bitterly wrote that "The nineteenth century is a century of cities. . . . Perhaps there was a time when a man could live in what the poet calls daily communication with nature and not starve his mind or dwarf his soul, but this isn't the century." Certain aspects of urban life such as the dictatorship of the clock, men acting in mass rather than as individuals, the excessive zeal in seeking material reward, and the acceptance of artificial values caused a poet to depict city residents as:

A curious and canny folk
who push and jostle and scheme and plot
in a mad conflict and unheeding crush.

A primary reason for the negative image of cities was the generally held belief that it was a poor environment in which to raise a family. The problems of delinquent and neglected children constantly reminded one of the failure of family life in the city. In addition to the lack of adequate recreation areas and the menace of physical danger, it was generally believed that the urban environment endangered or distorted children's lives in other ways. In 1880 when educator G. Stanley Hall tested two hundred first grade children from urban, middle-class homes on their knowledge of nature, he discovered a frightening ignorance of the subject. City children imagined a world where spools of thread grew

190

on bushes, where meat was dug from the ground, where potatoes were plucked from trees, where butter came from buttercups, and where cows barked "bow wow." Hall concluded that the city distorted life and those who never left it in childhood could not be normal.

Observers conditioned by traditional outlooks viewed the city as the site of social disorganization. Fundamental human institutions such as the family, the church, the schools, and the government underwent significant modification in large urban areas. This disorganization was sometimes only a complicated pattern or accommodation to conditions of a new environment. Nevertheless, the image of disorganization and dislocation became predominant in many people's minds. The decay of old forms and institutions left the individual in the city to his own devices. Some saw this as a marvelous opportunity to release man from traditional restraints and liberate his creative ability. However, others viewed the collapse of institutions with horror becaue it left man unprotected and isolated and therefore subject to deterioration. In short, large urban areas became the scene for the extremes of human existence.

Great music, art, science, and literature could be found there. However, the high rate of suicide, crime, alcoholism, and other forms of delinquency gave evidence of the extreme human failure in the city. The distinction of wealth and the obvious social divisions also gave the city an image as a place of wildly fluctuating life styles which only enhanced the negative reaction it had in the American mind.

While the dense population of large urban areas gave the individual a wider choice of people with whom to establish deeper personal relations, it also caused loneliness and social distance in crowded places. The image of the city as an impersonal environment lacking community spirit has evoked a large degree of anti-urban sentiment. The fragmented nature of urban life is exemplified by the statement of a Los Angeles housewife who said:

191

B. The City of the Mind

Why, I don't even know the name of my next door neighbor. I hear the water running in their bath tub as well or better than I hear it in my own tub. I know what they say and can tell what they are doing but I don't know what their name is and I have never cared to find out.

Throughout the history of Europe and Asia, cities were normally the place of refuge while the countryside was the scene of insecurity and exposure to violence. The United States, however, has been spared constant warfare on its own territory and instead violence, especially in the modern age, has been internalized. This internal conflict between different racial or ethnic groups within the population usually occurred in our cities, which therefore have become violent places.

American cities, especially the large ones in the Northeast, are constantly being "filled with unfamiliar people, acting in unfamiliar ways who are at once terrified and threatening." The great waves of immigration from Europe and the folk migration of southern Negroes have caused major dislocations in our urban centers. The resulting friction between different groups has sometimes led to massive violence such as the Draft Riot of 1863 and the race riots of the 1960s.

In part, violence is engendered by the nature of the city itself. Extended travel and promiscuous contacts are essential to urban life. There is a frequent mingling of men unknown to each other. Since most persons feel that the main danger of deviant social behavior comes from strangers there is no collective feeling of security in the city. The image of being a potential victim of violence haunts many residents of large central cities.

One research team in Boston interviewed one thousand homeowners, asking them what they considered to be the greatest urban problems. These homeowners felt that the greatest urban problems were improper behavior in public places, crime, violence, rebellious youth, racial tension, and public immorality. The problems of strife, conflict, and community failure were foremost in their minds. In other words, the central city has developed the negative image as a violent, unstable environment.

The question could be asked, if large cities developed so many negative images in the American mind why did they continue to grow? The answer, as Jefferson discovered, lies principally in the economic realities of the time. Up to the latter part of the twentieth century economic opportunities were to be found mainly in urban areas. The city was seen as one of the principal indicators of American material growth and economic progress. In effect, economic opportunity blocked the predominant anti-urban sentiment from becoming functional. We never bothered to correct the widespread negative impressions of urban life because there was never a need to do so. People were forced to overcome their hostility to large cities for economic gain.

Also, in the nineteenth and early part of the twentieth centuries many cities were filled with European peasant immigrants and rural American migrants. For both groups the city represented economic hope for the future. They appraised their new situations with standards developed in primitive rural or peasant societies from which they came. In most cases the American city, for all its hardships, was a distinct improvement over the life they had left behind. A low level of expectations and the lack of viable economic alternatives enabled them to survive in the tenements and ghettos of large cities.

Objectively today's cities are cleaner and healthier than they were at the turn of the century. However, as Stephen Thernstrom has pointed out, men are usually not motivated by the objective situation but rather by the discrepancy between what is and what is expected. The motion picture industry, radio, and television have raised the level of expectation of the common man to the point where even the improvements in urban life are not enough.

193

B. The City of the Mind

The rise in expectations along with the essentially negative view of the city have combined to help create the crisis of urban America today. Economic factors no longer protect the city as they once did. At one time, only large cities could provide the essential services that American industry required. Today, due to technological advances, industrial firms are no longer forced to rely on urban locations in order to operate successfully. Many firms have begun to move out of urban areas to suburban settings. While there are many concrete reasons for this growing trend, the one cited over and over again by business leaders is the negative image of the city as an unstable environment.

Another factor in the decline of central cities is that they are no longer the exclusive residence of culture and sophistication. Once urban civilization and provincial life were distinctly different. However, today through the use of mass education and the mass media the whole nation has become urbanized. There are no more "hicks" or "country bumpkins." We now find writers, artists, sculptors, musicians, and dramatists dispersed throughout the nation, especially on college campuses. As museums, theaters, libraries, and colleges in urban centers like New York and Newark find themselves in financial difficulty, art fairs, "summer" stock theaters, and other cultural centers are rapidly becoming permanent features of suburban life.

This suburban trend can also be seen in the area of popular recreation. Spectator sports were once an exclusive feature of large urban areas. Recently older cities such as New York, Buffalo, and Boston lost their football teams to suburban areas while Detroit is threatened with a similar fate. Thanks to the automobile, the trend of moving spectator sports out of older congested urban centers to the more modern, spacious, and safer haven of the suburbs will continue to grow.

Today neither economics nor culture stand in the way of Americans pursuing their suburban dream. It is now possible to live an urbane life in a suburban setting. The attractions of a single family detached house in a homogeneous setting, the illu-

194

sion of a restored family life, and a sense of community have always lured people to the suburbs. While the city provided freedom for personal behavior, the suburb offers institutional controls through zoning, school board meetings, and restricted recreational facilities which gives the individual a sense of regaining influence over his own destiny. Large cities have found it difficult to offer this type of community control because of their size, bureaucratic structure, and heterogeneous nature.

While the United States is now an urbanized nation, we are not on the way to becoming a nation of big cities. Cities with over one million residents have stabilized or decreased in population over the last several decades and will probably continue to do so. The breakdown of the modern American city has been occurring for a long time but it only became apparent with the series of revenue crises, riots, and municipal employee strikes of the 1960s which have alarmed the nation's leadership. After years of neglect we are now talking about the crisis of our cities. Politicians, church leaders, business executives, university administrators, and many others have made the urban crisis a popular theme for discussion.

Yet much of today's anxiety about cities does not spring from a positive attitude toward large urban centers but rather a concern that the problems are getting out of hand. A growing creditability gap between practice and rhetoric seems to be developing. For all their faults, the boss and the machine politician identified with the city while many of today's leaders refuse to share the urban experience of the people. Many officials who claim the city is a viable residence live in suburban areas. Many politicians who boost the urban public school system send their own children to private schools. These officials remind one of dedicated zoologists who are truly concerned but are reluctant to share the day-to-day experiences they claim are normal or beneficial. Under these conditions it is hard to convince people about the positive destiny of our cities.

Only if the underlying anti-urban sentiment is reversed

195

B. The City of the Mind

can we truly begin to resolve the problems of our large urban centers. Perhaps then we can give an affirmative answer to the poet's query:

One of the million that am I
One of the million wondering why
And what it is, and if it pays
This living in the city's ways.

C. the newcomers: intruders or invited guests?

19. migration: the revolving door of urban America

William A. Osborne

The growth of American cities can, paradoxically enough, be traced to the farm. It was the rural peoples of Europe as well as the United States who turned the trick. By their migration they had swelled American cities to such proportions that, by the turn of the century, the United States had transformed itself from a nation of farmers to a nation of city dwellers. Part of that development—immigration—is discussed elsewhere in this volume. Here our concern is domestic migration.

The American city has really been a revolving door in the migratory movements of this country. People were drawn to the city for many reasons, but the primary one was economic. Large groups of people moved to the city in search of a better way of life. This part of the migratory pattern was filled with tremendous difficulties because of the inherent problems of adjusting from a rural to an urban life style. Admittedly, the burden of accommodation to urban life was harder on immigrants but even native Americans strained to adjust to the new environment.

Yet for all the economic and social benefits the city could bestow, it did not always retain a stable population. The second phase of migration, the one we are most aware of now, is the move to the suburbs. The city was for many only a revolving door or staging area where people gained enough economic security to move on to "a better life" in the suburbs. This second phase of migration in most cases lacked the pain and pathos of the first. People moving to the suburbs do not generally seek economic gain but rather social status, security, family betterment, and the like. They readily fit into the pattern of life, and the problems of accommodation are usually small. Many people left in our urban areas are the ones who have failed to achieve the necessary degree of economic success or who are newly arrived and are beginning the long hard urban climb to economic betterment.

It is no accident that today American cities are being filled by blacks, Puerto Ricans, Chicanos, and other minority groups who are in search of economic success. Their quest along with the accompanying urban distress is a pattern familiar to both native Americans and immigrant Europeans who experienced the process a few decades before. Their cry to desegregate the suburbs is really an attempt to allow them to proceed to the second step of migration.

The transformation of America from a rural to an urban nation was in a way caused by an ultimatum from nature. Much of the migration from farm to city resulted from the "push" of drought, depleted soil, locusts, or plant disease. To this can be added the fluctuations of the business cycle and the inevitable and unpredictable effects of farm prices. The city, on the other hand, like the grass "on the other side of the fence" always seemed to offer jobs, and a job meant simply that at the end of just five or six days, labor, one received cash: week after week, year after year, wages on an almost guaranteed basis. To those who were young and single, this promise of economic liberation in contrast to the bland and unrewarded life of their parents was a most powerful magnet. Furthermore, the city has always had a certain allure for civilized man. Its anonymity, the promise of sexual adventure, the variety of recreational opportunity, all rendered accessible by the weekly wage, promised a more exciting life; and who is not drawn by such a promise? Thus there seems to be a push-pull relationship between country and the city as though urbanization of the whole nation was an inevitable process.

This inevitability hung, however, on one critical variable: work. Up to the nineteenth century, all western civilization despite its great cities, offered the overwhelming proportion of its people only one livelihood—farming. It was the Industrial Revolution and more specifically, the factory system which proved to be the turning point. Henceforth, the city could hold as many people as there were jobs. With the expansion of job opportunities, the drawing power of the city was enlarged. In the United States this development, although underway earlier, accelerated during and after the Civil War. Thereafter, those farmers who found themselves defeated by depleted soil, drought, or the prevailing economic system could head for the nearest city rather than moving further west for another gamble with the elements. Horace Greeley saw the picture clearly when he complained in an editorial in 1867, "We cannot all live in the cities yet nearly all seem determined to do so. Millions of acres . . . solicit cultivation . . . yet hundreds of thousands reject this and rush into the cities."

In retrospect, the settling of the vastness of the West and the resulting agricultural surplus was a collective success. For the natural reasons already cited however, countless millions of farmers experienced hardship if not failure on the land. Even today, government statistics classify forty percent of all farm families as "poor." Meanwhile, another development accelerated the pull relationship between city and country: the Agricultural Revolution. This comprised two main elements: scientific and technological. The first, the development of scientific farming, combined new techniques of soil fertilization with more hardy and fecund plant strains. The result was a marked increase in the yield per acre. Farm surpluses thus became, by the turn of the

201

C. The Newcomers: Intruders or Invited Guests?

century, a chronic national problem relieved only by the two world wars and the subsidy programs initiated under the New Deal.

The second element, the technological, can be dated with the invention and marketing of McCormick's reaper in the 1840s. But the more significant advances came over fifty years later when the internal combustion engine was adapted to farm use in the tractor. That same source of power was then applied, in the 1930s, to a machine called the combine, which performed the three tasks of cutting, threshing, and binding of grain in one operation. These and later adaptations of machinery to specific crops produced another surplus—this time it was manpower. Thus the Agricultural Revolution, in turning the nation into one of the world's major sources of food, also generated a reservoir of excess manpower.

From this reservoir, two migratory streams emerged; one headed for the city, the other followed the unmechanized harvest. The latter group of workers were in perpetual migration from the South, northward in the spring and back again in fall as northern harvests ran their course. The plight of these victims of the Agricultural Revolution was brought to the nation's attention by the television journalist Edward R. Murrow in the 1950s. His documentary, the "Harvest of Shame," stirred some ripples of concern and reform, but the successful farmers and farm corporations who need their cheap labor have successfully resisted the mild pressure for reform.

The other migration of rural people who headed for the city also had tragic overtones. Many white rural migrants found it difficult to adjust to an urban existence. The pace of life, lack of community, and other features of city existence were totally alien to them. The seasons no longer had any meaning and the natural horizon was lost amid the tall buildings of a man-made environment. Despite the hardship of rural life, an element of nostalgia was evident among these people. In California, state societies were formed where old neighbors and people from a similar background could come together at picnics, dances, and meetings. Just as the immigrants tended to cling together in urban ghettos, white American migrants found solace in an alien environment by trying to reconstruct part of their former lives through these associations.

Undoubtedly the most significant migratory stream to emerge from the pool of human surplus was the long but steady relocation of the black population. Over a period of perhaps sixty or seventy years, these people who had been predominantly rural and southern began to migrate to urban centers of the North. In 1910 approximately ninety percent of the Negro population lived in the southern and border states. Sixty years later that figure had dropped to about fifty-three percent. The effects of this migration on recent American history and the implications for the future warrant a closer look.

If the "heart-breaking nineties," with massive unemployment in the cities and disastrous debts, and low income for the farmers, was a time of trouble for the nation's white people, it was doubly so for the Negroes. By 1890, all the gains of Reconstruction had been erased, the franchise had been removed by the poll tax, the "grandfather clause," and the literacy test. Then the network of segregation statutes finally stripped them (de facto) of all rights. Even a Negro's right to life depended on the whim of any gang or mob of whites who might organize to avenge an alleged wrong or to make an example of some "uppity nigger." Inflation, low farm prices, and never-ending debt combined with the reign of terror to turn the eyes of Negro tenants, sharecroppers, and farmers northward for relief.

With the earnings that came at harvest time, Negro men in the 1890s began buying railroad tickets to Washington, D.C., or points north. Married or single, the men went first. Numbering perhaps a few thousand at first, the plan generally was to come back for the family or else with enough money to "get back'n yo feet." By 1914 the number of migrants approximated 50,000 annually and remained at that level for the duration of the war. The 1920 census revealed that for the decade, the South had lost over five percent of its black population.

More significant than the regional character of this migration was the urban aspect of the black exodus. The following table illustrates the enormous scope of this mass movement in recent years:

Proportion of Negroes in Each of the 30 Largest Cities,
1950, 1960, and Estimated 1965

	1950	1960	(Estimate)6 1965
New York, N.Y.	10	14	18
Chicago, Ill.	14	23	28
Los Angeles, Calif.	9	14	17
Philadelphia, Pa.	18	26	31
Detroit, Michigan	16	29	34
Baltimore, Md.	24	35	38
Houston, Texas	21	23	23
Cleveland, Ohio	16	29	34
Washington, D.C.	35	54	66
St. Louis, Mo.	18	29	36
Milwaukee, Wis.	3	8	11
San Francisco, Calif.	6	10	12
Boston, Mass.	5	9	13
Dallas, Texas	13	19	21
New Orleans, La.	32	37	41
Pittsburgh, Pa.	12	17	20
San Antonio, Texas	7	7	8
San Diego, Calif.	5	6	7
Seattle, Wash.	3	5	7
Buffalo, N.Y.	6	13	17

Cincinnati, Ohio	16	22	24
Memphis, Tenn.	37	37	40
Denver, Colo.	4	6	9
Atlanta, Ga.	37	38	44
Minneapolis, Minn.	1	2	4
Indianapolis, Ind.	15	21	23
Kansas City, Mo.	12	18	22
Columbus, Ohio	12	16	18
Phoenix, Ariz.	5	5	5
Newark, N.J.	17	34	47

[6] Except for Cleveland, Buffalo, Memphis, and Phoenix, for which a special census has been made in recent years, these are very rough estimations computed on the basis of the change in relative proportions of Negro births and deaths since 1960.

Source: U. S. Department of Commerce, Bureau of the Census.

As cited in *The Report of the National Advisory Commission on Civil Disorders*, New York, New York *Times* edition, 1968, p. 248.

Blacks not only had to undergo the hardships accompanying the process of urbanization but also were forced to bear the extra burden of second-class citizenship. Until recently, they were given no hope of assimilation or upward mobility in the general social strata. Whatever economic progress the city offered was always restricted in some way for Negroes. White migrants and immigrants could view the future with some hope. The inferior urban neighborhoods, housing, schools, and jobs that they were forced to endure might all be worth it if they or their children could escape them at some future date.

For blacks, however, the urban ghetto and inferior facilities seemed to be a permanent feature of life. Racial barriers seemed to block any hope for the future. The riots and demonstrations of

205

the 1950s and 1960s which struck Watts, Memphis, Atlanta, Cleveland, Chicago, Washington, New York, and numerous other smaller cities are probably the clearest articulation of what the blacks thought of conditions in their new urban residence. Here too, it seemed, they were getting the same "dirty deal" they got on the land.

Meanwhile the second stage of migration was well underway—the movement of whites from the city to the suburb. This is usually thought to be a recent phenomenon but in reality suburban migration is as old as cities. When American cities experienced tremendous growth in the nineteenth century they expanded geographically as well as in population density. Without exception every major American city grew by adjusting its boundaries. In fact if urban annexation had not taken place only New York City would have contained a population of over one million people, although it would have been confined to the Island of Manhattan. Thus, in part, cities were able to recapture suburban migrants while enlarging their geographic area.

The modern migration of whites to suburbia, complemented by an increasing black influx into the inner cities, does seem to support the warning of the President's Commission on Civil Disorders (1967); that the nation is polarizing itself along racial lines. While this may come to pass, it is not by design. The movement furthermore, seems to be economic rather than racial. For one thing, it predates the civil rights movement even in the modern period.

Popular national awareness of suburban growth dates from the end of World War II. "Levittown" became a symbol of the new middle-class suburb. The usual inhabitant in the newly developed suburb was the young veteran of World War II who, after the initial period of readjustment to civilian life, landed his first "big job" or promotion. Home ownership "with lots of room" inside and out was the goal. Mr. Levitt, with the generous assistance of federally guaranteed mortgages, provided the

206

means. The flight to the suburbs was underway by the late 1950s. More accurately, it was a move up on the social scale or the fulfillment of yearning by young parents for the safety, the spaciousness, the fresh air, in a word, the ideal atmosphere for raising children. It was not until the late 1960s that this heretofore steady migration of a successful middle-class population came to be called a "flight."

No doubt it did, for many, become a "flight" as the cities became prey to riots, epidemics of drugs, crime, and a host of other problems. Yet in contrast to the other migrations in American history, this one lacked the tragedy, the pain, and the anguish of most others. It was not, by comparison, a forced migration; on the contrary, it was and still is for the most part, a freely chosen move. Sprung from a set of family-oriented values, materialistic and child-centered, the suburban migration represents probably the first time in human history that so large a number of people have had the opportunity to freely search for a style of living rather than simply search for a livelihood. This inexperience may account for the crass materialism, hedonism, and ersatz esthetics which mark suburban life.

What is new about this latest suburban migration is that most cities have not been able to enlarge their boundaries to compensate for population losses. We are in the midst of one of the greatest migration movements in American history. Blacks and other deprived minorities continue to move into urban areas for economic gain while middle-class whites leave the cities in greater and greater numbers. The revolving door of urban migration now has taken on racial overtones. In part this may be traced to the inability of American cities to support an adequate life style for the white middle class in order to retain this vital segment of its population.

It is also due to the nature of today's suburbs. Those who migrate to the suburbs believe they leave the city and its problems behind them. Using restrictive zoning laws

207

and tightly controlled local governments (reinforced by their domination of the state legislatures), they seem determined to keep out the low-income groups. The suburbanites entice industry to their domain because of the tax benefits to local government. They then refuse any effort to provide adequate housing for the workers. Despite high educational levels, their ignorance of social change, economics, and constitutional developments is astounding. They fail to see that cities are not bound by political lines.

Urban, economic, and ecological systems are area-wide, if not regional in nature. The indigenous problems must have area or regional solutions. City and suburb are simply two parts of a larger system. One does not survive without the other. The challenge therefore facing the suburban migrant is to his creativity, his grasp of the real world, and ultimately his sense of values. If he fails to see the challenge in this light, the sinking city will pull down the suburbs with it. The epic of the rise and fall of American civilization will have terminated with the last migration—the flight to the suburbs.

20. xenophobia in America

Thomas J. Curran

President Franklin Delano Roosevelt once greeted the Daughters of the American Revolution with the salutation, "My fellow immigrants," much to the consternation of those dear, patriotic ladies. Another president, John F. Kennedy, could speak of the United States as a "nation of immigrants." Yet despite the polyglot population of America, there has always been an ambivalent feeling toward the newcomers: on the one hand welcome and on the other rejection. This tension between welcome and rejection can be found particularly in America's cities: the areas where the bulk of the immigrants landed and settled.

Xenophobia, which is a distrust of strangers because of the fear that their alien ways pose a threat to the culture of the native born, is endemic to most societies. In America these episodic outbursts took place initially as a reaction to the foreign born in the cities. While native American city dwellers were hostile to the immigrants in their midst, the xenophobic hatred of foreigners took on a wider meaning in rural areas where it became part of the anti-urban tradition in America.

While the Protestant English who settled this country were initially interested in populating their colonies, they generally passed laws against grants of citizenship to either Catholics or

C. The Newcomers: Intruders or Invited Guests?

Jews. This was a form of religious xenophobia, the belief that these religious creeds were anti-English, though in truth religious intolerance was practiced among and by the various Protestant sects. In seventeenth century Massachusetts, Mary Dyer was hanged for her persistence in preaching her "pestilent" doctrine of Quakerism in Congregationalist Massachusetts Bay Colony.

The Pennsylvania Quakers were quite upset in the eighteenth century with the tremendous influx of Protestant Germans. Benjamin Franklin in the 1750s spoke for many fellow Philadelphians when he wrote:

Those [Germans] who come hither are generally the most stupid of their own nation . . . not being used to liberty they know not how to make a modest use of it. And as Holbein says of the Hottentots, they are not esteemed men until they have shown their manhood by beating their mothers, so these seem not to think themselves free, till they can feel their liberty in abusing and insulting their teachers.

By far Franklin's most xenophobic outburst came in his *Observations Concerning the Increase of Mankind* (1751). In this pamphlet, he insisted that America was a white man's country, and it should be controlled by the Anglo-Saxons.

Franklin's approach became basic for future xenophobic movements. Each in its turn would denigrate their foreign born opponents by creating a stereotype that reflected the least desirable qualities of aliens plus an emphasis, sometimes implicit, on the racial superiority of the Anglo-Saxons.

When the new government was established under the Federal Constitution, the first desire was to increase the population of the country through a liberal naturalization act which was passed in 1790. This law allowed aliens to become eligible for citizenship after only a two-year waiting period. Since many of these newcomers voted against the Federalists, this only increased the hostility to foreigners within the ruling political party in the country. This was clearly evident when the Federalists pushed through the infamous Alien and Sedition Acts during the war scare period of 1798. As one Boston Federalist warned, "If some means are not adopted to prevent the indiscriminate admission of wild Irishmen and others to the right of suffrage, there will soon be an end to liberty and property."

This idea, to limit the political power of the immigrants, dominated the xenophobic organizations up to the Civil War period. In the 1870s and 1880s, the demand for exclusion arose and culminated successfully in the Chinese Exclusion Act (1882). Subsequent efforts would be made to restrict the admission of other immigrants as well. Again, most of these moves would originate in the cities.

The Hartford Convention of 1815, which was the Federalists' answer to the War of 1812, clearly indicated that the nativism of the Alien and Sedition Acts had not died. The convention called for a constitutional amendment that would bar all naturalized citizens from holding public office. In effect, it would extend the presidential requirement for American nativity found in the Federal Constitution to all other public offices.

The death of the Federalist party did not kill the xenophobic spirit in America. During the next hundred years, which may be termed a century of immigration (1820-1924) when close to 38 million immigrants came to these shores, many nativist-minded Americans felt impelled to support organizations which promised to fight the alien menace.

The American xenophobes thought that they belonged to a national community and were intent on preserving the character and integrity of the community by retaining control of it. As a result, they favored a more restrictive view of citizenship which they would not confer on the foreign born, or, at least, not confer readily. In this sense, we may certify them as conservatives.

Generally, the mistrust of foreigners appeared after a series

211

C. THE NEWCOMERS: INTRUDERS OR INVITED GUESTS?

of bewildering changes. In seeking an explanation for these changes the nativists found their answer in a foreign menace. One historian has shown that certain common themes persist in nineteenth century American nativist literature. He found that white, insecure Protestant Americans, reacting to confusing social changes and urbanization, felt impelled to unite against a common enemy who threatened their existence through some form of internal subversion.

As already noted, American xenophobia can be divided into two major movements. The first group up to the Civil War tried to control the power of the immigrants admitted to the United States. The second type, following the Civil War, emphasized the need to restrict the numbers or even exclude the immigration of foreigners altogether. The effort at control motivated the xenophobic Native American party of the 1830s, the American Republican party of the 1840s, and the Know Nothings of the 1850s.

All of these organizations began in the city and had their major support in the urban centers of the Atlantic seaboard—New York, Philadelphia, and Boston. The Know Nothings, however, did have strength in the rural areas as well. The second type of xenophobic movement was aimed at restricting the numbers and kinds of immigrants who were likely to seek entrance to the United States. For example, the anti-Chinese movement reached its pinnacle of power in the California Workingmen's party (1877-1880) and the Oriental Exclusion League (1905-1924).

In the first organized nativist groups, two aims appeared: the one directed at the religious beliefs of the immigrants and the second at their political power. Both religious and political nativism were basically conservative and reformist in the sense that they hoped to maintain the status quo or, at least, to mold society in the image of their Anglo-Saxon Protestant idea of the past.

For the most part, these nativists were sincere Americans, alarmed and confused at the changes taking place around them.

212

While there was an irrational element in the stereotypes and scapegoats that they created, it is also true that it was not unreasonable for them to protect themselves against the groups that they thought were damaging their community and destroying their sense of status. Generally, they were in the minority, but occasionally they would be reinforced by other Americans who were angered at specific grievances generated by the two major political parties. Almost inevitably, demagogues appeared who used the nativist creed to advance their own careers.

In the period from 1820-1860, immigration had profound political and social implications for the nation, though the eastern cities were the first to feel the impact of these newcomers. As immigration increased from .5 million in the decade 1830-1840, to almost 1.75 million in the succeeding decade, and to 2.5 million in the decade, of the 1850s, a feeling of alarm spread among some of the native born because the bulk of these foreigners were not only Roman Catholics but also of Irish and German descent.

Among the native born urban dwellers, reaction to the Irish immigrant was generally much harsher than to other foreigners. The Irishman was poor, clannish, priest-ridden, and a drunk, according to the nativists. And they remained, by and large, in the cities. Then, too, the Irish quickly played a role in Jacksonian politics.

Philip Hone, former Mayor of New York City and a wealthy Whig merchant, echoed the sentiment of many others in the 1830s when he described the political power of the Irish in the following manner. "These Irishmen, strangers among us, without a feeling of patriotism or affection in common with American citizens, decide the elections in the city of New York. They make Presidents and Governors, and they send men to represent us in the councils of the nation. . . . " The more demagogic editors of the Philadelphia *Sun* and the future nativist Congressman, Lewis Charles Levin, insisted that the Irish Catholic vote is organized to overthrow American liberty.

Anti-Catholicism was a factor in the xenophobia of the ante-

213

C. The Newcomers: Intruders or Invited Guests?

bellum period. Beginning with the writings of the New York City artist Samuel Finley Breese Morse, of telegraph fame, a series of anti-Catholic tracts appeared culminating in the work of Maria Monk and her *Awful Disclosures*. Maria, an alleged nun, claimed to have escaped from a Montreal convent where innocent girls were forced to submit to priests who gained access to the convent via secret tunnels. Those nuns who resisted were killed. The children born of those meetings were baptized, then strangled and thrown into a lime pit. The baptized infants, free of all sin, would go directly to heaven where they would intercede for those who baptized them.

Maria's readers were given a heady mixture of sex and religion. Maria Monk's mother reported that she was a wild child who had damaged her brain as a youngster by inserting a pencil in her ear and trying to force it out the other side. But her successful book, which has sold more copies than any other publication in America except the Bible, encouraged imitation.

In the 1830s and 1840s nativist political parties were able to use the fear of foreigners to elect their candidates for mayor in Boston and New York. In all instances, these groups tried to appeal to the reform element: they emphasized the increased corruption, crime, and welfare costs, all of which they placed at the door of the Irish Catholics. In New York, they were able to point with horror to the actual use of Catholic political power. Bishop John Hughes, the Irish-born leader of New York's Catholics, set up a political ticket in the election of 1841. He endorsed those who favored public aid to parochial schools. This marriage of politics and religion was a mistake because it gave concrete grounds with which to fan nativists' fears.

But despite their success, most nativist parties speedily declined. Many politicians believed it was a wiser policy to try to win the naturalized voters than to antagonize them. Then, too, despite the promise of reform, the performances of the nativist elected officials left a good deal to be desired. Perhaps, the most

214

important reasons, though was the fact that the nativists were accused of church burnings (1844 in Philadelphia) and of favoring a policy of proscription against the foreign born. The belief was still strong that immigrants were necessary to the economic growth and development of the country. This attitude became so pervasive that the nativists had to go underground.

This shift to secrecy in the Know Nothing movement of the 1850s was an indication of weakness. The Know Nothings initially developed their secret lodges first in New York City and then to the other cities of the country. Finally this movement spread to the rural areas where its anti-Catholicism found some listeners. In the rural areas, too, its conservative emphasis on the past—a past without these urban immigrants—won many supporters.

For example, a former Congregational minister and a prominent literary celebrity elected to statewide office by the Know Nothings, Joel T. Headley, explained his own anti-urban bias. He spoke for many when he condemned the activism he found rampant in New York City: "The mad excitement after gain," he held, augered "sadly for the race, and the growing urbanization would have a harmful effect upon the people. God has spread out the earth to be inhabited," he asserted " . . . not . . . to have man shut himself up in city walls. . . . Every large city on the face of the earth has sunk into ruin and gone down, too, from the degeneracy, corruption and crime of its inhabitants." But factories and cities continued to grow.

The Know Nothings were both helped and hindered by two factors: first, the disruption of the other political parties over the issue of slavery and its extension and secondly, an increase in the amount of anti-Catholic propaganda in 1850s. These factors appeared to so strengthen the movement that it threw off secrecy and participated in the presidential election of 1856 by nominating the former President Millard Fillmore. The slavery issue drove many Whigs and Democrats out of their own parties, par-

215

ticularly among southern Whigs who, along with some others, tried to substitute the issue of immigration for that of slavery. They tried to escape from the slavery extension issue, which had a strong Negrophobic bias, and replace it with the threat of the foreign born, particularly the Irish Catholics.

The Civil War, by and large, temporarily abated the outbursts against the foreign born. Over 500 thousand foreign-born soldiers served in the Union Army. Xenophobia, though muted, did not entirely disappear from America in the 1860s. A dormant anti-Semitism surfaced at this time. The former Know Nothing, General Ulysses S. Grant in December, 1862, even went so far as to expel the Jews from his military jurisdiction because he unjustly believed they were all smugglers. Lincoln rescinded the

During this period in the cities of California, particularly San Francisco, the increased numbers of Chinese immigrants caused an anti-Chinese movement to develop. The Chinese came for much the same reason as other immigrants: to improve their economic conditions. Often they came under indenture, in Chinese K'u-li (coolie). Thus in 1862, anti-coolie clubs were formed. Basically, the anti-coolie movement was based on religious, racial, and economic grounds. John Chinaman was a heathen, a "yellow belly," a "moon-eyed leper." Economically he worked harder, longer, and for less money, so that he was viewed favorably by employers and with hostility by labor. Chinese immigration was never extensive but since it was concentrated in certain areas of the country, it appeared to menace the economic security of the white worker. For instance, half the factory jobs in San Francisco in 1875 were held by Chinese. When wage rates fell, white workers blamed their Chinese competitors.

In California, the Irish-born workers became the leaders of the xenophobic Workingmen's party of California organized in 1877. It was led by Denis Kearney, a teamster, who was born in

216

County Cork, Ireland. Kearney, a demagogic speaker, always insisted in his speeches that the "Chinese must go!" In 1882 the campaign was successful and for the first time the immigration gates were closed to a specific racial group. But the Asiatic Exclusion League of San Francisco was still not satisfied. Nor was American labor. A staunch supporter of the Exclusion Act was the American Federation of Labor which was organized in 1881. One of their great fears was that the Asian hordes might inundate the American labor market.

Obviously, some regulation of immigration was required if the nation's industrial classes were to be able to organize effective trade unions, but the racial emphasis for rejection of the Chinese and then the Japanese helped institutionalize the belief in the superiority of the white, Nordic race. This idea was now applied to the increased numbers of immigrants from southern and eastern Europe who inundated the cities of America. The Immigration Restriction League was opposed to these immigrants not only because they were considered racially inferior, but also because large numbers of them were Catholics and Jews.

To fight the menace of Catholicism, the American Protective Association was formed in 1887. Strictly speaking, it was not xenophobic, since it did admit the foreign born. It was founded in the city of Clinton, Iowa, the largest manufacturing town in that state where two-fifths of the population were foreign born. The basic theme of this movement was opposition to the Catholic conspiracy to subvert America. It also reacted to the corrupt municipal politics in which the foreign born were seemingly engaged. Thus it was not unlike the previous anti-Catholic movements, except that it did not set up its own political party but instead operated mostly through the Republican party. In 1893 some members of the A.P.A. were convinced that the Catholic conspiracy was at hand. They believed that Pope Leo XIII was coming to the United States on December 8, 1893, at which time the Catholics in the cities would rise up in rebellion. When the

217

C. The Newcomers: Intruders or Invited Guests?

expected coup did not occur, the A.P.A. insisted that their vigilance had prevented it. By 1896, the movement's energies had dissipated.

A new group, the Immigration Restriction League was organized in 1894 in Boston, Massachusetts. Its main purpose was indicated by its name. It had the support of some outstanding men: Senator Henry Cabot Lodge, Prescott Hall, and Edwin A. Ross to name a few. Their instrument of restriction was the literacy test which would avoid the label of proscription. It seemed sensible to emphasize the need for people to be able to read and write. Most of the immigrants from southern and eastern Europe, however, came from areas where education was almost nonexistent. The thrust was anti-Semitic, anti-Catholic, and pro-Nordic.

Xenophobia was now slipping into racism. And once again, the proponents of restrictions pointed with horror to the city ghettos with their little Italy, little Russia, and little Poland—all symbols of clannishness. They placed great stress on the increased crime, poverty, and welfare costs. They asked, could America benefit from such groups? Their campaign successfully culminated in the passage of the Literacy Act of 1917. World War I, however, had already halted major immigration into the United States.

In 1915, yet another nationalistic organization with racist overtones came into existence, the Ku Klux Klan. This organization had more in common with previous nativist organizations that it did with the Reconstruction Ku Klux Klan. Normally, the Klan has been viewed as a rural organization reacting against urbanized America with its Catholics, Jews, blacks, and immigrants. Actually as a recent historian of the Klan has pointed out the roots of the Klan can be found in the expanding cities as well as in the declining farms and villages. Again, as with other xenophobic organizations, the city Klan was the reaction of people frightened, dislocated, and uprooted by the constant changes taking place in urbanized America. It was the urban leaders of the Klan who provided the leadership and financial resources for the movement. Once again, as with other xenophobic organizations, many people were attracted to the Klan because it promised to do something about corruption in the cities: the prostitution, the violation of the prohibition laws, and the "alien" parochial schools.

By 1925, the Klan reached its peak and began to decline. But it certainly joined the Immigration Restriction League in supporting the racist Quota Laws of 1921 and 1924 which closed the open gates for European immigrants as the Exclusion Act of 1882 had for the Chinese. Certainly the Klan was the last of the purely xenophobic organizations in America, with its animosity directed against the foreign born. Of course, this statement does not deny the hostility to native born Jews, Catholics, and Negroes. But it does say that xenophobia on an organized basis was dead. The Christian Front and the America First movements of the 1930s were more nationalistic and directed against outside enemies.

Still frightened, troubled Americans upset at the changes that beset them, did not disappear from America's cities with the Quota Laws. Now new migrants, blacks, Puerto Ricans, and Mexican-Americans became the focus of fear as they moved into the American cities to supply the unskilled labor that was needed in industrial America. Again stereotypes were created, largely in industrial America. Again stereotypes were created as these newcomers were blamed for crime and the rising welfare costs.

21. the transplanted Americans: immigrants in an urban world

Ronald H. Bayor

The growth and development of most American cities is closely related to the flow of immigrants to America's shores. Immigrants enabled the city to expand and to industrialize but also encumbered the urban areas with new problems such as overcrowding, large-scale poverty, epidemics, and the need for new city services. Few cities were prepared to deal with the mass of immigrants who arrived in the nineteenth and twentieth centuries. Native contemporaries of the immigrants often asked why immigrants tended to settle in cities when rural areas seemed to offer both opportunity and living space. The answer to this must be sought by examining the immigrant's background and adjustment problems.

Immigration actually began with the first European settlers arriving in America, but large-scale immigration, involving hundreds of thousands of people a year, was a nineteenth and twentieth century phenomenon. The reasons for coming were as varied as the immigrants but tended to be a combination of disgust with the old world and hope for a better life in the new. By looking at four major groups—the Irish, Germans, Jews, and Italians—we can detail most of the causes for immigration.

Ronald H. Bayor

The Irish came to America basically because of economic factors. Life in Ireland was difficult. Many of the Irish who were rent-paying tenants on lands owned by absentee English landlords were driven off their farms when the landlord no longer thought it either politically or economically profitable to keep them there. Emigration therefore had already begun when a major catastrophe occurred. The potato crop, upon which the Irish farmer was dependent for food, failed. The years 1845 to 1849 were years of famine forcing many Irish to leave for other lands. By 1864, approximately two and one-half million Irish had left their homeland.

The German and Italian migrations were similar to the Irish in that economic problems were the major push factor. Many German farmers, in an effort to modernize their farms, bought machinery and mortgaged their farms in the process. When crop failures occurred in the 1840s and 1850s, the farmers lost their land. Rather than start anew in the German area, many of these people decided to emigrate. With them came a number of German artisans displaced economically by the introduction of machinery into German factories.

For the Italians it was a combination of tenant farming, extreme poverty, and decreasing crop prices that pushed these people to emigrate. With the farmer, as in Germany, came the artisans, the professionals, and the clergy. Whole towns sometimes emigrated together.

The Jews experienced a combination of economic, religious, and political problems. The majority of Jews in eastern Europe were under the control of Russia with lesser numbers in Rumania and the Austro-Hungarian Empire. Restrictions on Jewish religious life and on what occupations they could enter were part of the oppressive system found in Russia and Rumania. Coupled with this was violence directed at Jews which reached peaks in the years 1881-1882, 1891, and 1905-1906. A debilitating poverty plus a restricted existence forced many eastern European

221

C. The Newcomers: Intruders or Invited Guests?

Jews to emigrate. Between 1890 and 1920, over one third of the Jews in eastern Europe decided to make the journey to the United States.

In all these cases of migration the problems in Europe plus the concept of a better life in the United States pushed and pulled these people to leave their homes and seek this better life. Whatever their reasons for coming however, most immigrants found their way into cities and remained there, even though most of them had been farmers in Europe. It should be noted that this was part of a general rural to urban trend taking place in Europe and America simultaneously. The Irish were as prone to go to London as to New York. The native American farmer also felt that the city offered a better future.

The movement to cities arose from a number of causes, most of which the immigrant had little control over. Before the development of regular passenger service for immigrants around 1850, most of these people arrived in America by way of merchant ships which brought American raw materials to Europe and returned with European manufactured goods and immigrants. This situation arose because manufactured goods were less bulky than raw materials. Therefore merchant ships going from Europe to the United States filled their empty cargo spaces with immigrants.

Hastily constructed passenger quarters provided poor living conditions for the immigrants on their long journey. However, as the competition for passengers intensified, the price of a ticket fell, and immigration increased regardless of the conditions on board. Since trade was particularly intense between Liverpool in England and New York, many of the Irish came to the new world by this route. Other Irish immigrants, leaving from port cities in Ireland, went first to the Canadian maritime provinces and then to Boston and other New England cities. The ships making these journeys were mainly lumber and cotton carriers, not intended for passenger service, but the result of their sailings was to concentrate the Irish in the New England and New York areas.

The Germans exhibited a similar settlement pattern based on trade routes. German immigration was dependent on tobacco ships sailing from Bremen to Baltimore and cotton ships sailing from Le Havre to New Orleans. Liverpool also served as a port of departure for Germans destined for settlement in New York. As a result of trade routes few German immigrants landed or settled in New England. In this way, the choice of one city over another or one region of the country over another as a first settlement area was not up to these immigrants.

Whether to remain in the first settlement area also was not always a voluntary choice of the immigrant. The Irish, arriving in a more destitute state than most immigrants, were also more likely to remain in the first urban area that they reached. The Germans, in contrast, had the financial ability to move further inland either to rural sections or to such growing cities as Cincinnati, St. Louis, or Milwaukee. Inland cities which were the terminal points for rail and water transportation also became immigrant centers particularly as transportation improved and fares were lowered.

Although money was required to purchase farmland or move inland, it is unlikely that some of these immigrants would have wanted a rural life even if they had the necessary financial resources. People who had been small farmers in Europe often were disgusted with that type of life. There also was a lack of knowledge about American farming techniques. Therefore the decision of many former farmers was to remain in the cities. New York, Baltimore, St. Louis, Cincinnati, and Milwaukee all had large German populations.

Similar immigration patterns were exhibited by the late nineteenth and early twentieth century immigrants, mainly southern and eastern Europeans. By this period steamship

223

C. The Newcomers: Intruders or Invited Guests?

passenger service for immigrants was available and had replaced the trade routes and sailing ships. This eliminated many of the hazards of crossing the Atlantic in merchant sailing ships, but poor conditions continued such as overcrowding, inadequately ventilated steerage quarters, and epidemics on board.

The urban concentration also continued. Immigrants tended to be drawn to the same city ports as before. The steamship lines operating in the immigrant traffic visited a larger number of European ports. It was then possible to obtain passage to the United States from almost any port in Europe. However, these lines still deposited their human cargoes in such immigrant centers as Boston and New York. Many of these immigrants, arriving poor, were unable to move inland. Those that did went to cities like Chicago or Cleveland which were growing industrial centers. As other sections of the country industrialized, they began to attract immigrants. The distaste for a rural life was still evident for the bulk of immigrants arriving at this time.

Besides trade routes, financial problems, and a disgust with rural life, there were other reasons for the immigrant's attachment to cities. For immigrants arriving with little money, the first thing to do was to find employment. Urban centers in general, and certain cities in particular, offered the immigrant better job opportunities and higher wages than could be found in the rural areas. The immigrant was interested in making money fast, both for himself and for members of his family abroad.

Employment suitable for immigrants was also more easily found in the city. For immigrants who were unskilled or semi-skilled, the industrializing city with its newly mechanized factories offered work which required the simplest of skills. In New York, Italians and Jews entered the clothing industry, and in Chicago, Poles and Bohemians entered the meat packing and steel industries. Cities that had large immigrant populations soon expanded their industrial development. Boston was a commercial center when the Irish arrived. When factories were mechanized the Irish were able to turn Boston into an industrial center particularly in relation to the shoe and textile industries. Skilled immigrants usually congregated in areas which were centers for their craft. For example, British textile workers mainly went to cities involved in textile manufacturing.

Finally, the city offered to the immigrant the company of his fellows through the development of the ethnic colony or ghetto. As immigrants arrived in cities, they began to concentrate in certain areas. As these ethnic ghettos grew they became centers for the cultural life of each group. The area was usually near a factory or business district; long hours and low wages kept the immigrants near their places of work. Being near expanding business districts, the ethnic colony was usually a slum with the worst housing in the city, yet it also provided certain benefits for the immigrant.

The growth of these ethnic colonies was in part due to a feeling of alienation from the mainstream of American society. This provoked a desire to recreate the old world existence by congregating among familiar people. America was a new experience for the immigrant, and even more so was the city. Although critics of these ghettos assailed them for slowing the assimilation process, the ethnic colony was a stepping stone to life in American society, a way to adjust to the new world and to the city slowly and among your own people. Rather than perpetuate old world traits, the ghettos tended to Americanize the immigrant at a faster pace than had he been in an isolated rural setting. The immigrant thought that he was recreating the old world when in reality he was assimilating into the new.

There were many forces in the ghetto which speeded this process. The immigrant newspapers, written in the language of the old world, was one ghetto institution which taught the immigrant about America in the simplest manner possible, in his own language. The schools enabled the children of the ghetto to learn more about American life and bring this knowledge home to their parents. Benevolent societies helped the immigrant in a number of ways to adjust. Some provided sickness benefits and paid funeral expenses, which were important matters to a poverty-striken people. Other organizations cared for orphaned children or were involved in the relief of the poor. Beside economic security some of these organizations such as fraternal lodges and athletic clubs gave the immigrant a place to find companionship with people in similar circumstances. The religious life of the old world was kept intact in numerous churches and synagogues, which also served as a source of comfort to the immigrant. For these reasons the ethnic colony was important in assimilating the immigrant into American life and also made the city a more attractive place to live.

All cities which had immigrants saw these ghettos emerge and also saw them move. The German and Irish populations in New York moved and formed new colonies when their original areas of settlement were taken over by Jews and Italians. The same process occurred in Chicago when Poles and Bohemians moved into German and Scandinavian areas. The ghetto was a fact of life in the city and one which was far more beneficial than the critics could ever imagine.

The city and the ghetto, of course, had their faults providing nothing but a life of misery and despair for many immigrants. Part of the problem was that few cities were prepared for the newcomers. New York grew from a population of 166 thousand in 1825 to 630 thousand in 1855. The increase, although not entirely due to immigration, exceeded anything the city could provide in housing. Boston, Chicago, and other cities experienced similar housing shortages. The result was the overuse of all available land. Shacks were built in backyards and alleys, and ten families crowded in where there was only one before. Ventilation and sanitation were inadequate, and the city was well on its way to creating large slum areas.

Close quarters and unsanitary conditions brought with them disease. Boston before mass immigration had eliminated many of its health problems. However, with the emergence of Irish slum areas epidemics appeared once more, particularly cholera and smallpox. Tuberculosis began to take many lives again. Infant mortality rates rose to new heights. The death rate among the Irish was the highest in Boston. The reactions of the cities to these new problems did little to improve the situation. Inadequate medical service, lack of sanitation services, and continued poverty kept disease and mortality rates high. The city simply was not able to cope with a large, poor population.

For some immigrants, rather than physical illness, the despairs of slum living and the unsettling experience of migration became too much for their minds. The insanity rate was higher among immigrants than among the native born. Suicide was a problem as was alcoholism. Crime also was a matter of concern both to the immigrants and the general city population. Caught in poverty with their recognized ways of life altered, some immigrants turned to crime to escape their environment.

Native Americans in the cities tended to blame the new problems on the immigrants. Rather than finding ways to relieve the poverty which produced the crime or the lack of housing resulting in poor health, the immigrant was often attacked for having transformed peaceful cities into large slum and crime centers. Each group which arrived in American cities was subsequently blamed for the cities' problems and failures. The immigrants were aware that they were not particularly welcomed. Despite the hostile attitude of native Americans and the slum conditions, the bulk of immigrants continued to come to urban areas bypassing the rural sections.

Some attempts were made to change the settlement pattern.

227

C. The Newcomers: Intruders or Invited Guests?

Organizations arose dedicated to diverting the immigrant to American rural areas. The Irish Catholic Colonization Association and the Hebrew Emigrant Aid Society were two such organizations which tried to set up ethnic communities away from the cities. Most of the settlements failed. There was no strong interest in leaving the city. The land was, from old world experience, a symbol of poverty and suffering. Efforts to collect money among the immigrants to support these rural colonization ventures also failed. Of course, some immigrants were successful as farmers and went mainly to rural sections. Scandinavians, for example, settled to a greater extent in farm areas than in cities. However, for the majority of immigrants, the rural life never elicited much interest.

The city, with its faults, remained the immigrant center. It was the first settlement for most immigrants, the area which provided the best job opportunities, and also the one which offered a growing ethnic colony filled with cultural and other activities which reminded them of the old world while they were adjusting to the new.

22. ethnicity in America's changing cities

Eugene Kusielewicz

Today, we are at long last becoming aware of the ethnic factor, not merely as the mortar that kept old urban neighborhoods intact but also as part of the future of our cities. The awakening is a painfully slow one, for in book after book on urban affairs, we still find little or no reference to ethnics or ethnic problems. Yet in our urban areas across the United States, it is largely these ethnics who are struggling to prevent the further decay of our cities. If these ethnics, these Italians, Poles, Greeks, Slavs and others, were to follow the exodus of the white, Anglo-Saxon, Protestants and affluent Jews who have fled the cities before their inundation by blacks, few whites would be left. The consequences of such a movement would be tragic indeed. Because they have remained behind, it is the ethnics who are forced to find solutions to problems raised in living with blacks, solutions arising from life, from day to day encounters, and not from the sociological gymnastics of the liberal WASPS and Jews who sit in the comfort of their affluent suburbs.

Regrettably, this liberal establishment brands the ethnics as racist, without conceding that there might be some legitimacy to their reactions. Yet, unless we attempt to understand the

C. The Newcomers: Intruders or Invited Guests?

ethnic and his problems with the same compassion given to the black, we will simply alienate him and put off any meaningful solution to black-white relations for another generation or more. And unless we consider ethnic needs as well as black needs in our cities, the future of our cities is in jeopardy.

One reason we are so little aware of ethnicity is the difficulty in defining it. To a degree, one can say that all Americans are ethnics. However the greater part of those coming from England, Ireland, and Germany, particularly those who have come to the United States before the great economic immigrations of the 1880s, have long since been assimilated and find no need to identify with their kind. Thus, by and large we mean the immigrants, the children and grandchildren of those whom Michael Novak termed PIGS (Poles, Italians, Greeks, and Slavs). In his penetrating study entitled *The Rise of the Unmeltable Ethnics* (subtitled *The New Political Force of the Seventies*), we find perhaps the best book ever written on the subject.

However, not all members of these groups can really be called ethnics. Rather we use the term to describe those individuals who find a need to identify with their ethnic heritage. Usually these are first, second, or third generation Americans. By and large they are Catholic, though large numbers of southern and eastern Slavs are Orthodox, particularly the Russians, Ukrainians, Serbs, and Bulgars. In most cases their educational experience is below the national norm. They usually are physical laborers or blue collar workers, and live in our major urban centers. In all they number some forty to fifty million of our fellow Americans.

The difficulty in defining them has caused serious problems for students of ethnicity. Peter Binzen, for example, who has written *Whitetown U.S.A.* (subtitled *A First Hand Study of How the "Silent Majority" Lives, Learns, Works, and Thinks*) actually lived and taught in the ethnic neighborhoods of

230

Philadelphia. This was made possible by a grant from the Carnegie Foundation which enabled him to take a leave of absence from the Philadelphia *Bulletin*. Despite the excellent reviews his work received, he fails to see the difference between White owners, Working Americans, Forgotten Americans, Ethnic Americans, and the Silent Majority, terms which are used interchangeably throughout his work. There are many points of similarity, but there are also points of difference. The result is the hodge podge that is *Whitetown U.S.A.*

Another reason why we are so little aware of ethnicity is the lack of first hand studies on ethnic Americans. The case of the Italian Americans is typical. To this day we are still lacking an adequate history of their experience, even though they number some 20 million persons. And it will be years before their history, as well as that of their fellow ethnics, will be written.

The belated but growing awareness of ethnic Americans has led a number of major foundations to invest some funds in exploring these fields. This in turn has led a number of educational opportunists to transform themselves into ethnic specialists producing so called authoritative studies on ethnicity. It seems that as long as the project submitted agreed with the dominant philosophy of its foundation sponsor, major deficiencies were overlooked. As a result we have studies of ethnic communities that make a mockery of scholarship.

Peter Binzen, for example, picked up some scattered facts on ethnics and then began generalizing on them. The Irish, he discovered, formed fifty-seven percent of the convicts in the Boston House of Correction in 1862. He then jumps to the conclusion that criminal behavior was rampant among all immigrant groups. If this was part of the immigrant experience, then why do the ethnics refuse to understand the problems of the blacks? Obviously because they are racists. The Irish may have formed a large part of the prison population in the past, and indeed this may have also been characteristic of some

231

other ethnic groups in our cities, but it is not characteristic of all ethnic groups. Given the experience of the Chinese, the Poles, and the Swedes, such a generalization is utter nonsense.

Binzen goes on to link the Irish with riot, pointing out that the Irish have caused riots in nearly every major American city between 1830 and 1870, inferring that this too was typical behavior for all immigrant groups. On the basis of wild generalizations such as these the social planners are attempting to solve the major problems of the cities.

Another example of faulty generalization is found in the work of Andrew Greeley, whose studies on ethnicity, thanks to a quarter million dollar grant from the Ford Foundation, are considered by the misinformed as the last word in this field. Greeley has in fact gone beyond what Binzen has attempted. He actually did the impossible and devised a standardized test to determine which ethnic groups are most racist, antisemitic, alcoholic, and so on.

Ethnic groups are different in thought patterns, value judgments, goals, historical conditioning, life styles, and so on. To an Ukrainian American, the staff of life is most likely wheat. To a Mexican American, it is corn, and to a Chinese American, it is rice.

To a black American a ghetto may be a place of horror. To a Polish American it may be a place of security, a haven from the dehumanizing and debasing aspects of American life. The attitude of Italian Americans toward the Catholic Church is noticeably different from that of Irish Americans. The WASPS who were not personally affected by the inhumanity of the German concentration camps might not fully appreciate the reaction of Jewish Americans to the condition of their coreligionists in the Soviet Union.

Each ethnic group is different, and within each ethnic group there are differences among subgroups. This is basic to ethnicity. How then can one devise a standardized set of

232

questions on which to compare the attitudes of these groups? Since we know so little about the ethnic groups under consideration, this quest is impossible. This basic premise makes nonsense of Andrew Greeley's work.

A question asked of those interviewed to determine if they were racists or not, was: "Should the Negroes have separate schools?" If one answered "yes," he was listed as a racist. The conclusion might be valid for some groups, but it is questionable for Polish Americans. For more than 100 years during the Polish Partitions, when the only schools Poles were permitted to attend were Russian or German, the Poles fought long and hard for their own separate schools. In America, where most public and parochial schools taught the children of the newly arrived immigrants to be ashamed of their national origins and heritage, the Polish Americans went out and established over 700 schools of their own. To many of them, therefore, separate schools are good. If they were good for them, then might not they be good for Negroes as well? Segments of the Polish American community might indeed be racist, but they should not be judged so on the basis of such evidence.

Another example of the gross inadequacy of Andrew Greeley's approach can be seen in his basis for determining the anti-Semitism of the ethnics: their reply to the question: "Do the Jews have too much power?" In the 1962 4th Assembly District Democratic primary election in Brooklyn every candidate put up for office by the regular Democratic organization was Jewish. This was done despite the fact that the area was ethnically mixed. Throughout the area, in which a large number of Poles lived, the cry went up: "The Jews have too much power." For this, charges of anti-Semitism were hurled at the protestors, especially the Poles.

A rival slate was organized reflecting the ethnic composition of the neighborhood. There was an Italian, an Irishman, a

233

C. The Newcomers: Intruders or Invited Guests?

Puerto Rican, a Pole, and a Jew. In the election that followed, the Poles voted three or four to one for the Jewish candidate for the Assembly whom they believed to be the abler of the two candidates even though his opponent was of Polish descent. Poles in the area still by and large believe that Jews have too much power because of their virtual monopoly of local political offices. On the basis of this case however, how valid is it to draw conclusions about anti-Semitism?

In fact, given events as they developed in Poland one would be surprised to learn that there was not a great deal of anti-Semitism among some segments of the Polish population. However, Greeley's standardized test ignores historical perspectives and local conditions in order to obtain standardized results.

That the Binzens and Greeleys have made errors is in large part due to the almost complete absence of materials on ethnicity. To a degree, one can excuse their errors as inevitable in pioneering works. However, the condescension with which they treat ethnics is another matter. Regrettably the few accounts they had to work with were largely primitive and *filio-pietistic*. Ethnic studies exist in only a handful of schools in the United States. Even Catholic universities to whose denomination the greater part of ethnic America belongs have overlooked them. In many of the Catholic universities, black studies programs have been instituted, but strangely, ethnic studies have been ignored. Perhaps this is the result of the Church's determined policy to eradicate ethnicity and to turn all these "smelly PIGS" into healthy wholesome Americans.

With so few materials, it is not surprising that ethnic problems are almost completely ignored in the university classroom, even in those where attention is given to current problems. In *The Restless Americans* (subtitled *The Challenge of Change in American History*) by Rozwenc, Martin, and Sandler, the latest of the current problems-oriented textbooks

234

in American history, for example, the problems of blacks and Indians each are treated in special sections of their own. But the forty to fifty million ethnic Americans rate no more attention than the Chicanos or the Japanese. There is not even a single reference in the index to the Italians, some 20 million people, nor to the Irish, the Greeks, or the Slavs. The only reference in the index to Poles points to them as racists— a conclusion reached on the basis of Greeley's findings. How can we possibly hope to understand the problems of our cities, particularly as they affect blacks, when we completely ignore the other side of the coin?

It is largely to correct this lack of information that the Schweikert-Pucinski Ethnic Studies Bill was adopted by the United States Congress. However, one wonders if the results of this bill will be any more effective than many of the foundation grants made for these purposes in the past. Whereas blacks were consulted in the establishment of guidelines for the utilization of the funds allocated for programs related to them, the Department of Health, Education and Welfare has thus far failed to consult the ethnic communities in the establishment of guidelines for the disposition of funds to be made available as a result of the Schweikert-Pucinski Bill. What we can probably expect, therefore, is more Greeleys and Binzens, and a further multiplication of misinformation.

Another factor that is responsible for our lack of sensitivity to ethnics is their low profile. Rarely are they seen protesting or demonstrating in our cities. Aside from the fact that demonstrations are alien to most of them, few have the freedom to demonstrate, a luxury that is restricted to the affluent, students, and unemployed. While the armchair liberal, the student, and many blacks can appear at meetings and rallies, few ethnics can. Until such time as the labor unions to which ethnic Americans belong demand for their members a certain number of days off with pay for political or social activism

235

so that the voice of this "silent majority" can be heard, this condition will not change. Ethnics ought to place this demand in the forefront of the new contracts their leaders are negotiating. Regrettably, just as some ethnics have almost no say in their Church or their government, so too they have no say in their unions. When Joseph Yablonski fought, among other things, to secure recognition for the ethnic elements in the United Mineworkers of America, he and his family were murdered.

Another factor that also is responsible for this lack of sensitivity to ethnicity are the various stereotypes the media have been responsible for, stereotypes as horrendous as any racist America has directed against the blacks or anti-Semites have directed against the Jews. Regrettably, it is in large part black and Jewish comedians who are responsible for the current rash of Polish jokes. Stereotypes of the Poles as anti-Semites, reflected even in the writings of so popular an author as Leon Uris, have caused many Jews to turn against anything Polish.

Some years ago when a Pole ran for Mayor of Chicago on the Republican ticket, large segments of the Jewish community refused to vote for him on the basis that all Poles were anti-Semitic and therefore not to be trusted. The news was brought to him by his son-in-law and campaign worker, who happened to be Jewish himself. Even Edmund Muskie had to play down his Polish origin. He avoided visiting Poland while on a pre-election trip to Europe, rather than possibly offend or lose any of his supporters.

So deeply ingrained is this stereotype among large segments of the Jewish community that they accept it as fact, and refuse to consider the possibility that they themselves may have contributed to these anti-Semitic reactions where they do exist. Italian Americans fare even worse than do Polish Americans, for it has become almost axiomatic in America that all Italians are members of the Mafia. So damaging is this stereotype that

236

one of the world's largest Catholic universities was unwilling to establish an Italian Institute for fear that some of the money might come from Mafia sources. Even today many Italian Americans believe that the absence of any Italian Americans on this University's Board of Trustees, is due to this particular stereotype, despite the fact that Italian Americans are the largest segment of the university's faculty and student body, and the largest single constituency of the diocese in which the university is located.

The misinformation about ethnics has had a serious impact especially in urban areas. Typical is the reaction of Dr. Norman Drachler, the superintendent of the Detroit Public Schools, who was interviewed by Peter Binzen. The city is one in which Poles form one of the largest minority groups. So little did Dr. Drachler know this constituency that he stated the following: "In the so-called Polish corridors we lose mileage and we lose it consistently." He meant, says Binzen, that those areas vote against school tax increases. "They're concerned," Dr. Drachler continued, "that every dollar goes to the Negro." Such a view is myopic at the very least.

Polish Americans have for years supported their own parochial school system. Naturally they oppose additional taxation to support another school system. Especially one which humiliated their children, demeaned their culture, and from which they will derive little benefit. Prior to the black inundation of the cities, when Polish Americans also voted against school taxes, the liberal establishment found the root of this attitude in the failure of Polish Americans to appreciate the importance of education. Dr. Drachler's knowledge of the ethnic factor in his city is typical of most city administrators. How can they effectively administer their cities if they are so misinformed about one of their largest constituencies?

Another example of the consequences of this misinformation is the biased attitude of the Kerner Commission. This commission did great service in pointing to many problems concerning blacks, but consistent with the simplistic approach of the liberal establishment, everything is evaluated in terms of black and white. In table after table, conclusions are reached solely on the basis of race. Since the average white income, education, and other indicators of social and material advancement far exceed that of blacks, it would seem that white ethnics have little to complain about. Yet no one seems to ask if all ethnic groups share in this white affluence we all hear about.

True, it would be difficult to secure statistics for all the ethnic groupings, but unless such statistics are obtained, conclusions reached will be faulty and solutions based on them will often be worthless. For example, if whites are better educated than blacks, as the Kerner Commission tells us, then why do more blacks, both numerically and proportionately, go on to higher education than do Polish Americans? If blacks have less access to political power than whites, then why are some 2 million Italian Americans in New York City virtually excluded from any significant office in the administration of their city? Racial statistics are constantly used to advance the interests of blacks at the expense of white ethnic Americans, many of whom never have shared in the white affluence of America except on paper.

The misconception about white ethnic Americans has been institutionalized in the new Museum of Immigration, built at the base of the Statue of Liberty. The initial proposal almost completely excluded the post-1880 immigrants, especially the Italians, Jews, and Poles. A distinguished panel of immigration historians headed by Oscar Handlin was assembled to correct the original inadequacies. And indeed, some shortcomings were corrected: attention was given to blacks and Jews, each of whom received an entire exhibit area. Though some attention is now paid to Italians and Poles, given their numbers, they are almost completely ignored.

Other groups are treated even worse. Though there are about

the same number of Chinese and Ukrainians in America, the picturesqueness of the Chinese merits them an entire display area, while the Ukrainians, who have what apparently are less desirable facial characteristics and eating habits are virtually excluded.

What is even more surprising is the complete absence of any materials relating to the history of Catholics in America, the largest of the immigrant churches. What will be the reaction of Catholics when they see the large display area devoted to Judaism, and no area devoted to their church? Yet, even after this potential source of anti-Semitism was drawn to the attention of the Department of the Interior, the authorities there refused to correct the situation. If the leadership in the United States government is so insensitive to the religious feelings of men, is it any surprise that they, the media, or the Kerner Commission are equally insensitive to the ethnic factor in our cities?

The ethnic Americans in our cities today are angry Americans. By and large they have little or no effective political power. The Democratic party, to which the greater part had traditionally given its allegiance, at its 1972 convention, virtually excluded them, depriving them of whatever voice they had had. They see the liberal establishment championing the cause of the blacks, at what seems their expense. They see neighborhood after neighborhood in which they have invested millions in churches, schools, cultural and social centers destroyed as increasing numbers of blacks and other minorities move in.

They are angry at a media that twists truth and treats them as a group of semiliterate primitives. They are angry at the courts which are destroying their neighborhood schools and along with them that sense of community spirit the neighborhood school serves to maintain. They are also angry with the courts for destroying the little security they can offer their children.

Unlike the affluent liberal who can provide first-rate education and trust funds, the only tangible asset many ethnic Americans can give their children is an assured place in the union.

239

With the introduction of quotas based on race alone, this too is being taken away from him. He is angry at his church, if he is a Catholic, for demeaning his heritage and preventing him from having any voice in church affairs.

Though Poles and Italians form over sixty percent of the Catholic population in the United States, they are virtually excluded from its hierarchy. What is particularly galling to them is that in many of the parochial schools they built in which Italian or Polish studies were prohibited, black studies are now being introduced. They are angry at their universities which establish black studies programs, but which refuse to do anything meaningful for ethnic studies. They are angry with a political system that demands of them the highest qualifications and performance but overlooks these criteria for others solely on the basis of race. They cannot understand this double standard. If blacks are entitled to ten percent representation in the Democratic Convention because they form ten percent of the population, should not Italian Americans deserve equal representation because they are as large?

Ethnic Americans are angry with a society that will react to situations only when people demonstrate or burn. Finding it difficult to demonstrate and being too practical to burn their own cities, ethnic Americans may fall prey to extremist political ideologies. Unless their problems are given the attention they deserve, it may not merely be our cities that will be in transition but our entire political system as well.

23. the New York barrio: cultures in conflict

Robert A. Martinez

The Puerto Rican living in New York City today is caught in a web of poverty and racism. His poor occupational status results in subsistence level income, and his low income condemns his children to limited educational opportunities. This in turn condemns his offspring to grinding poverty. Thus a vicious circle of economic deprivation is established.

When one adds racism to the problem of poverty, it becomes even more difficult to break through the web. Dr. Eduardo Seda Bonilla, Director of Puerto Rican studies at Hunter College, has observed that:

> the conditions that followed from being placed in a non-white racial category is the single most important factor determining the adaptation of Puerto Rican migrants in New York. If this categorization had not taken place, Puerto Rican adaptation would have followed the patterns set by other immigration groups within the melting pot.

In other words, the European immigrant groups which arrived in New York during an earlier era were able to adopt the

C. The Newcomers: Intruders or Invited Guests?

American culture as their own. They then gained acceptance into the mainstream of American life. Such is not the case with Puerto Ricans in New York. Because of their diverse racial backgrounds (which can be any combination of European, Taino Indian, and black African), the Puerto Rican finds that he is not as easily accepted by the dominant culture of New York. An imposed racial stigma, therefore, reinforces existing cultural differences. Since Puerto Ricans are denied admission to the American mainstream on racial grounds, they seek accommodation in a Puerto Rican identity even if it has been diluted by living on the mainland for several generations.

In a time when we have been made aware of the American Negro's plight, we have remained almost totally unaware of the fact that in job status, family income, housing, and educational achievement, the Puerto Rican is below the level attained by blacks. The Department of Labor's statistics show that for men between the ages of twenty-four and fifty-four the rate of unemployed Puerto Ricans is 7.9 percent while for blacks the figure is 4.9 percent and for whites 2.7 percent. The figure for Puerto Rican women in New York in the same age group is 3.8 percent unemployed as compared with 4.7 percent for blacks and 2.8 percent for whites. A possible explanation for the lower figure for Puerto Rican women, according to the Labor Department, can be found in the fact that they tend more readily than women generally to withdraw from the labor force upon losing their jobs.

A comparison of figures for those between the ages of sixteen and twenty-five seems to substantiate this. For Puerto Rican women between sixteen and twenty-five the unemployed rate is 10.9 percent while for blacks and whites the figures are 6.4 percent and 3.7 percent respectively. For men in the same age bracket, the rate of unemployment for Puerto Ricans is 9.2 percent as compared with 6.4 percent for blacks and 3.5 percent for whites.

Puerto Rican efforts to break out of this poverty circle are complicated by their low levels of educational achievement. For example, among Puerto Rican men between the ages of eighteen and thirty-four in the New York labor force, only twenty-five percent have four years of high school or more as compared with seventy-one percent for mainlanders, which includes blacks and whites. The figure for women of the same age group is somewhat more encouraging at fifty-two percent for Puerto Ricans as compared with seventy-nine percent for mainlanders. For those Puerto Ricans thirty-five years and over, the educational gap is far greater in the local labor market. For Puerto Rican men of this age, only ten percent have four years of high school or more as compared with fifty-five percent for mainlanders. The figure for Puerto Rican women in this age bracket is fifteen percent as compared with sixty percent for mainland women. Worse yet, fifty-three percent of all New York Puerto Ricans over thirty-four years of age have not completed elementary school.

Oddly enough few mainlanders are aware of this dilemma. What they are aware of, or think they are aware of, are the problems that the Puerto Ricans create for the city at large; that is welfare, crime, and drugs. Yet, as Father Joseph Fitzpatrick, Fordham University's eminent sociologist, points out, "It is not so much the problems that Puerto Ricans create for New York as it is the problems that New York creates for them."

This poverty and racist cycle is especially sad when one considers that Puerto Ricans came to New York for a better life! First they came in small numbers in the 1920s and 1930s. Then during the post-war years a much larger influx occurred. Industry on the mainland, particularly in New York, offered the Puerto Rican greater opportunities for economic improvement. The recession period of the 1950s hit the island even harder than the country at large so that greater numbers than ever before flocked to New York in search of economic relief. By the 1960s, with cheaper air rates and a positive upswing in the American economy, the numbers began to hit record highs.

243

C. The Newcomers: Intruders or Invited Guests?

Many became alarmed at this "invasion" and expressed a desire to stop these Puerto Ricans who, in their eyes, were only coming for welfare. What many New Yorkers forgot was that the Puerto Rican was not an immigrant. Unlike the European immigrants of earlier years, the Puerto Rican was a migrant. That is, he was one moving freely within his own country.

To some the Puerto Ricans seemed different, indeed strange. Their cultural differences—customs, language, philosophy, and racial attitudes—made them the new underdogs and objects of ridicule. There was no place for them except in urban slums, those bleak landscapes of run-down tenements, garbage strewn lots, and mean streets. Yet Puerto Ricans continue to come in droves because the dream of the 1920s and 1930s persisted. That dream was to come to New York, make money, learn a trade, and go home to Puerto Rico. The dream still lives because Puerto Rico is an island with a population density eleven times that of the United States, an unemployment rate of fourteen percent and a per capita income of only about $1,000 a year. The latest count shows that there are 1,586,397 Puerto Ricans in the United States (up from 855,724 in the 1960 census) with nearly a million of them in New York City. This means that Puerto Ricans constitute eleven percent of the city's population.

They came to New York for a better life. Yet the reality of New York kills physically and spiritually. Even the weather of New York kills. Puerto Ricans did not understand New York's fierce winters. They had seen snow only in American movies. The cold overwhelmed those who came dressed for the tropics. The cold weather also seemed to erode the spirit. The male was emasculated because he lacked employable skills for New York's labor market and his wife was forced to assume the dominant role of bread winner. To make matters worse his culture came into conflict with the dominant one on the mainland. To see this more clearly, let us consider the Puerto Rican's social concept of the male role.

Robert A. Martinez

To the liberated, emancipated, urban mainlander, *machismo*, which might be very loosely translated as male chauvinism, is easily dismissed as an archaic Latin "hang up." Yet to the Puerto Rican male the question of dominant masculinity is no laughing matter. For him, male dominance is an important social characteristic. Women who work and earn more money than men offend the Puerto Rican male ego. To resort to welfare is a humiliating experience and the male begins to lose respect as a husband and father. Social and psychological pressures mount once his wife and children begin to lose respect for him. The hold he had over his family in Puerto Rico is gone in New York. Now the wife becomes more independent and emancipated in the wake of her new role, more than the social norms of Puerto Rico would ever have allowed. The children see their father constantly at home, brooding, edgy, and perhaps even unkempt. It is not long before the family falls apart.

René Marqués, observing this development, wrote a socially significant play, "La Víspera del Hombre" (The Eve of Man) in which he portrays a man who leaves Puerto Rico as the head of his family with the intent of a better life for all. However, the urban American way of life found in New York manages to destroy his world and he returns to the island completely broken and abandoned by his family. Traditions such as *machismo* and institutions such as the family are an inherent part of the Puerto Rican way of life. However, these vital elements are weakened in the process of Americanization and usually destroyed in the urban environment of New York which is hostile to almost all traditions and institutions.

To achieve a more sympathetic understanding of this cultural conflict, a quick look at the history of the island and its peculiar development is needed. The island was a colony of Spain from 1493, when Columbus set foot there, until 1898, when as a result of the Spanish-American War, it became a possession of the United States. The four centuries of Spanish rule is clearly evi-

C. The Newcomers: Intruders or Invited Guests?

dent in all the cultural expressions of Puerto Rico; its music, language, literature, and religion. A peculiar aspect of Puerto Rico's development that now accounts for the ethnological and spiritual structure of the population is seen in the early mixtures of Spanish and African inputs with those of the native Indians of the island, the Tainos.

The Spanish culture remained dominant even after the United States occupation. English was taught in the schools of Puerto Rico when the United States became the ruling political force of the island, but it has never been adopted as the language of the island. In order to understand the culture of Puerto Rico it is imperative to know the Spanish language, since all of the available sources are written or expressed orally in that language. The music, folklore, plastic arts, and social institutions of Puerto Rico are all characterized by a strong Spanish flavor.

The Puerto Rican family, the prime example of a social institution seen in the Spanish cultural frame of reference, is of a patriarchal and extended nature. Grandparents, aunts, uncles, and cousins to the third degree along with godparents are all considered important forces within the family structure. The father is the one who sets the norms for the whole family and is respected by all of its members. The wife, daughters, and sons have particular roles to play and norms to abide by, not the least of which is the *machismo* concept for males and the question of honor (*La honra*) or the cult of virginity for girls.

Many problems arise from the Puerto Rican family structure. The generation gap that occurs in Puerto Rican families in New York is in part really a cultural gap. The young people disregard some of the things their parents believed in and held dear. Spiritualism is now an object of ridicule, as well as religion itself. In Puerto Rico, where eighty-five percent of the population is Roman Catholic, religion plays an incredibly important role in everyday life. It is not an institutionalized form of Catholicism but one practiced on a personal basis where its center is the

246

Robert A. Martinez

home. In New York, as in most American urban centers, religion cannot seem to maintain its strength. The young begin to break away from older religious practices and this in turn further erodes the family structure.

Parental control in New York is not the same as it was on the island. Young girls no longer pay strict attention to their mother's home instruction in domestic skills or allow themselves to be chaperoned by elders in public. Here less respect is shown to the elderly. Grandma, who was always asked for her blessing by the young before they left the house in Puerto Rico, is now ignored or disregarded as old and unknowing in New York. To continue this lovely old custom of the blessing is seen as old fashioned. The young go their own way in the city. They assume the language and dress of other New York youngsters. They even imitate the social behavior patterns of their New York counterparts with respect to dating, attitudes toward school and the police, and gang structures.

Yet the Puerto Rican youngster is not just another "kid" raised from the streets of New York, for as we noted, he has a racial stigma to contend with. So while the urban atmosphere of New York destroyed their past it did not incorporate them into the American mainstream. The young suffer a unique cultural conflict which is better stated as an identity crisis. Because they have adopted the language and varied customs of the mainland youth, they refuse to speak Spanish at home and alienation increases. When they are old enough to know, that despite all their "assimilation," they are still singled out as "P.R's" and that they are really alienated from the urban society at large as well, the crisis is compounded. Perhaps this double alienation of Americanization and urbanization provides one explanation for the present renaissance of street gangs among Puerto Rican youngsters in New York.

A multitude of other problems confront the Puerto Rican in New York. On the educational front, the situation is still critical.

To understand why nine out of ten Puerto Ricans over the age of twenty-five never finished high school, we must keep in mind the socioeconomic conditions of the Puerto Rican community and its many interrelated problems. Only by viewing the educational problems of Puerto Ricans in this context can one fully comprehend their poor performances in the mainland schools. An examination of reading and math scores shows that Puerto Rican children are from two and one-half to four years behind white students; and pretty much the same lag is seen when compared with scores for blacks. Ignoring the problem, or misinterpreting the scores to mean hopelessness, does not help. Obviously the problem of communication and the failure of the young to develop writing and comprehensive reading skills is complicated by the city school system's failure to realistically deal with bilingual education. Since language is the main avenue of communication, all subject instruction suffers, thus lowering the overall academic achievement of students.

This may account for the fact that among those Puerto Ricans finishing high school in New York, ninety percent have been getting a general diploma, eight percent completing vocational courses of study, and less than two percent of those receiving academic diplomas going on to college. The school system has not only failed New York's young Puerto Ricans in the classroom but also in the guidance office. There exists an inadequacy of counseling services in the city schools with heavy concentrations of Puerto Rican children. The ignorance of many Puerto Rican parents regarding the availability of free vocational and guidance facilities, along with an ignorance of overall city school procedures (still bureaucratic beyond belief) compounds the situation. Thus the needs of almost a quarter of a million children go unheeded, as evidenced by the current threat to end whatever bilingual education does exist.

Although we are told that the need for bilingual education is not pressing, Spanish, it seems to me, is here to stay. This city, like Montreal, is a bilingual city. The input of Puerto Rican culture had made it so. The importance of the Puerto Rican presence can be seen in the quantity and quality of mass media available in Spanish—two television networks, three radio stations, an equal number of newspapers, and a rather impressive list of magazines and periodicals.

For hundreds of thousands of Puerto Ricans living in *El Barrio*, the situation is still desperate. Puerto Ricans are at the bottom of the city's social and economic ladder. In a recent study comparing annual wage increases, Puerto Ricans had gained only $49 in their annual income, earning an average income of $3,949 as compared to $7,635 for whites with a net gain of $927 for the year.

These statistics are all the more deplorable in light of the fact that Puerto Ricans have larger families than mainland Americans. Reliance on social welfare increases because one cannot support a large family in New York City on an income of less than $4,000 a year. Therefore, the number of Puerto Ricans receiving relief rose from 29.5 percent of the welfare rolls in 1959 to 33 percent in 1967 and is presently about 35 percent. Some estimates state that for 40 percent of the city's Puerto Ricans receiving some form of public assistance, most of it is supplementing the low wages paid to Puerto Rican heads of households. Low wages are still paid in sweatshops and factories with unrepresentative unions. For example, the leadership of the International Ladies Garment Workers Union does not reflect the overwhelming numbers of Puerto Rican workers in the industry.

The problem of narcotics, along with the re-emergence of street gangs and gang warfare are other serious problems in *El Barrio*. Narcotics addiction on the island of Puerto Rico may be seen as a reversed cultural impact. That is, the social blight of narcotics was unknown in Puerto Rico until those contaminated by it in New York returned to the island introducing the social disease there.

249

C. The Newcomers: Intruders or Invited Guests?

These discouraging factors all point to the sordid side of Puerto Rican life in New York. What then are the prospects for a brighter future? One is that the Puerto Rican has endured prior difficulties and he will endure in New York. The reason he will endure is because the Puerto Rican has no time for self-pity. There are many in business for themselves; from grocery stores to trucking concerns and an ever-increasing number are going into the professions—teaching, law, and medicine. An economic fact of life in *El Barrio* has been the Puerto Rican's determination to have a part, no matter how small, in his community's business.

For the young, despite the shortcomings of the city school system, there are increasing numbers going on to higher learning. A 1970 study by the City University of New York shows that 7,785 Puerto Rican students are part of that institution (probably owing to the advantages of open enrollment), 1,085 in private colleges in New York City, 300 in state colleges and 950 in out-of-state colleges. This is encouraging since the leadership of tomorrow comes out of today's colleges.

Dr. Ramirez de Arellano, one of Puerto Rico's leading intellectuals and the island's poet laureate, has said, "Despite all, there is a place for scholarship. We need intellectuals who will be constructive spokesmen for the needs of Puerto Ricans in New York City." That is not to say that we do not have such leadership now. We just need more as the problems have become more complex. Puerto Ricans can proudly point to a fine tradition of intellectual leadership. Names like Salvador Brau, Eugenio Maria de Hostos, and Albizu Campos are part of that outstanding leadership of the recent past. Today one can produce an equally impressive list of Puerto Rican leaders in all fields.

The situation is still difficult for Puerto Ricans and will continue to be as long as the socioeconomic problems persist, the ignorant racial attitudes hinder their progress, and the system remains unresponsive to their needs. However, the goal of upward social mobility is the one reality that the Puerto Rican

250

understands. Why else did he come to the mainland's urban centers! Puerto Ricans are increasingly aware of their political power. They showed this in the near victory they provided for Herman Badillo in the Democratic mayoral primary of 1973. The voice of nearly a million cannot be ignored, especially when one considers that today's young generation is politically oriented. So the hope is in the young and with luck they will succeed. But how much easier it would be for them if all came to understand more fully the problems of *El Barrio* and helped to remove the causes of low educational achievement, crime, drugs, and unemployment. The solutions are not easy but they would be more easily attained if those of the so-called establishment stopped and realized that they were dealing with human beings who have much to offer this city, given the chance.

While the processes of Americanization and urbanization have had a tremendous impact on Puerto Rican migrants, the forces of change are not all one sided. New York will never be the same again. Besides making it a bilingual center and influencing its political leadership, Puerto Ricans have also altered its cultural atmosphere. Already *El Barrio* has made its mark on this city; its music and flamboyance, its sense of the exotic as one shops in the neighborhood *bodegas* for *plátanos* and *lechón* or into the local *botánica* for herbs and spiritual advice. *Carnecerias, barbariás, restarantes, joyerías* and so forth are all part of the charm. Who can deny the enrichment that all this has brought to the city?

Puerto Ricans also have sought institutional changes within the city. Through the efforts of concerned young Puerto Rican New Yorkers, the city and its institutions have begun establishing much needed programs. Consequently, any concluding optimism is not unfounded because the young now study the problems, seek answers, and in some cases provide the necessary solutions.

24. Harlem: an urban ghetto and symbol of black self-fulfillment

John Henrik Clarke

Harlem is more than a community; it is really a city within a city. Its influence extends beyond city, state, or sectional boundaries because Harlem is the nerve center of black America. In many ways it is unique. Harlem is one of the few large black communities that is not on the "other side" of town. Rather it is located in the heart of the richest piece of real estate in America —Manhattan Island. Harlem is also a frame of mind with international implications. It is the headquarters of cults, self-proclaimed kings, and pretenders. It is the intellectual and spiritual home of the African people in the Western World. Some of the most important men and movements in America's black urban ghettos have developed in Harlem. It is probably the most written about and least understood community in the world.

Negro intellectuals have tried to grasp its meaning in many different ways. Roi Ottley felt that Harlem is:

The fountainhead of mass movements. From it flows the progressive vitality of Negro life. Harlem is, as well, a cross section of life in black America—a little from here, there and everywhere. It is at once the capital of clowns, cults and cabarets, and the cultural and intel-

lectual hub of the Negro world. By turns Harlem is provincial, worldly, cosmopolitan and naive—sometimes
cynical. From here, though, the Negro looks upon the
world with audacious eyes. . . . To grasp the inner mean-
ings of life in black America, one must put his finger on
the pulse of Harlem.

Claude McKay called it a "Negro Metropolis" and added:
"Harlem is the most interesting sample of black humanity marching along with white humanity." James Weldon Johnson found it
different from any other black settlement in the northern United
States. He believed it to be an extremely healthy and attractive
community and worried whether Negroes would be able to
"always hold it as a residential section." Johnson's optimism
allowed him to view Harlem as "the great mecca for the sight-
seer, the pleasure-seeker, the curious, the adventurous, the
enterprising, the ambitious and the talented of the whole Negro
world: for the lure of it has reached down to every island of the
Carib Sea and has penetrated into Africa."
Harlem has been called, and may well be, the cultural and
intellectual capital of the black race in the western world. It has
also been described in less complimentary terms such as: "a
cancer in the heart of a city" and "a large-scale laboratory experiment in the race problem." Some of the most colorful and dynamic personalities in the black world have used Harlem as a
vantage point, a platform, and proving ground for their ideas and
ambitions. The "Back-to-Africa" movement and the more vocal
aspects of black nationalism found a greater acceptance in Harlem than in any other place.
The development of Harlem as the mecca of black America
is a development of recent history. The mass exodus and settlement of blacks in Harlem did not begin until 1900. At the turn of
the century, large numbers of blacks began to leave the farms and
the cities of the South to search for employment opportunities

253

and a better way of life in the cities of the North and along the eastern seaboard of the United States. In the process Harlem was transformed from a white neighborhood into a black metropolis and, subsequently, into the culture capital of the black world. The conclusion of the First World War did not end the large migration from the South. This exodus removed thousands of black Americans from the insulated, self-contained atmosphere of the agricultural South and placed them in a throbbing northern urban society with problems more acute than they had ever encountered.

The migration, urban life, and the events of the twentieth century, such as the First World War, helped to reorient black thought in America. Blacks began to demand recognition for their artistic and cultural heritage while also seeking to gain control over their economic and political destiny. Harlem became the focal point for this black renaissance. As thousands of Negroes continued to move into Harlem, the community became a new force in the politics of New York.

Black Americans' almost religious devotion to the Republican party at first hampered their effectiveness in the politics of New York. The Republican party was sure of the black vote and did not feel compelled to cater to it. At the same time the leaders of the Democratic party did not make any serious attempt to win the support of the black voters in Harlem. The activity of Harlem's first major politicians changed this situation and started both parties catering to black voters.

In 1898, Edward E. Lee, known as the "Chief," helped to establish the United Colored Democracy as a black subdivision of the Democratic party. The Harlem community, still mainly Republican, denounced Lee and his followers. Democrats found it advantageous to reward Lee and his small group by giving them a measure of political patronage. James D. Carr, a Harlem lawyer who had graduated from Columbia University in 1885, was appointed assistant district attorney while Lee himself, was made sheriff. More and better appointments followed.

254

The Republicans had to take note of this development, and early in the twentieth century the first significant black politician in the city rose in their party's ranks. His name was Charles W. Anderson. Anderson, a self-educated and self-made man, was born in Oxford, Ohio, a year after the Civil War ended and came to New York City at the age of twenty. He immediately became active in local Republican politics. In 1890, he was elected president of the Young Men's Colored Republican Club of New York County. As a reward, he was appointed to the position of gauger in a district office of the Internal Revenue Service. From this not too important position, Anderson became "the recognized colored Republican leader of New York." He quickly rose to more important positions until he was appointed to what was undoubtedly the most responsible federal office held by any black politician in the early twentieth century: Collector of Internal Revenue for the Second New York District—the Wall Street District.

Anderson was an astute and effective community politican who had the welfare of the entire Harlem community at heart. He refused to involve himself in the bitter philosophical conflict between Booker T. Washington and W.E.B. DuBois over the future of black Americans and in fact was a friend to both men. Anderson left philosophy to others and concentrated on improving the race by using his influence to find more and better-paying jobs for black citizens. More than any other politician before him, Anderson made certain that the people of Harlem received their share of what politicians call "the little plums"—the political appointee jobs. He was responsible for a major breakthrough in municipal employment when Samuel J. Battle was appointed as the first black policeman in New York City history.

With Anderson working within the Republican party and the Harvard-educated Ferdinand Q. Morton now leading the United Colored Democracy, blacks became part of the political process of the city. In addition to this, Marcus Garvey had begun to win support for black solidarity through his "Back-to-Africa" move-

255

ment. These competing forces were not content with minor patronage for they realized that blacks, like other groups, had a right to gain political control over their community. Therefore they united in a campaign to create a black district leadership for Harlem. After this was achieved, black politicians raised their sights and aimed at creating a congressional district for Harlem.

Fortunately for blacks, Harlem had an abundance of talented men to lead the fight for political recognition. In addition to Anderson and Morton, other early participants in this campaign were: Fred R. Moore, editor and publisher of *The New York Age*; Thomas Fortune, former editor of *The Age*, then editor of the Garvey publications; Edward A. Johnson, Harlem's first assemblyman; and the militant socialist, nationalist, and Garveyite, Hubert H. Harrison. The fight to create a new congressional district in Harlem coincided with the rising popularity of the most dynamic black personality of the century—Marcus Garvey.

The appearance of the Garvey movement was perfectly timed. Blacks had eagerly participated in the World War I drive to make the world "safe for democracy." They believed that their contribution combined with the lofty ideals of the war would finally earn them an equal place in America. However, the broken promises of the post-war period produced a widespread cynicism among the black population, some of whom began to lose faith in the future. Starting in the streets of Harlem, Garvey spread the word of hope by preaching a kind of black nationalism which had never before been heard in this country. Though his ideas were highly controversial, even among blacks, there is no doubt of his importance. In his book, *Marching Blacks*, Adam Clayton Powell, Jr. wrote: "Marcus Garvey was one of the greatest mass leaders of all time. He was misunderstood and maligned, but he brought to the Negro people for the first time a sense of pride in being black."

Not only was Harlem the scene of black growth in politics and philosophical outlooks, it was literally the home of black self-fulfillment in all areas of American life. Naturally it was in Harlem that the black cultural explosion referred to as "The Negro Renaissance," or "The Harlem Literary Renaissance," began. It was born around 1920 and developed during the artificial prosperity and gayety that followed the First World War. In 1921 an all-black variety show called "Shuffle Along" opened at the 63rd Street Theater in New York City. This show, that played to packed houses night after night, brought to public attention a large number of black performing artists for the first time. It opened doors for other black performers in other areas of the theater, including drama. Throughout the Twenties, as Langston Hughes has said, "The Negro was in vogue." White interest in black people, especially in black artists, writers, and performers, became a national pastime. The Harlem community remained the focal point for this development for more than a decade. It became the new entertainment arena, literally a magnet drawing masses of white people to its night clubs. People came uptown to experience a kind of pseudosocial equality with blacks even though white night club owners still did not welcome "Negro patronage."

Recognition of the creativity within the foremost "Negro community" in America was guaranteed when in 1925, Alain Locke expanded the special Harlem issue of the magazine, *Survey Graphic*, which he edited, into the anthology, *The New Negro*. This book, recently reissued in paperback, is a milestone and a guide to Afro-American thought, literature, and art in the middle Twenties. The announced objective of the volume was "to register the transformation of the inner and outer life of the Negro in America that had so significantly taken place in the last few preceding years," but the book went far beyond this achievement. The poet and teacher Robert Hayden, in his introduction of the 1968 edition of this work published by Atheneum stated it "was the definitive presentation of the artistic and social goals of the New Negro movement." "Perhaps," he said, "it is no exaggeration to say that this book helped to create the movement. Cer-

257

tainly it had the effect of a manifesto when it appeared, and it remains an invaluable document of the cultural aspects of the Negro struggle as they were revealed by the work of artists and writers in Harlem during the 1920s." Professor Hayden further observed that "the New Negro movement had no formal organization, and it was more aesthetic and philosophical—more metaphysical, let us say—than political."

Locke, himself, believed that, "The New Negro must be seen in the perspective of a New World, and especially a New America." He extended the point by saying, "Europe seething in a dozen centers with emergent nationalities, Palestine full of a renascent Judaism—these are no more alive with the progressive forces of our era than the quickened centers of the lives of black folk. America seeking a new spiritual expansion and artistic maturity, trying to found an American literature, a national art, and national music implies a Negro-American culture seeking the same satisfactions and objectives."

Locke observed that his generation of black writers and artists had opened new doors and asked new questions that could not be ignored. He saw the Harlem Literary Renaissance as a significant sign of racial awakening on a national and perhaps even a world scale. Within the pages of the book, *The New Negro*, he brought together the essence of the creative writing talent of the 1920s. Many of these writers were being introduced to a large general audience for the first time. His choices had long range significance.

Most of the writers whose work is included in the book went on to fulfill the promise that was evident in their early offerings. Albert C. Barnes called attention to the role of "Negro Art in America" and reminded us that the black artist "has in superlative measure that fire and light which, coming from within, bathes his whole world, colors his images and impels him to expression." "The Negro," he says, "is a poet by birth." William Stanley Braithwaite, in his essay on "The Negro in American Literature," made the same point another way. In the section on fiction, Rudolph Fisher, Jean Toomar, and Zora Neale Hurston are represented, among others.

This literary movement and its participants were soon "discovered" by the previously mentioned assortment of white celebrities, pseudoliterary figures with good publishing connections, and some moderately wealthy liberal whites who had wandered from their social moorings. They sponsored some black writers and opened doors for others. Most of these well-wishers were somewhat paternalistic and possessive about the particular writers they favored, and some of them became overnight "authorities" on the new literature and its creators.

The Harlem Renaissance has a meaning generally missed by most people who write about it. This movement had indigenous roots, and it could have existed without the concern and interest of white people. This concern, often overstated, gave the movement a broader and more colorful base, and it may have extended its life span. The movement was the natural and logical result of years of neglect, suppression, and degradation. Black Americans were projecting themselves as human beings and demanding that their profound humaneness be accepted. It was the first time a large number of black writers, artists, and intellectuals took a unified walk into the North American sun.

Physically and spiritually, blacks had made Harlem uniquely their own. Store-front churches, and restaurants specializing in "soul food" marked the area. The Harlem community became the land of opportunity for new cults as well as for leaders of older established religious organizations, such as the Abyssinian Baptist Church. George Wilson Becton, first of the famous cult leaders to excite the imagination and stir the enthusiasm of the entire Harlem community, died and left the field open to Father Divine, who expanded the domain of his Kingdom of Peace and found a way to feed Harlem's hungry people at a price they could pay.

259

C. The Newcomers: Intruders or Invited Guests?

While local political gains were made by black leaders, Harlem was really a kind of underdeveloped area dominated mainly by messenger boys for the larger and richer political machine bosses in downtown New York City. There were two outstanding exceptions: Benjamin J. Davis, Jr. and Reverend Adam Clayton Powell, Jr. Fiercely independent, both men were destined to enlarge their role beyond the community and became spokesmen for the black population of the city. In 1943, under proportional representation, a progressive and democratic form of election, Davis was elected to the New York City Council to fill the seat vacated by Adam Clayton Powell, Jr., who had been elected to Congress. In the City Council Davis, a man of outspoken views and affiliations, was a thorn in the side of machine politicians who were determined to silence him in order to get him out of the City Council and out of Harlem.

Finally, these forces succeeded in bringing down their prey. First, proportional representation was abolished. Before his last term had expired, Davis was barred from the City Council because he had been convicted under the Smith Act. Then in 1951, the Supreme Court upheld the Smith Act, and Davis and his comrades were sent to prison. In prison, Ben Davis continued his lifelong fight against Jim Crow and second-class citizenship. The long prison terms diminished his effectiveness but not his popularity in the Harlem community.

Adam Clayton Powell, Jr., was born into controversy and comfort. For more than thirty years, this self-proclaimed "Disciple of Protest," was the most colorful and sometimes the most effective politician in black America. In Washington, reporters and legislators competed to denounce him. In Harlem and in other black communities, he was the deliverer of the word—spokesman of the black oppressed. As the Congressman from the 18th District in Harlem, he was the creator of a political mystique and a dramatic enigma. This mystique and this enigma stand in the way of every attempt at making an objective appraisal of the

260

adventurous career of Reverend Adam Clayton Powell, Jr. Harlem is not a self-contained community, a fact which has both favorable and undesirable aspects. On the positive side, Harlem's politicians, religious leaders, artists, writers, and businessmen have influence beyond the community. Economically, however, it is owned and controlled by outsiders. It is a black community with a white economic heartbeat. Of the major retail outlets, national chains, and local merchants, only a handful are black owned. In the raging battle for integration and equal job opportunities for blacks, little is heard about the blacks' long fight to gain control of their community. A system of pure economic colonialism exists in the Harlem community. This colonialism extends into politics, religion, and every money-making endeavor that touches the life of a Harlem resident.

This exploitation has helped to produce the phenomenon known as black nationalism. This phenomenon brings into focus the conflicts, frustrations, and crises encountered by Harlem's inhabitants, both outside their immediate environment and among themselves. For over half a century of Harlem's existence, various local groups within the community have been planning and fighting to free the people of this—the world's most famous ghetto—from outside control. The creation of HARYOU-ACT (Harlem Youth Opportunities Unlimited) in 1964, made some people of the community believe that this was possible. The announced objective of the HARYOU-ACT programs was to place persistent emphasis and insistence upon social action, rather than dependence upon mere social service. The ultimate goal was to develop in central Harlem a community of excellence through the concern and initiative of the people of the community.

The basic guide for the project was a monumental document, called "Youth in the Ghetto . . . A Study of the Consequences of Powerlessness and a Blueprint for Change." The proposed "Blueprint for Change" was a landmark in creative research and astute planning. In the preface to this document, the Board of

C. The Newcomers: Intruders or Invited Guests?

Directors and the Executive Committee of HARYOU-ACT made the following collective statement:

This study is completed at an historic moment in American life. A century after Emancipation and a decade after the *Brown Decision*, Negro Americans still wait on the fulfillment of great hopes. Meanwhile, the flags of newly sovereign peoples flying before the United Nations buildings symbolize the fact that freedom and equality have come to twice as many peoples as were in the family of nations only two decades ago. The glacial slowness with which freedom and equality come to the minorities within our own nation heightens the contrast, converts hopes into expectations, and expectations into demands. The American Revolution waits to be completed.

It is in this context that the present study of Central Harlem is to be understood and interpreted. Massive deterioration of the fabric of society and its institutions is indicated by the findings of this study. Such massive deterioration calls for corrective action on a scale to match the magnitude of the problem. As America moves forward, the heart and core of the largest Negro community in the world will be able to play its part in this forward movement only as the debilitating and degrading effects of a deteriorating ghetto are effectively countered. To enable Central Harlem to play its part in the realization of the American Dream will be to bring the full realization of that dream a little closer.

Three major components of HARYOU-ACT were developed as the vehicles for dynamic social change: The Community Action Institute, the Neighborhood Boards, and Harlem Youth Unlimited. The main functions of these components are to

262

suggest, select, and refine the type of services which particular families and individuals might require; and at the same time, to provide the training, orientation, and specific skills necessary for sustained and successful community action.

In the area of political action, the intent of HARYOU-ACT was to show the people of Harlem how they can force governmental agencies to respond to their needs. The intent was also to show that this involves knowledge both of the formal political institutions, and of the groups and individuals who, for one reason or another, actually—or might potentially—determine and influence what occurs within the political structure. For Harlem, this was meant to be a way of discovering its political self and how to make the most of it. Unfortunately, the bright dreams of HARYOU-ACT faded before community support could be marshaled behind them. Many times the agency was harassed by lengthy investigations that proved nothing of consequence. By the end of 1968, HARYOU-ACT was only a shell of its former self.

Harlem, that six-square-mile area in Manhattan's geographical center containing over half of New York's million-plus black people, continues to grow and grapple with its problems. It continues to be a community in transition, searching for its proper place in the Black Revolution.

contributors

Frank J. Coppa is Associate Professor of History at St. John's University. He received his Ph.D. from the Catholic University of America and is the author of several volumes including: *Planning, Protectionism, and Politics in Liberal Italy* (1971) and *From Vienna to Vietnam: War and Peace in the Modern World* (1969). His articles have appeared in *The Journal of Modern History, The Journal of Economic History, The Catholic Historical Review* and *The Journal of Church and State.* Dr. Coppa's reviews appear frequently in *The American Historical Review.* He has presented papers before a number of learned societies including the American Historical Association, the Catholic Historical Association and the Columbia University Seminar on Modern Italy. He has participated in a number of radio and television series which examined the Italian experience in America.

A Fulbright scholar, Dr. Coppa has received several university grants to continue his research. His biography of Count Camillo di Cavour is scheduled to appear shortly in a Twayne edition.

Philip C. Dolce is Assistant Professor of History at Bergen Community College. He received his Ph.D. from Fordham University and his articles have appeared in *Humanitas* and the *Journal of the History of the Behavioral Sciences.* He is a member of the Columbia University Seminar on the City and is on the editorial board of the *Journal of Social History.*

Dr. Dolce has received grants from the Harry S. Truman Library Institute and St. John's University to complete his book entitled *Newbold Morris: A Patrician in Politics.* Dr. Dolce also is coediting a book entitled *The Transformation of American Society: The Old Culture vs. The New in the Twentieth Century.* He created and directed the WPAT radio series "Race to the Suburbs: The American Dream and Dilemma."

Ronald Bayor is Assistant Professor of History at the Georgia Institute of Technology. He received his Ph.D. from the University of Pennsylvania and is the coeditor of *A Documentary History of New York City* which is forthcoming from Quadrangle Books.

His work has appeared in the *International Migration Review* and the *American Jewish Historical Quarterly*. He is currently working on a book dealing with ethnic conflict in New York City. He is a member of the Columbia University Seminar on the City.

John Henrik Clarke is Associate Professor in the Department of Black and Puerto Rican Studies at Hunter College. He received his education at New York University.

Professor Clarke is a founding member of the Black Academy of Arts and Letters and is the editor of *Freedomways Magazine*. He is the author of a number of books including *Rebellion in Rhyme; The Lives of Great African Chiefs; Harlem, U.S.A.;* and *William Styron's Nat Turner: Ten Black Writers Respond*. His latest book is *Malcolm X: The Man and His Time*.

Professor Clarke was the coordinator for the CBS-TV Black Heritage series and Director of the Heritage Teaching Program for HARYOU. He has been invited to lecture at numerous institutions on three continents.

Thomas J. Curran is Associate Professor of History at St. John's University. He received his Ph.D. from Columbia University and his articles have been published in *The New York Historical Society Quarterly, The International Migration Review, Humanitas,* and the *Wyoming Review*. He served as the academic coordinator of the CBS television series, "The Evolution of Cities" as well as the NBC television series "The Ethnic American: Experience and Impact."

Dr. Curran is completing two books for publication next year, *The Know Nothings* (St. Martin's Press), and *Xenophobia and Immigration* (Twayne).

Vincent J. Falzone is Assistant Professor of History at St.

267

John's University. He received his Ph.D. from the University of Maryland.

Craig Fisher is Associate Professor of History at Long Island University. He received his Ph.D. from Cornell University and his articles have appeared in *Studies in Medieval and Renaissance History, Magistri Terrarum, Modern Language Notes,* and The *Catholic Encyclopedia.* He delivered a paper before the Pacific Coast Branch of the American Historical Association.

Currently he is conducting research on an edition of verse and prose of the *Chronicle of Perugia* written by Boniface of Verona about 1300 A.D.

Richard Harmond is Associate Professor of History at St. John's University. He received his Ph.D. from Columbia University and his work has appeared in *The Journal of American History,* the *Journal of Social History* and *The Historical Collections of the Essex Institute.* He has presented papers before the Long Island Historical Symposium, the Beverly Historical Society and the Marist College Seminar. He is currently coediting a book entitled *The Transformation of American Society: The Old Culture vs. the New in the Twentieth Century.*

Winston L. Kirby is the Director of the Television Center and a member of the Communications Arts Faculty at St. John's University. He received his education at Brown and Columbia Universities. He has over thirty years experience in mass communications including positions with the National Broadcasting Company and the American Broadcasting Company.

Mr. Kirby served as the Director of Radio and Television at Columbia University. Among the many programs he helped produce was *Black Heritage: A History of Afro-Americans* awarded a citation of merit by the New York Chapter of the

National Academy of Arts and Sciences. He has served as an Assistant to the President at Ramapo College of New Jersey where he was responsible for public affairs, development, and special assignments.

At St. John's University he was responsible for presenting the CBS television series "The Evolution of Cities" as well as the NBC television series "The Ethnic American: Experience and Impact."

Theodore P. Kovaleff is Assistant Professor of History at St. John's University. He received his Ph.D. from New York University and his articles have appeared in *The Journal of Church and State* and the *Intercollegiate Review*.

Dr. Eugene Kusielewicz is Associate Professor of History at St. John's University and President of the Kosciuszko Foundation. He received his Ph.D. from Fordham University and is the author of *The Cultural Condition of the Polish American Community,* and *The Meaning of the Polish Millennium.* He has contributed articles to *The Journal of Central European Affairs, The American Slavic and East European Review, The Polish Review, Polish American Studies, Thought Patterns, The Russian Review,* and *East Europe.*

Dr. Kusielewicz is a former President of the Polish American Historical Association. A founder and assistant editor of the newspaper, *Polish American World,* he was for several years an associate editor of *Polish American Studies.*

A member of the Advisory Committee of the American Jewish Committee's National Project on Ethnic America, he served for two years as a member of the Advisory Board of the Jozef Pilsudski Institute for Research in the Modern History of Poland. He is presently on the advisory boards of the Polish American Historical Association and the Polish Institute of Arts and Sciences in America. His book, *Teschen Dispute,* is soon to be published.

Edward J. Manetta is Professor of Art and Chairman of the Department of Fine Arts at St. John's University. He completed his graduate studies at Carnegie Mellon University and the John Herron School of Art at Indiana University.

He has had exhibitions of his paintings at the Royal Society Galleries in Birmingham, England, The Raven Galleries in Detroit, the Leiber Galleries in Indianapolis, the Pennsylvania Academy in Philadelphia, the Cincinnati Art Museum, the Wichita Art Museum, the National Academy of Design in New York, the Contemporary Christian Gallery in New York, and many others.

Professor Manetta's paintings form part of the following private collections: the Ford Motor Company, RCA Corporation, Ball State Art Museum, Indianapolis Art League Foundation, and many others. He has received several honors and awards in recognition of his work including a Fulbright Exchange Fellowship, a Huntington Hartford Foundation Fellowship, a Millikan Travel and Study Scholarship, and a Shell Foundation Research Grant.

Professor Robert Martinez is Instructor of History and head of the Puerto Rican Studies program at Baruch College of the City University of New York.

William A. Osborne is a Professor of Sociology and Anthropology at St. John's University. He received his Ph.D. from Columbia University and is the author of the *Segregated Covenant.* His articles have appeared in *The Journal for the Scientific Study of Religion, Cross Currents,* and in *The History of the Catholic Church in North America* edited by James Gleason.

270

He has presented papers before the Eastern Sociological Society, the Society for the Scientific Study of Religion, the Religious Research Association, and the Association for the Study of Negro History and Culture.

Dr. Osborne has served as a consultant to many organizations including Notre Dame University's Institute for the Study of Man, the New York State Department of Education, the Bishop's Commission on Peace and World Justice, and the National Conference on Religion and Race. He is a senior consultant to Foy, Falcier Associates.

Anne Paolucci is University Research Professor at St. John's University and editor of *The Review of National Literatures*. She received her Ph.D. from Columbia University and is the author of many books including *Hegel on Tragedy, Pirandello, A Short History of American Drama, Classical Influences in Shakespearean Tragedy*, and *From Tension to Tonic: The Plays of Edward Albee*.

Her articles have appeared in *Ararat, The Massachusetts Review, Italica, Shakespeare Encomium, Comparative Literature, Classical Journal, Promethean* and many other journals. Dr. Paolucci has published her poems in *Forum Italicum, Balsam's Ass, Literature East and West,* and *The Kenyan Review*. She has written two plays and has produced and directed several others.

Dr. Paolucci has received a drama award for her play *Minions of the Race*, and the AMITA award as the Outstanding Woman in Literature, a Fulbright Fellowship, as well as research grants in Oriental Literature.

Daniel R. Smith is Instructor of African History at Iona College. Educated at Iona College and St. John's University, his field of specialization is African History.

271

Jacob Sodden is Assistant Professor of Sociology at St. John's University. He received his Ph.D. from New York University. Active in community affairs in New York City, he is the Vice Chairman of Community Board Seven in the Bronx as well as the Concourse Neighborhood Action Program. He is currently writing a book entitled *The Sociology of Transportation.*

Richard Stalter is Assistant Professor of Biology at St. John's University. he received his Ph.D. from the University of South Carolina and has published articles in the *South Carolina Academy of Science Bulletin, The ASB Bulletin, Ecology, Castanea,* Plant Science Bulletin, *The American Fern Journal, American Forests,* and the *Journal of the Elisha Mitchel Scientific Society.*
A Baruch Fellow, he has received grants from Sigma Xi and the Piedmont Center. Dr. Stalter is currently conducting research on the Zonation of Vegetation in the Long Island Marshes.

suggested readings

General Works on the City and Urbanization

Abrams, Charles. *The City is the Frontier.* New York, 1965.

Breese, Gerald. *Urbanization in Newly Developing Countries.* Englewood Cliffs, 1966.

Briggs, Asa. *Victorian Cities.* Chicago, 1955.

Cole, William E. *Urban Society.* New York, 1958.

Cox, Kevin R. *Conflict, Power, and Politics in the City: A Geographic View.* New York, 1973.

Dickenson, R. E. *The West European City.* London, 1962.

Dixon, Roland B. *The Building of Cultures.* New York, 1928.

Geddes, Patrick. *Cities in Evolution.* London, 1915.

Ghurye, Govind S. *Cities and Civilization.* New York, 1962.

Gordon, Mitchell. *Sick Cities: Psychology and Pathology of American Urban Life.* Baltimore, 1965.

Gottman, Jean. *Megalopolis.* Cambridge, 1961.

Gutkind, E. A. *International History of City Development.* New York, 1964-71. 6 vols.

Hall, P. *The World Cities.* New York, 1966.

Handlin, Oscar and Burchard, John, eds. *The Historian and the City.* Boston, 1963.

Little, Kenneth. *Some Contemporary Trends in African Urbanization.* Evanston, Ill., 1966.

MacIver, R. M. *Society: Its Structure and Changes.* New York, 1932.

McKelvey, Blake. *The Urbanization of America, 1860-1915.* New Brunswick, 1968a.

———. *The Emergence of Metropolitan America, 1915-1966.* New Brunswick, 1968b.

Mumford, Lewis. *The Culture of Cities.* New York, 1938.

———. *The City in History.* New York, 1961.

———. *Technics and Civilization.* New York, 1963.

Petrie, W. F. *The Revolutions of Civilization.* London, 1911.

Schlesinger, Arthur M. *The Rise of the City 1878-1898.* New York, 1938.

Schneider, Hermann. *The History of World Civilization from Prehistoric Times to the Middle Ages*. New York, 1931.
Spengler, Oswald. *The Decline of the West*. New York, 1928.
———. *Man and Technics*. New York, 1932.
Weber, Adna F. *The Growth of Cities in the Nineteenth Century*. New York, 1899.
Weber, Max. *The City*. New York, 1958.

I. Early Urbanization and the Dawn of Civilization

Alighieri, Dante. *The Divine Comedy*, tr. Henry Carey. New York, 1908.

Augustine, Saint. *The Political Writing of St. Augustine*, ed. Henry Paolucci, Chicago, 1962.

———. *The Confessions of St. Augustine*, ed. Ernest Rhys. New York, 1907.

Bautier, Robert Henri. *The Economic Development of Medieval Europe*. New York, 1970.

Beresford, Maurice. *New Towns of the Middle Ages*. New York, 1927.

Blunt, Anthony. *Artistic Theory in Italy 1450-1600*. London, 1940.

Boissonade, P. *Life and Work in the Middle Ages*. New York, 1927.

Butler, W. F. *The Lombard Communes*. New York, 1906.

Cellini, Benvenuto. *Autobiography*. Tr. John A. Symonds, Garden City, New York, 1961.

Clark, Sir George. *The Seventeenth Century*. New York, 1961.

Coulton, G. G. *The Medieval Village*. Cambridge, 1926.

Cox, Oliver. "The Preindustrial City Reconsidered," in *The Historian and the City*, ed. Handlin and Burchard.

De Coulanges, Numa Denis and Fuste. *The Ancient City: A Study of the Religions, Laws and Institutions of Greece and Rome*. Garden City, N.Y., 1970.

De Roover, Raymond. *The Rise and Decline of the Medici Bank 1397-1495*. New York, 1966.

Dickens, Charles. *Bleak House*, ed. Morton Zabel. Boston, 1956.

Ellul, Jacques. *The Meaning of the City*. New York, 1970.

Ferguson, W. K. *Europe in Transition 1300-1520*. Boston, 1962.

Gage, John. *Life in Italy at the Time of the Medici*. London, 1968.

Goldwin, Robert, ed. *A Nation of Cities*. Chicago, 1966.

Gombrich, E. H. *The Story of Art*. London, 1956.

Gross, C. *The Guild Merchant*. Oxford, 1890. 2 vols.

Haskins, C. H. *Medieval Culture*. Oxford, 1929.

Heydenreich, L. H. *Leonardo da Vinci*. New York, 1954.

Hexter, J. H. *et al.*, eds. *The Traditions of the Western World*. Chicago, 1967.

Holmes, George. *The Florentine Enlightenment 1400-50*. London, 1969.

Kitto, H. D. F. *The Greeks*. Baltimore, 1957.

Koffka, Kurt. *The Growth of the Mind*. New York, 1965.

Laslett, Peter. *The World We Have Lost*. New York, 1965.

Lopez, Robert S. "The Crossroads Within the Wall," in *The Historian and the City*, ed. Handlin and Burchard.

MacKenrich, Paul. *The Mute Stones Speak: The Story of Archaeology in Italy*. New York, 1960.

Mahon, D. *Studies in Seicento Art and Theory*. London, 1947.

McCurdy, Edward. *Leonardo da Vinci's Notebooks*. New York, 1923.

Moller, Herbert, ed. *Population Movements in Modern European History*. New York, 1964.

Moote, Lloyd A. *The Seventeenth Century: Europe in Ferment*. Lexington, Massachusetts, 1970.

Mundy, John H. and Riesenberg, Peter. *The Medieval Town*. Princeton, 1958.

Ogg, Frederick A. *Economic Development of Modern Europe*. New York, 1932.

Pirenne, Henri. *Medieval Cities*. Princeton, 1925.

Plumb, J. H. *The Italian Renaissance*. New York, 1961.

Saalman, Howard. *Medieval Cities*. New York, 1968.

Sedgwick, H. D. *Italy in the Thirteenth Century*. Boston, 1912.

Sjoberg, Gideon. "The Preindustrial City." *American Journal of Sociology*, January, 1955.

———. *The Preindustrial City*. Glencoe, Ill., 1961.

Stephenson, C. *Borough and Town*. Cambridge, 1932.

Symonds, J. A. *The Life of Michelangelo Buonarroti*. London, 1892.

Thomson, James. *The City of Dreadful Night*. London, 1880.

Vassari, Giorgio. *Lives of the Painters, Sculptors and Architects*. London, 1927.

Venturi, L. *History of Art Criticism*. New York, 1936.

Waley, Daniel. *The Italian City-Republics*. New York, 1969.

Weber, Eugene, ed. *Paths to the Present*. New York, 1968.

Wilson, James Q., ed. *The Metropolitan Enigma*. Cambridge, Mass., 1968.

Wittkower, R. *Architectural Principles in the Age of Humanism*. London, 1952.

II. Industrialization and Urbanization: the Emergence of the Modern City

Ashton, Thomas S. *The Industrial Revolution, 1760-1830.* London, 1948.

Belandier, Georges. *Ambiguous Africa: Cultures in Collision.* New York, 1966.

Bowden, Witt *et al. Economic History of Europe since 1750.* New York, 1937.

Bridenbaugh, Carl. *Colonial Craftsmen.* New York, 1950.

Bruchey, Stuart. *The Roots of American Economic Growth.* New York, 1972.

Carosso, Vincent P. *Investment Banking in America.* Cambridge, Mass., 1970.

Clapham, J. H. *The Economic Development of France and Germany 1815-1914.* Cambridge, 1961.

Clark, Victor. *History of Manufactures in the United States.* New York, 1929.

Deane, Phyllis. *The First Industrial Revolution.* Cambridge, 1965.

Fishlow, Albert. *American Railroads and the Transformation of the Antebellum Economy.* Cambridge, Mass., 1965.

Fogel, Robert. *Railroads and American Economic Growth.* Baltimore, 1964.

Forster, Robert and Forster, Elborg. *European Society in the Eighteenth Century.* New York, 1969.

Goodrich, Carter *et al. Canals and American Economic Growth,* New York, 1961.

Gutkind, Peter. "The African Urban Milieu: A Force in Rapid Change," *Civilization.* 12:167-95.

Hammond, J. L. and Hammond, Barbara. *The Rise of Modern Industry*. London, 1925.

Heaton, Herbert. *The Economic History of Europe*. New York, 1948.

Henderson, W. O. *The Industrial Revolution in Europe*. Chicago, 1961.

———. *Britain and Industrial Europe, 1750-1870*. New York, 1965.

Jenkins, George. "Africa as it Urbanizes: An Overview of Current Research," *Urban Affairs Quarterly*. 2:66-80.

Jones, J. D. Rheinallt. "The Effects of Urbanization in South and Central Africa," *African Affairs*. 52:37-44.

Knowles, L. C. A. *The Industrial and Commercial Revolutions in Great Britain During the Nineteenth Century*. New York, 1968.

Kuczynski, Jurgen. *The Rise of the Working Class*. New York, 1967.

Kuper, Hilda, ed. *Urbanization and Migration in West Africa*. Los Angeles, 1965.

Landes, D. S. *The Unbound Prometheus: Technological Change and Industrial Development in Western Europe from 1750 to the Present*. Cambridge, 1969.

Langer, William L. *Political and Social Upheaval 1832-1852*. New York, 1969.

Little, Kenneth. *West African Urbanization: A Study of Voluntary Association in Social Change*. Cambridge, 1965.

Lorimer, Frank. *Demographic Information on Tropical Africa*. Boston, 1961.

Lorwin, Val R. *Labor and Working Conditions in Modern Europe*. New York, 1967.

Maboqunje, Akin L. "Urbanization and Change," *The African Experience*. Edited by John Paden and Edward Soja. Evanston, Ill., 1970.

Miner, Horace, ed. *The City in Modern Africa*. London, 1967.

280

Morazé, Charles. *The Triumph of the Middle Classes.* New York, 1968.

Morris, Richard B. *Government and Labor in Early America.* New York, 1946.

Mountjoy, Alan B. *Industrialization and Underdeveloped Countries.* Chicago, 1970.

North, Douglas C. *The Economic Growth of the United States.* New York, 1961.

Oram, Nigel, *Towns in Africa.* London, 1965.

Pike, E. Ryston. *"Hard Times:" Human Documents of the Industrial Revolution.* New York, 1966.

Pollard, S. and Holmes, C., eds. *The Process of Industrialization 1750-1870.* New York, 1968.

Postan, M. M. and Habakkuk, H. J. *The Industrial Revolution and After.* Cambridge, 1965.

Rosenberg, Nathan. *Technology and American Economic Growth: 1607-1861.* New York, 1965.

Rude, George. *The Crowd in History, 1730-1884.* New York, 1964.

Singer, Charles *et al. History of Technology.* Oxford, 1954-58. 5vv.

Taylor, Philip A. M., ed. *The Industrial Revolution in Britain: Triumph or Disaster?* Boston, 1965.

Thompson, E. P. *The Making of the English Working Class.* New York, 1963.

Toynbee, Arnold. *The Industrial Revolution.* Boston, 1956.

Tuma, Elias H. *European Economic History.* New York, 1971.

Wrigley, E. A. *Industrial Growth and Population Change.* Cambridge, 1962.

III. The Impact of Urbanization in the United States: An American Revolution in the Making

A. Problems of the Asphalt Environment

Abbot, Edith. *The Tenements of Chicago, 1908-1935*. Chicago, 1936.

Abrams, Charles. *The City is the Frontier*. New York, 1965.

Boughey, H. S. *Man and the Environment*. New York, 1971.

Callow, Alexander B., Jr. *The Tweed Ring*. New York, 1965.

Campbell, R. R. and Wade, J. L. *Society and Environment: The Coming Collision*. Boston, 1972.

Carson, Rachael. *Silent Spring*. Boston, 1962.

Daubenmire, R. F. *Plants and the Environment*. New York, 1947.

Dorsett, Lyle W. *The Pendergast Machine*. New York, 1968.

Duncan, O. D. "Social Organizations and the Ecosystem" in R. E. L. Ferris, ed. *Handbook of Modern Sociology*. Chicago, 1964.

Ehrenfeld, D. W. *Biological Conservation*. New York, 1970.

Ernest, Robert. *Immigrant Life in New York City, 1825-1863*. New York, 1949.

Fair, M., and Geyer, J. *Water and Waste Water Treatment*. New York, 1958.

Greer, Scott. "Traffic, Transportation and the Problems of the Metropolis," in Merton and Nisbet, eds. *Contemporary Social Problems*. New York, 1961.

Handlin, Oscar. *Boston's Immigrants, A Study in Acculturation*. Cambridge, revised ed. 1959.

Hawley, A. H. *Human Ecology: A Theory of Community Structure*. New York, 1950.

Holli, Melvin G. *Reform in Detroit: Hazen S. Pingree and Urban Politics.* New York, 1969.

Hutmacher, J. Joseph. "Charles Evans Hughes and Charles Francis Murphy: "The Metamorphosis of Progressivism," *New York History,* 44:28-34.

Johnson, H. D. *No Deposit No Return.* Reading, Mass., 1970.

Kormandy, E. J. *Concepts of Ecology.* Englewood Cliffs, N.J., 1969.

Leinwand, Gerald. *The Traffic Jam.* New York, 1969.

Lubove, Roy. *The Progressives and the Slums, Tenement House Reform in New York City, 1890-1917.* Pittsburgh, 1962.

Merton, Robert K. *Social Theory and Social Structure.* New York, 1957.

Miller, Zane L. *Boss Cox's Cincinnati: Urban Politics in the Progressive Era.* New York, 1968.

Mumford, Lewis: *The Highway and the City.* New York, 1953.

Murin, William. *Mass Transit Policy Planning.* Lexington, Mass., 1971.

O'Connor, Edwin. *The Last Hurrah.* New York, 1956.

Odum, E. P. *Ecology.* New York, 1963.

———. *Fundamentals of Ecology.* Philadelphia, 1971.

Oosting, H. J. *The Study of Plant Communities.* San Francisco, 1965.

Osofsky, Gilbert. *Harlem: The Making of a Ghetto, Negro New York, 1890-1930.* New York, 1966.

Owen, Wilfred. *The Accessible City.* Washington, D.C., 1972.

———. *The Metropolitan Transportation Problem.* Garden City, New York, 1966.

Pell, Clairborne. *Megalopolis Unbound: The Supercity and the Transportation of Tommorrow.* New York, 1966.

Reid, G. K. *Ecology of Inland Waters and Estuaries.* New York, 1961.

Riis, Jacob. *The Children of the Poor.* New York, 1892.

———. *How the Other Half Lives: Studies Among the Tenements of New York.* New York, 1891.

Riordan, William L. *Plunkitt of Tammany Hall*. New York, 1948.
Rischin, Moses. *The Promised City, New York's Jews, 1870-1914*. Cambridge, Mass., 1962.
Royko, Mike. *Boss: Richard J. Daley of Chicago*. New York, 1971.
Schlivek, Louis. *Men in Metropolis*. New York, 1965.
Schneider, Kenneth R. *Autokind vs. Mankind*. New York, 1971.
Smerk, George M., ed. *Readings in Urban Transportation*. Bloomington, Indiana, 1968.
Smith, R. L. *Ecology and Field Biology*. New York, 1966.
Stalter, J. T. *Boss Rule: Portraits in City Politics*. New York, 1935.
Stave, Bruce M. *The New Deal and the Last Hurrah: Pittsburgh Machine Politics*. Pittsburgh, 1970.
Stone, Tabor R. *Beyond the Automobile: Reshaping the Transportation Environment*. Englewood Cliffs, N.J., 1971.
Tarr, Joel A. *A Study in Boss Politics: William Lorimer of Chicago*. Urbana, Ill., 1971.
Turk, A. J., and Wittes, J. H. *Ecology Pollution Environment*. Philadelphia, 1972.
Warren, C. E. *Biology and Water Pollution Control*. Philadelphia, 1971.
Weiss, Nancy Joan. *Charles Francis Murphy, 1858-1924: Respectability and Responsibility in Tammany Politics*. Northampton, Mass., 1968.
Zink, Harold. *City Bosses in the United States: A Study of Twenty Municipal Bosses*. Durham, N.C., 1930.

B. The City of the Mind: Recreation, Education, Communication, and the Urban Image

Barnow, Erik. *The Image Empire: A History of Broadcasting*. New York, 1970.
Boyle, Robert H. *Sport-Mirror of American Life*. Boston, 1963.
Burns, James A., and Kohlbrenner, Bernard J. *A History of Catholic Education in the United States*. New York, 1937.

Caillois, Roger. *Man, Play and Games.* New York, 1961.

Chaney, David C. *Process of Mass Communication.* New York, 1972.

Clark, Kenneth. *Dark Ghetto: Dilemmas of Social Power.* New York, 1965.

Cooper, David. *The Death of the Family.* New York, 1971.

Cox, Harvey. *The Secular City.* New York, 1965.

Cozens, Frederick W., and Stumpf, Florence S. *Sports in American Life.* Chicago, 1953.

De Fleur, Melvin L. *Theories of Mass Communications.* New York, second ed., 1970.

Dentler, R. A. and Warshauer, M. E. *Big City Drop-outs and Illiterates.* New York, 1965.

Dulles, Foster Rhea. *America Learns to Play.* Gloucester, Mass., 1959.

Fogelson, Robert M., *The Fragmented Metropolis: Los Angeles 1850-1930.* Cambridge, Mass., 1967.

Franklin, John Hope. *From Slavery to Freedom: A History of Negro Americans.* New York, 1967.

Glaab, Charles N. "The Historian and the American Urban Tradition," *Wisconsin Magazine of History,* 46:13-25.

—— and Brown, A. Theodore. *A History of Urban America.* New York, 1967.

Goode, William. *World Revolution and Family Patterns.* New York, 1963.

Greer, Scott. *The Emerging City: Myth and Reality.* New York, 1962.

Handlin, Oscar. "The Modern City as a Field of Historical Study," in *The Historian and the City,* ed. Handlin and Burchard, Cambridge, Mass.

Higham, John. "The Reorientation of American Culture in the 1890s," in John Higham, ed. *Writing American History.* Bloomington, Ill., 1970.

Hollingshead, August, and Redlick, Fred. *Social Class and Mental Illness.* New York, 1958.

285

Kaplan, Max. *Leisure in America–A Social Inquiry*. New York, 1960.

Kimball, Solon. *Family and Community in Ireland*. Cambridge, Mass., 1968.

Kramer, John, ed. *North American Suburbs: Politics, Diversity, and Change*. Berkeley, California, 1972.

Langner, Thomas, and Michaels, John. *Life Stress and Mental Health*. New York, 1963.

Lannie, Vincent. *Public Money and Parochial Education: Bishop Hughes, Governor Seward, and the New York School Controversy*. New York, 1968.

Lynch, Kevin. *The Image of the City*. Cambridge, Mass., 1960.

Mayer, Martin. *About Television*. New York, 1972.

McLuhan, Marshall. *Understanding Media: The Extensions of Man*. New York, 1964.

Menke, Frank G. *The Encyclopedia of Sports*. South Brunswick, N.J., rev. ed., 1969.

Nash, Jay B. *Philosophy of Leisure and Recreation*. St. Louis, 1953.

Neumeyer, Martin H., and Esther S. *Leisure and Recreation*. New York, 1958.

Ottley, Roi, and Weatherby, William J., eds. *The Negro in New York:An Informal Social-History, 1626-1940*. New York, 1967.

Otto, Herbert. *The Family in Search of a Future*. New York, 1969.

Piven, Frances, and Cloward, Richard. *Regulating the Poor*. New York, 1972.

Reiss, Ira. *The Social Context of Premarital Sexual Permissiveness*. New York, 1967.

River, William L., and Schramm, Wilbur. *Responsibility in Mass Communications*. New York, rev. ed., 1969.

Rourke, Francis E. "Urbanism and American Democracy," *Ethics*, 74:255-68.

Scheiner, Seth. *Negro Mecca: A History of the Negro in New York City, 1865-1920.* New York, 1965.

Schramm, Wilbur. *Mass Communications.* Urbana, Ill., 1960.

Sherman, Richard B., ed. *The Negro and the City.* Englewood Cliffs, New Jersey, 1970.

Silberman, Charles. *Crisis in Black and White.* New York, 1966.

Sizer, Theodore R. "The Schools in the City," in James Q. Wilson, ed. *The Metropolitan Enigma.* Garden City, N.Y., 1970.

Srole, Leo *et al. Mental Health in the Metropolis.* New York, 1962.

Steiner, Jesse Frederick. *Americans at Play.* New York, reprinted, 1970.

Stevens, William. *The Family in Cross Cultural Perspective.* New York, 1963.

Strauss, Anselm L. *Images of the American City.* New York, 1961.

Szasz, Thomas. *The Myth of Mental Illness.* New York, 1961.

Thernstrom, Stephan, "Urbanization, Migration, and Social Mobility in Late Nineteenth-Century America," in Barton J. Bernstein, ed. *Towards a New Past: Dissenting Essays in American History.* New York, 1968.

Tunis, John S. *The American Way in Sport.* New York, 1958.

Wade, Richard C. "Violence in the Cities: A Historical View," reprinted in Kenneth T. Jackson and Stanley K. Schultz, eds. *Cities in American History.* New York, 1972.

Walker, Robert H. "The Poet and the Rise of the City," *Mississippi Valley Historical Review.* 46:85-99.

Weisz, Howard. "Irish-American Attitudes and the Americanization of the English Language Parochial School," *New York History,* 53:157-76.

White, Morton and Lucia. *The Intellectual Versus the City: From Thomas Jefferson to Frank Lloyd Wright.* Cambridge, Mass., 1962.

287

Wirth, Louis. "Urbanism as a Way of Life," *American Journal of Sociology*, 44:1-24.

C. The New Comers: Intruders or Invited Guests?

Allport, Gordon W. *The Nature of Prejudice*. New York, 1954.

Banner, James M., Jr. *To the Hartford Convention: The Federalists and the Origins of Party Politics in Massachusetts, 1789-1815*. New York, 1970.

Bender, Laurenta, and Nichtern, Sol. "Two Puerto Rican Boys in New York City," in Georgene Seward, ed. *Clinical Studies in Culture Conflict*. New York, 1958.

Billington, Ray Allen. *The Protestant Crusade: A Study of the Origins of American Nativism*. New York, 1938.

Binzen, Peter. *Whitetown U.S.A., A First Hand Study of How the "Silent Majority" Lives, Learns, Works and Thinks.* New York, 1970.

Clark, Kenneth B. *Dark Ghetto: Dilemmas of Social Power.* New York, 1965.

Clarke, John Henrik, ed. *Harlem: A Community in Transition.* New York, 1969.

——, ed. *Harlem U.S.A.* New York, 1971.

——, ed. *Harlem: Voices From the Soul of Black America.* New York, 1970.

——, ed. *Malcolm X: The Man and His Times.* New York, 1969.

Cochran, Thomas Childs. *The Puerto Rican Businessman: A Study in Cultural Change.* Philadelphia, 1959.

Coolidge, Mary Roberts. *Chinese Immigration.* New York, reprinted, 1969.

Davis, David Brion. "Some Themes of Counter-Subversion: An Analysis of Anti-Masonic, Anti-Catholic and Anti-Mormon Literature," *Mississippi Valley Historical Review*, 47:205-29.

DeConde, Alexander. *Half Bitter, Half Sweet: An Excursion into Italian American History.* New York, 1971.

Ernst, Robert. *Immigrant Life in New York City, 1825-1863.* New York, 1949.

Fitzpatrick, Joseph P. "The Adjustment of Puerto Ricans to New York City," in Milton L. Barron, ed. *Minorities in a Changing World.* New York, 1967.

Friedman, Murray, ed. *Overcoming Middle Class Rage.* Philadelphia, 1971.

Gans, Herbert J. *The Urban Villagers: Group and Class in the Life of Italian-Americans.* New York, 1962.

Glazer, Nathan, and Moynihan, Daniel Patrick. *Beyond the Melting Pot: The Negroes, Puerto Ricans, Jews, Italians, and Irish of New York City.* Cambridge, Mass., 2nd ed., 1970.

Gordon, Milton. *Assimilation in American Life: The Role of Race, Religion, and National Origins.* New York, 1964.

Gossett, Thomas F. *Race: History of an Idea in America.* Dallas, 1955.

Greeley, Andrew M. *Why Can't They Be Like Us? America's White Ethnic Groups.* New York, 1971.

Handlin, Oscar. *Boston's Immigrants, A Study in Acculturation.* Cambridge, Mass., rev. ed., 1959.

———. *The Newcomers: Negroes and Puerto Ricans in a Changing Metropolis.* Garden City, N.Y., 1962.

———. *The Uprooted.* Boston, 1951.

Hansen, Marcus Lee. *The Atlantic Migration, 1607-1860.* Cambridge, Mass., 1940.

Herberg, Will. *Protestant–Catholic–Jew.* New York, 1955.

Higham, John. *Strangers in the Land: Patterns of American Nativism, 1860-1925.* New Brunswick, N.J., 1955.

Jackson, Kenneth T. "Metropolitan Government Versus Suburban Autonomy: Politics on the Crabgrass Frontier," in Kenneth T. Jackson and Stanley K. Schultz, eds. *Cities in American History.* New York, 1972.

Jaffe, A. J., ed. *Puerto Rican Population of New York City.* New York, 1954.

Lewis, Oscar. *La Vida.* New York, 1966.

Lincoln, C. Eric. *The Black Muslims in America.* Boston, 1961.

Lipset, Seymour Martin, and Raab, Earl. *The Politics of Unreason: Right-Wing Extremism in America, 1790-1970.* New York, 1970.

Locke, Alain, ed. *The New Negro.* New York, reprinted, 1969.

Lopreato, Joseph. *Italian Americans.* New York, 1970.

Mayerson, Charlotte Leon. *Two Blocks Apart.* New York, 1966.

McKay, Claude. *Harlem: Negro Metropolis.* New York, reprinted, 1968.

McWilliams, Carey. *North From Mexico.* New York, 1948.

Meier, August, and Rudwick, Elliot. *From Plantation to Ghetto.* New York, 1966.

Moore, Joan W., and Grebley, Leo. *Pre-Mexican American People.* New York, 1970.

Nelli, Humbert S. *The Italians in Chicago, 1880-1930: A Study in Ethnic Mobility.* New York, 1970.

Novak, Michael. *The Rise of the Unmeltable Ethnics: The New Political Force of the Seventies.* New York, 1972.

Osofsky, Gilbert. *Harlem: The Making of a Ghetto.* New York, 1965.

Proper, Emerson Edward. *Colonial Immigration Laws: A Study of the Regulation of Immigration by the English Colonies in America.* New York, 1900.

Report of the National Advisory Commission on Civil Disorders. New York, New York *Times* edition, 1968.

Rischin, Moses. *The Promised City, New York's Jews, 1870-1914.* Cambridge, Mass., 1962.

Seda-Bonilla, Eduardo. "Social Structure and Race Relations," in *Social Forces,* 40:141-48.

Shannon, Fred A. *The Farmer's Last Frontier.* New York, 1945.

Smith, James Norton. *Freedom's Fetters: The Alien and Sedition Laws and American Civil Liberties.* New York, 1956.
Steffens, Lincoln. *The Shame of the Cities.* New York, 1904.
Steinbeck, John. *Grapes of Wrath.* New York, 1939.
Thomas, William I., and Znaniecki, Florjan. *The Polish Peasant in Europe and America.* Chicago, 1918.
Wagner, Nathaniel N. and Haug, Marsha J. eds. *Chicanos: Social and Psychological Perspectives.* Saint Louis, 1971.
Ward, David. *Cities and Immigrants, A Geography of Change in Nineteenth Century America.* New York, 1971.
Young, Bernice Elizabeth. *Harlem: The Story of a Changing Community.* New York, 1972.